ROMANTICISM, LYRICISM, AND HISTORY

ROMANTICISM, LYRICISM, AND HISTORY

Sarah M. Zimmerman

STATE UNIVERSITY OF NEW YORK PRESS

T5152

A portion of chapter 2 is reprinted by permission of the
University Press of Kentucky. Engravings on pages 45, 46, and the cover are
reproduced by permission of Department of Rare Books and Special
Collections, Princeton University Library. Selections from the poetry and
prose of John Clare © Eric Robinson 1996, 1989, 1984, 1985, are
reproduced by permission of Curtis Brown Ltd., London

Published by
State University of New York Press
© 1999 State University of New Y ork
All rights reserved
Printed in the United States of America

For information, address the State University of New York Press,
State University Plaza, Albany, NY 12246

Marketing by Dana Yanulavich
Production by Bernadine Dawes

Library of Congress Cataloging-in-Publication Data

Zimmerman, Sarah MacKenzie.
    Romanticism, lyricism, and history / Sarah M. Zimmerman.
        p.   cm.
    Includes bibliographical references and index.
    ISBN 0-7914-4109-1 (hc. : alk. paper). — ISBN 0-7914-4110-5 (pbk.
alk. paper)
    1. English poetry—19th century—History and criticism.
    2. Wordsworth, William, 1770–1850—Criticism and interpretation.
    3. Literature and history—Great Britain—History—19th century.
    4. Liberature and history—Great Britain—History—18th century.
    5. Clare, John, 1793–1864—Criticism and interpretation. 6. Smith,
Charlotte Turner, 1749–1806—Poetic works. 7. Wordsworth, Dorothy,
1771–1855. 8. Romanticism—Great Britain. I. Title.
PR590.Z37   1999
821'.709145—dc21   99-10644
                                                                        CIP

1   2   3   4   5   6   7   8   9   10

For my family—
Jay, Isabel, Jay, and Chad

Contents

Preface

This study investigates the Romantic lyric's possibilities for engaging reading audiences on matters both private and public. The topic itself challenges a persistent, if often unstated, equation of the mode with the personal as opposed to the social, and with the autobiographical as opposed to the historical. I argue instead that Romantic lyricism is more accurately a vehicle for collapsing these distinctions, and that in fact the mode's great appeal to contemporaneous readers was its capacity for submitting the seemingly private reflections of an autobiographical speaker to public view. Given this persuasive potential, the mode facilitated a greater range of impulses— political as well as meditative or emotional—than has yet been sufficiently acknowledged.

Romantic lyricism has been central to critical understandings of the period, and was for a long time virtually identified with it. Although recent historical approaches have inflected the other major genres, key underlying assumptions about Romantic lyricism have remained surprisingly stable since John Stuart Mill's pithy definitions in "What is Poetry?" (1833). Drawing largely on his reading of William Wordsworth, Mill severs "eloquence"—which seeks a social world—from "poetry," which turns away from that same world. He thereby invests the lyric with an aura of detachment from quotidian concerns and a defining drive toward transcendence. In an important if not immediately apparent sense, this view has persisted well into the 1990s, leaving intact key tenets of such critics as M. H. Abrams and Northrop Frye, who cast Romantic lyricism as an inward-looking form. Abrams and Frye accept as necessary the ways in which the poet "turns his back on his audience"; influential Romantic new historical critiques have, in effect, reinforced this paradigm by elaborating the ideological implications of a desire for transcendence without interrogating the preeminence of that desire in characterizing the period's lyric impulses. For Abrams, the mode's privacy works toward a spiritual self-renewal; for new historicists, this orientation coincides with the repression of traumatic social events. Yet these critics agree that Romantic lyricism relinquishes sociohistorical immediacy for the sake of a cultivated disinterestedness. What we have lost in this contentious critical history is a clear view of the myriad ways in which many of the period's lyric poems display a pronounced "eloquence" that writers understood and employed, and that contemporaneous readers and critics seized upon as compelling.

In several landmark studies that appeared across two decades, Abrams defined a canonical view of Romantic lyricism as the primary poetic vehicle for a "spirit of the age": *The Mirror and the Lamp* (1953), "English Romanticism: The Spirit of the Age" (1963), "Structure and Style in the Greater Romantic Lyric" (1965), and *Natural Supernaturalism* (1972). These works' cumulative account of Romantic lyricism has retained a hold on the critical imagination, which is operative even when Abrams's influence is not explicitly recognized, since his claims have been so thoroughly absorbed into working perceptions of the mode. By the same token, we have often lost sight of Abrams's own assiduous circumspection in defining Romantic lyricism and the flexibility of his definitions. Despite his clear interest in championing Romanticism as a field worthy of scholarly and pedagogical attention after its stern critique by T. S. Eliot and some of the New Critics, Abrams defines his terms with marked care—he describes the "greater Romantic lyric" rather than Romantic lyricism—and he cites in almost encyclopedic detail the exceptions to all of his rules. It is thus a testament to the immense persuasiveness of Abrams's models that these qualifications have frequently been obscured in the subsequent appropriation and contestation of his key terms.

Abrams's massive critical and rhetorical endeavor has demanded equally grand reimaginings of Romanticism by those who would challenge his view of the field. The most important of these efforts have been a feminist critique of gendered power relations in the period's canonical lyrics and models of them, and a new historical critique of the ideological investment of certain tenets—introspection, transcendence, the aesthetic, and an attraction to the natural world—long deemed central to Romanticism. These paradigms and counterparadigms comprise what Eliot might have termed a monumental critical history of the Romantic lyric. They have been sharply inveighed contests, since what was at stake for a long time was, in effect, a definition of the period itself. Abrams influentially defined the "greater Romantic lyric" around an exchange of hopes—of social revolution for poetic renovation—on the part of Samuel Taylor Coleridge and Wordsworth in the aftermath of the French Revolution. New historicism has in turn represented the Romantic lyric as suppressing historical trauma in the service of an ideology of the imagination and the aesthetic.

Yet a different historical approach to the period's lyric poems is possible, one that I will argue is better suited to catching the subtle indirection of the mode's capacity for social engagement. If the period's lyric poems are read only in relation to major historical events and judged according to a mimetic standard of reference to them, then very few indeed of the period's lyric poems seem responsive to their social contexts. This study recommends instead situating the period's lyric poems not only in relation to its major events but also within their myriad local contexts, including the biographical matrices of the poet's career; the literary marketplace and the processes of book production; relevant cultural traditions, such as the cult of sensibility; literary works' critical reception in the period's thriving periodical culture; and readers' consumption of poems in newspapers, miscellanies, periodicals, annuals, and individually bound volumes and their responses to those poems—in poems and letters submitted to periodical editors, and in private letters, diaries, and memoirs. This study is predicated upon the notion that the period's various reading audiences—critics, middle- and upper-class patrons, other writers, and readers—can tell us more than we have asked about the Romantic lyric's rhetorical possibilities.

John Clare's poetry provides a particularly clear argument that gauging the social responsiveness of lyric poems requires close attention to local contexts (such as his economic dependence upon his patrons) as well as to national events (parliamentary enclosure). Since Clare's more explicit poetic statements against enclosure were monitored by his patrons, it becomes necessary to read his lyrics within the context of his promotion as "the Northamptonshire peasant." Because of his acute dependence upon his patrons and publishers, he could not address enclosure directly without risking a contest over those lines. Yet by heightening a conventional sense of the poet's strong affection for his natural environment and lamenting any changes to its scenes, Clare manages to convey a subtle but powerful critique of enclosure's devastating alterations. His poems demonstrate how a feature common to many of the period's lyric poems—the poet's strong attraction to rural scenes—may be weighted with political significance in a period of intensified parliamentary enclosure and rural resistance to it. In a historical materialist project that informs this study, Walter Benjamin provides a theoretical imperative for a close consideration of such local contexts, along with major social events: "A chronicler who recites events without distinguishing between major and minor ones acts in accordance with the following truth: nothing that has ever happened should be regarded as lost for history."[1] This perspective is vital for reading the political valences of lyric poems by writers such as Charlotte Smith, Clare, and—at some moments in his career—William Wordsworth, who could quite literally not afford directly to address the period's most volatile social events.

Numerous lyric poems in the period directly address social concerns—some canonical, such as William Blake's *Songs of Innocence and of Experience*, and others increasingly prominent, such as Percy Bysshe Shelley's 1819 political poems. I am concerned instead with poems that seem to resist historical engagement and thereby to uphold conventional views of the mode as inherently asocial. My critical object thus approximates what was once called "high Romantic lyricism": poems that feature an autobiographical and often solitary or self-absorbed speaker whose subjectivity is often elaborated via the processes of remembrance and meditation and poems that emphasize the speaker's affinity for natural surroundings and interest in the possibilities of transcendence.[2] My central claim is that these qualities need not add up to a familiar account of a Romantic lyricism in retreat from the social into the self and the aesthetic. This kind of reassessment was spurred by my sense that, in a field newly rich with a variety of writers and genres, Romantic lyricism has become an antiquated critical object, a synecdoche for an older version of the period that featured from four to six canonical poets and a handful of lyric poems. In criticism of the period, Romantic lyricism is frequently referred to as a kind of shorthand for the most conservative impulses of canonical Romanticism. The mode has been characterized almost allegorically, as embodying in poetic form certain tenets that once defined our view of the period's literary production: a solitary, implicitly masculine poet alienated from his social surroundings, looking inward and upward (in Frye's model), into a personal past and beyond a quotidian realm.

Some of the freshest insights into Romantic lyricism have been provided by recent attention to noncanonical poets. A number of critics have reapproached Romantic lyricism by defining a variety of lyrical practices as alternative to a canonical (often Wordsworthian) model, and thus one brand of "high Romantic lyricism" no longer dominates the critical imagination of the period's lyric poetry; we now have a vivid sense of the vast output of lyric poetry in this era. This panoramic view is being gradually but dramatically articulated by a number of critics in the wake of the field's early feminist arguments, which influentially gestured toward a field of women's poetry waiting to be remembered, studied, and theorized.[3] Working-class poets like Clare, too, receive increasing attention. Yet even though the field seems newly populated by varied lyric practices, key assumptions about Romantic lyricism remain intact.[4] My study participates in this ongoing effort to reimagine Romantic lyricism in the aftermath of these challenges to the once narrow canon of Romantic lyricism. I would, however, situate my project in the next stage of this reevaluation of the canon: my aim is to rethink canonical paradigms not only because they have excluded so many poets but also because they have trained our focus on canonical figures in limiting ways. An adequate reassessment of Romantic lyricism requires not only including poets ignored in conventional paradigms but also rethinking those paradigms and in order to reread canonical poets. Thus, I return to Wordsworth by reading him alongside three noncanonical contemporaries—Charlotte Smith, Dorothy Wordsworth, and John Clare—who shed light on each other's and on Wordsworth's poetic concerns and strategies.

William Wordsworth assumes an important role in this study precisely because he is still a key figure in definitions and debates about Romantic lyricism. His preeminence in defining the mode began in the collaborative relationship with Coleridge, with the latter's vexed and painful relinquishment of the role of poet in favor of Wordsworth's rising star. Abrams gives Coleridge precedence in developing the "greater Romantic lyric" in "Structure and Style," but it is Wordsworth to whom Abrams (in *Natural Supernaturalism*) and his successors have turned in contesting Romantic lyricism. As Jerome McGann explains in his landmark reimagining of Abrams's "Romanticism," Wordsworth's "works—like his position in the Romantic Movement—are normative and, in every sense, exemplary."[5] It is important not to leave Wordsworthian lyricism intact as a canonical monolith against which to define different brands of lyricism, for to be "alternative" is still to be excluded from centers of definitional power. My aim in rethinking Romantic lyricism without reinscribing a center and periphery distinction is to introduce noncanonical writers more fully into our view of the period while allowing those writers to render canonical lyrics markedly less familiar. When William Wordsworth is read within a diverse field of the period's lyric practices—a field that includes Smith as an acknowledged predecessor, Dorothy Wordsworth as a well-positioned contemporary, and Clare as an inheritor of a Wordsworthian poetics—his lyricism looks far more heterogeneous than canonical paradigms of Romantic lyricism have suggested. Together, the four writers in this study span the development of Romantic lyricism, from the late eighteenth century to the early Victorian era, and reflect a range of the period's lyric practices: canonical and noncanonical; male and female; and landed gentry, middle class, and working class.

Chapter 1 undertakes my study's first aim: to chart the gradual, often contentious development of a canonical view of Romantic lyricism, beginning with William Wordsworth's own shifting definitions and moving toward a Romantic new historicism richly informed by deconstruction, especially in the work of Marjorie Levinson and Alan

Liu. These critics have described the ideological workings of some of the period's canonized lyrics by theorizing an autobiographical impulse that strives to define an autonomous poetic self, one that transcends quotidian temporality and especially the cause-and-effect of history's narratives.[6] I will argue, however, that their accounts of the lyric overlook the genre's capacity for a more profound ambivalence and discount its pursuit of less-otherworldly aims. After outlining the contours of these prominent debates about Romantic lyricism, I turn to the task of developing an account of the mode as a popular poetic vehicle in the period for multiple and often complex treatments of both personal and social concerns. In doing so, I draw on Benjamin's historical materialism to incorporate a more skeptical account of the workings of subjectivity than has generally informed definitions of Romantic lyricism. Benjamin's emphasis on the imbrication of social experience and memory informs my argument against a conventional equation of the poet's act of recollection with a retreat from a political present to a personal past.

Chapter 2 charts Smith's discovery that the most introspective lyric poetry can be a compelling vehicle for social critique. In *Elegiac Sonnets*, her autobiographical poet's absorption in private sorrows operates with a theatrical dynamic to engage reading audiences in the substance of her meditations, which shift repeatedly and easily between personal and social dilemmas. Because the period's more introspective lyrics rarely address readers directly, it has been largely assumed that the poet-reader relationship is peripheral to the mode's workings. Smith's sonnets demonstrate how an autobiographical speaker could generate a cult of personality, which might then be employed for social topics. Smith's striking popular success demonstrates how lyric poems may captivate readers and respond to social themes precisely by enhancing a feature often deemed to preclude the speaker's awareness of such concerns: that figure's turn away from readers in mournful contemplation of personal sorrows. Smith shows how, when the poet is a familiar figure from a tradition of sensibility—an abandoned mother—even the most contemplative lyric poetry becomes politically inflected. Her sympathetic self-portrait in the sonnets won partisans to whom she would later make her case for other social sufferers, including French émigrés. In *The Emigrants*,

Smith publicly identifies her poet with the persons arriving on her native Sussex shores as fellow exiles, thereby lending them some of the sympathetic appeal that she had garnered for herself.

Chapter 3 reads the early development of a canonical model of Romantic lyricism in William Wordsworth's career, beginning with his investigation in *Lyrical Ballads* of a lyric poetics that might win readers receptive to his poetic "experiments" with the scenes and events of rural working-class existence and the poet's emotional and reflective responses to them. I outline how this optimistic venture into the literary marketplace was followed by his gradual substitution of an ideal, transhistorical "People" for the all too present reading "Public" that he had failed to find in sufficient numbers, an exchange formally announced in the 1815 Essay, Supplementary to the Preface. I focus on Wordsworth's central role in producing a canonical model of Romantic lyricism drawn largely from his poems, from his prose criticism, and from readings of his career. According to Frye's canonical account of a poet happily unaware and independent of the literary marketplace, Wordsworth arrives at his mature poetic form in the lyricism of "Tintern Abbey" and *The Prelude*, poems characterized by introspection turned to psychological maturity. Yet *Lyrical Ballads* testifies to Wordsworth's early confidence in the lyric's potential both for engaging readers and for treating social themes, and I argue for the vexed persistence of this faith in the lyric's rhetorical capacity long after the optimistic predictions of this collaborative venture were first made.

Chapter 4 focuses on Dorothy Wordsworth's perceptive and instructive treatment in her prose works and letters of the implications of the poet's dependence on reading audiences in an increasingly anonymous literary marketplace. She helps to crystallize a critical understanding of the rhetorical potential of Romantic lyricism simply by assuming that it is operative, and therefore an object for investigation and concern. In the *Alfoxden Journal* and *Grasmere Journals*, *The Narrative of George and Sarah Green*, and in letters articulating her reasons against publishing her own works, Dorothy Wordsworth fosters an understanding of the liabilities of the lyric stance with which she experimented along with her brother and Coleridge. By participating in William's career, even as she considered publishing her own works, she develops a sharp sense of the costs of a lyric poetics that foregrounds the poet: capitalizing on the personal appeal of an autobiographical speaker also subjects that figure to public scrutiny, which constitutes a kind of exposure particularly risky for women writers and male writers who were dependent for their primary income on literary production. She also recognizes that she would put not only herself at risk: in deciding against publication of the *Narrative*, she considers the submission of impoverished rural scenes and their inhabitants to the curiosity and aesthetic pleasure of middle- and upper-class reading audiences. She is thus quite wary of the same rhetorical potential that Clare embraces in order to make a case against enclosure: its facility in presenting natural scenes to reading audiences with a persuasive immediacy underwritten by the writer's personal responses to those scenes.

Clare's lyric poems demonstrate how an aspect of Romantic lyricism generally assumed to preclude its capacity for social engagement might address the volatile issue of parliamentary enclosure. Chapter 5 describes how his speaker's intense identification with his natural surroundings in many of his poems constitutes not an exclusion of social concerns, but rather a furthering of Clare's case against enclosure. Unlike William Wordsworth, whose descriptions of natural scenes are generally more evocative than empirical, Clare emphasizes the particular and the local in order to register a pressing awareness of those scenes and thereby to protest their destruction. After establishing this poetic strategy in poems such as "Helpstone" and "Remembrances," Clare turns this poetic strategy upon himself in the wake of his perceived neglect by patrons, friends, and readers—and the onset of insanity. Several important late poems and prose fragments take the poet as the object of his own meditations, in an effort to preserve a stable sense of self that was jeopardized by the obscurity that followed his initial literary success and by the increasing mental deterioration of his last thirty years.

My first chapter examines the development of a canonical understanding of Romantic lyricism that, for a long time, kept Clare on the field's margins. We have been hampered by a persistent desire for a single, definitional key to understanding a lyric mode that has been so closely associated with the period's central mythologies. The rich, fraught history of these critical efforts can now provide valuable insights into the mode's uses. A legacy of sharp disagreements about the nature of Romantic lyricism proves instructive about the mode's rhetorical power. For the impassioned tenor that has long characterized debates about Romantic lyricism testifies to just how much is at stake in the mode's "eloquence."

Acknowledgments

In writing this book, I have acquired that rare kind of debt which is a pleasure both to recall and publicly to acknowledge. U. C. Knoepflmacher and Esther Schor were this study's first readers; their early responses continued to inform its progress even as it assumed a new shape. Susan J. Wolfson has generously shared with me, as with many other students of Romanticism, the benefit of her encyclopedic knowledge of the field's critical history and her keen understanding of poetic form.

This study represents in part a continuation of inquiries begun in the classrooms of Daniel Kiefer and K. K. Collins and then sustained in years since as friends and colleagues. John Shoptaw's course in Lyric Theory at Princeton University laid some of the groundwork for inquiries pursued here.

Both this book and the process of completing it owe far more than will readily be apparent to conversations that ranged well beyond Romantic lyricism with Anne-Lise François, Jenna Hayward, Allan Hepburn, and Ginger Strand. Writing this book would have been a much poorer experience without the seemingly limitless resources of Robert L. Mack's literary knowledge and humor, and his unerring and immensely humane sense of perspective.

I have been fortunate in finding as readers for various portions of the book Stephen C. Behrendt, Bridget Keegan, Zachary Leader,

Harriet Kramer Linkin, and Eric Robinson. My readers for SUNY Press provided detailed, engaged, and thoroughly helpful responses. Among my colleagues at Madison who have shared their time and critical insights are Robert S. Baker, Bruce Burgett, Heather Dubrow, Gordon N. Hutner, Lynn Keller, Jacques Lezra, Eric Rothstein, Jonathan Veitch, Howard D. Weinbrot, and Joseph Wiesenfarth. Several colleagues at Madison provided even more. During the period when I wrote much of the book, I benefited immeasurably by having Susan Stanford Friedman as both "official" mentor and unofficial source of inspiration. Dale M. Bauer was, first, a guiding force during an early, crucial reimagining of the book's argument. As a different book emerged, she contributed to that process her unmatched energy, her editorial astuteness, and her rare sense of friendship. Susan David Bernstein has been no less than a sustaining presence. She provided throughout both thoughtful and timely readings of much of the manuscript and also her own fine example of critical circumspection.

This study began during a summer's research in England supported by a Donald and Mary Hyde Short-Term Fellowship for Research Abroad. At Madison, I have received several summers' support to complete the book from the Graduate School Research Committee. The Department of Rare Books and Special Collections at Princeton University Library granted permission to use as illustrations two engravings from the eighth edition of Charlotte Smith's *Elegiac Sonnets*. I am indebted as well to the University of Wisconsin's Memorial Library, and particularly to Jill Rosenshield and Yvonne Schofer.

The University Press of Kentucky has allowed me to reprint a portion of chapter 2, which appeared in *Romanticism and Women Poets: Opening the Doors of Reception*. Both the collection's editors, Harriet Kramer Linkin and Stephen C. Behrendt, and the volume's two readers responded to the essay in ways that in turn helped me to reshape the chapter. I am grateful both to James Peltz and Bernadine Dawes at SUNY Press for making the publication process efficient and productive.

My greatest debts have also been the most sustaining; it is predictable Romantic logic that they would prove hardest to articulate. For once I will simply borrow one of the period's literary conventions—that of the ineffable—without interrogating it, and dedicate this book to my parents, Isabel and Jay, and to my brother Jay. Chad L. Edgar has been at once the best reader and engaged colleague, and the most constant companion that I could have desired.

Standard References

Unless otherwise noted, quotations from Charlotte Smith's poems, notes, and prefaces are from *The Poems of Charlotte Smith*, ed. Stuart Curran (New York: Oxford University Press, 1993). Quotations from William Wordsworth's poems and notes to them in *Lyrical Ballads* are from *Lyrical Ballads, and Other Poems, 1797–1800*, ed. James Butler and Karen Green (Ithaca: Cornell University Press, 1992). Quotations from his prose works are from *The Prose Works of William Wordsworth*, ed. W. J. B. Owen and Jane Worthington Smyser, 3 vols. (Oxford: Clarendon Press, 1974).

All quotations from the letters of William and Dorothy Wordsworth are from *The Letters of William and Dorothy Wordsworth*, ed. Ernest de Selincourt, 2d ed., vol. 1: *The Early Years, 1787–1805*, revised by Chester L. Shaver (Oxford: Clarendon Press, 1967). Vol. 2: *The Middle Years, Part I, 1806–1811*, revised by Mary Moorman, 1969. Vol. 4: *The Later Years, Part I, 1821–1828*, revised by Alan G. Hill, 1978. Vol. 5: *The Later Years, Part II, 1829–1834*, revised by Alan G. Hill, 1979. Vol. 6: *The Later Years, Part III, 1835–1839*, revised by Alan G. Hill, 1982. Text and notes refer to this series as *Wordsworth Letters*, followed by the volume number and page number.

For the sake of clarity, I have sometimes cited Dorothy Wordsworth's prose works parenthetically by the following abbreviations.

Quotations from the *Alfoxden Journal (AJ)* and *Grasmere Journals (GJ)* are from, respectively, Mary Moorman's *Journals of Dorothy Wordsworth*, 2d ed. (Oxford: Oxford University Press, 1971) and Pamela Woof's *The Grasmere Journals* (Oxford: Oxford University Press, 1993). Quotations from *George and Sarah Green: A Narrative (N)*, are from Ernest de Selincourt's edition (Oxford: Clarendon Press, 1936). Within the body of the text, I refer to the *Narrative* by its more familiar title, *The Narrative of George and Sarah Green.*

All quotations from John Clare's poems are from the following editions. *The Early Poems of John Clare, 1804–1822*, ed. Eric Robinson and David Powell, 2 vols. (Oxford: Clarendon Press, 1989). *The Later Poems of John Clare, 1837–1864*, ed. Eric Robinson and David Powell, 2 vols. (Oxford: Clarendon Press, 1984). *John Clare*, ed. Eric Robinson and David Powell, The Oxford Authors (Oxford: Oxford University Press, 1984). Copyright Eric Robinson 1996, 1989, 1985, 1984. Reproduced by permission of Curtis Brown Ltd., London. Quotations from Clare's letters are from *The Letters of John Clare*, ed. Mark Storey (Oxford: Clarendon Press, 1985).

ONE

The History of an Aura: Romantic Lyricism and the Millennium that Didn't Come

Poetry and eloquence are both alike the expression or uttering forth of feeling. But if we may be excused the seeming affectation of the antithesis, we should say that eloquence is *heard*, poetry is *over*heard. Eloquence supposes an audience; the peculiarity of poetry appears to us to lie in the poet's utter unconsciousness of a listener. Poetry is feeling confessing itself to itself, in moments of solitude, and bodying itself forth in symbols which are the nearest possible representations of the feeling in the exact shape in which it exists in the poet's mind. Eloquence is feeling pouring itself forth to other minds, courting their sympathy, or endeavoring to influence their belief, or move them to passion or to action.

—John Stuart Mill, "What is Poetry?" (1833)

In 1833, John Stuart Mill described his ideal poet, a portrait that, this book argues, has never been sufficiently revised, a circumstance that testifies to Mill's "eloquence" and to our investment in poets who lack it. Mill's grand gesture of severing poetry from eloquence inaugurates a critical history of divorcing lyricism from rhetorical—and by extension, social—concerns. Eloquence—as a rhetorical strategy—betrays a desire for intervention by moving auditors to feeling, to thought, and sometimes to action. Mill's distinction is immensely important to subsequent definitions of Romantic lyricism, since to divide eloquence from poetry isolates the poet from an audience and from social engagement. Mill, of course, was not alone in insisting that the poet is recognizable by the quality of intense introspection.[1] But his claim has been particularly influential for twentieth-century critics of Romanticism, informing prominent paradigms by Northrop Frye and M. H. Abrams. Important vestiges of these critics' tenacious models have in turn survived dramatic

1

changes in critical approaches and assumptions: thoroughly critiqued by feminist and Romantic new historicist critics, an emphasis on disinterestedness and transcendence continues to haunt critical accounts of the mode. For despite sharp disagreements about the political and ethical import of the aesthetic solace that the mode is said to provide, critics have generally agreed on a series of equations that define the form: solitary = asocial, sincere = antitheatrical, introspective = disengaged. This chapter addresses the limitations of models based on antithetical characteristics, first, by questioning their implicit claims of a capable subjectivity, and second, by considering the mode's potential for social engagement by situating poems in the specific contexts of their composition, publication, and reception.

I do not claim that there are not reactionary strains in many of the period's lyric poems, nor do I question that Romantic lyricism, with its focus on interiority, may facilitate a withdrawal into the self, away from social scenes. Rather, I contend that these impulses are rarely pure, and, moreover, that they should not be associated with any one poetic mode. I argue instead for a recognition of the range of impulses—emotional, psychological, and political—of which Romantic lyricism is capable, and for a keener critical sense of its strong rhetorical appeal. This view requires a more circumspect understanding of a mode that has traditionally inspired impassioned critical responses, and thus encouraged sharply and polemically defined canonical models. As Mill's definitions make clear, paradigms of Romantic lyricism have always comprised more than formal features, or even a set of common practices: they have encoded a certain view of the period, a version associated with a poetics of privacy, which is now understood to be fundamental to the Romantic ideology. Canonical models of Romantic lyricism have been an important site for contesting approaches to the field. The result has been a certain lack of critical circumspection that has rendered definitions of the mode increasingly inflexible. For Abrams's candid acknowledgment of his own identification with the Romantic poets was followed by the demystifications of a generation of new historical critics who wanted to distinguish themselves from Abrams's generation, and so from the poets themselves. Jerome McGann describes his new historical project as motivated by the conviction that "the scholarship and criticism of Romanticism and its works are dominated by a Romantic Ideology, by an uncritical absorption in Romanticism's own self-representations."[2] This critique has been salient in disrupting an identificatory strain in Romanticist criticism, but it also imposes a model of counter- or dis-identification that is haunted by a similar impulse to advocacy. In the wake of this successful new historical critique, we can now afford a less polemical approach to the period's poets and poems.

Even as new historicism has critiqued the ideological implications of a poetics of interiority and transcendence codified in Abrams's model, the terms of that critique have ironically reinforced an equation of a poetic mode with these extraformal qualities. The strictness of canonical paradigms has created something of a crisis in the wake of a broadening of the Romantic canon to include women writers and other marginalized figures, such as John Clare. Their greater prominence has made the prescriptive nature of conventional paradigms of the mode seem even more narrowly and polemically defined to reflect a particular view of the field. It is a cliché that Romanticism is concerned with psychological subtlety, yet formal paradigms have not adequately reflected the implications of this critical commonplace. New historicism complicated Abrams's influential model of the "greater Romantic lyric" by revealing political betrayal to be the underside of a desire for transcendence. But our approaches to Romantic lyricism will only be sufficiently complex when they comprehend the full range of responses—political and psychological—possible for a form closely associated with subjectivity. A more circumspect view of Romantic lyricism would acknowledge its capacity for solipsism and sympathetic identification, privatization and historical consciousness.

Defining lyricism has been an inexact science for good reason, since the mode's uses vary tremendously between, and within, different periods and cultures. Critics attempting to define the lyric have often settled for succinctness, by focusing on a quality deemed central, such as brevity or a historical association with music.[3] Yet there has been a greater consensus on Romantic lyricism, because it has so often been defined by extraformal qualities associated with a "spirit of the age." Romantic lyricism has seemed tied to an older version of the period, even as canonical, periodic, and generic boundaries have been expanded and their heuristic uses challenged. Thus W. R. Johnson's valuable 1982 argument about the lyric—he reminds us that its roots in Greek and Latin poems are rhetorical, and thereby social—pointedly excludes the Romantic lyric: "The poet has removed himself (or has been removed) from a world into a private vision of nature in which he sees himself reflected." In his view, Romantic lyricism actually heralds "the death of lyric" as an engaged genre.[4] Recent treatments of the lyric in other literary fields presume the mode's openness to the social world, while the public and performative aspects of Romantic lyricism have received little such attention.[5]

Recently, there have been calls for rethinking a prevailing view of Romantic lyricism.[6] Yet why revise this model when the field's periodic, generic, and canonical boundaries have also been challenged? First, questioning received models of one of the period's key modes can help further to obscure canonical distinctions between writers. And there are other reasons for continuing to talk about "Romantic lyricism." The history of critical definitions of the mode is highly instructive about critical history itself: because Romantic lyricism has been viewed so obdurately as the period's poetic "norm," accounts of it have long been charged sites for interpretive debates. Generational continuities and points of contention alike are rendered particularly visible in feminist and new historicist inquiries into the gender and social politics of Romanticism, partly because so many of these critics have self-consciously situated their models in relation to earlier accounts. For example, Frye explicitly incorporates Mill's description of lyric poetry as "*over*heard" into his portrait of the poet turning his back on an audience, and Abrams acknowledges his use of Mill's premium on "feeling" in his definition of the "greater Romantic lyric." In her treatment of Wordsworth's "Ode: Intimations of Immortality," Marjorie Levinson discusses her uses of Abrams's paradigm, elaborating how his focus on subjectivity informs her new historical account of the ideology of the Wordsworthian self. The specifics of these continuities are instructive. Yet the most important lesson of these generational debates is that their product has been, ironically, a remarkable consensus in defining Romantic lyricism's key impulses.

This prominent tradition of critical self-reflexivity also points, however, toward the means of its own critique. Abrams himself opens the way to reconsidering his immensely influential paradigm by acknowledging its investment with specific biographical and historical meaning. In a rare and candid autobiographical aside in *Natural Supernaturalism*, he registers an identification with Wordsworth's despair after the French Revolution. Abrams's aside is a frank and generous recognition of how our critical understandings of the mode have been shaped by the pressures of historical incident and personal exigency. He aligns his own experience of acute political disappointment with Wordsworth's, via the mediating figure of W. H. Auden. He cites Auden's "New Year Letter of 1940":

> Herschel Baker has rightly said that Wordsworth's *Prelude* recorded 'the spiritual biography of his generation.' Auden, writing in 1940, reminds us that it also anticipated remarkably the spiritual biography of Auden's own generation, and mine:
> We hoped; we waited for the day
> The State would wither clean away,
> Expecting the Millennium
> That theory promised us would come,
> It didn't.

We can hear in Abrams's paradigmatic account of Wordsworth's crisis an echo of similar reckonings made by a postwar generation of critics: "The great Romantic works were not written at the height of revolutionary hope but out of the experience of partial or total disenchantment with the revolutionary promise."[7]

Focusing on Abrams's generation, E. P. Thompson extends Abrams's point to speculate upon a critical generation's identification with the Romantic poets: "The glib comparisons rise up, and they lie beneath the surface when unstated." These parallels include "[t]he French and Russian revolutions; the Coalitions and N.A.T.O.; the Spanish insurrection and Hungary, 1956; Godwinism and Marxism." Thompson concedes that, "[s]crupulously examined, most of these comparisons break down," yet I agree with him that suggestive "parallels remain."[8] In the case of Romantic lyricism, Abrams's and Thompson's metacritical analyses draw attention to how successive generations of critics sought the qualities of disinterestedness and transcendence associated with the mode. They have thereby confirmed the value of the mode's aesthetic consolations for political disappointments. Thus, models of Romantic lyricism have encouraged a particular view of Wordsworth's turn from political activism: the advent of his mature lyricism is viewed as ratifying the poet's substitution of imaginative for political concerns.

The cost of equating Romantic lyricism with a politics of disengagement has been an understanding of the mode's facility for registering diverse and ambivalent political impulses. This price applies particularly to Wordsworth, who has been the key exemplar of Mill's, Abrams's, and Romantic new historicists' models. Because a generation of critics identified strongly with his political disillusionment and focused on Wordsworth's rejection of revolutionary hopes, we have lost sight of the complexity of his relinquishment of radical sympathies in the wake of the Terror and French imperialism. Writing in 1969, Thompson claims: "So obsessed was a recent generation of critics with similar experiences of disenchantment in their own time" that we have focused on Wordsworth's doubts and overlooked his continued "affirmation" of political ideals that may have lasted until the end of the Napoleonic Wars.[9] Although contemporary Romantic criticism is alert to the ideological conflicts, contradictions, and instabilities of any political stance, that poststructuralist and postmodern awareness has, oddly, worked to reify expectations of Romantic lyricism as inherently antimaterialist.

Examining the canonical definitions of Wordsworth, Mill, and Abrams within the contexts of their careers discovers a suggestive congruence: each turned to the work of defining the mode in the wake of disillusionment with political activism. Recovering from very different social crises, each of these critics follows a path from political engagement, to disillusion, to a desire for an aesthetic remedy to sociohistorical trauma. Within these contexts, the poetic form each associates with a pure, aesthetic arena comes to seem less transcendent, and more embedded in particular moments in the lives of influential poets and critics. Abrams's candor provides one answer to why definitions of Romantic lyricism have been so sharply contested: the mode's association with the transcendence of partisan strife, human suffering, and the constraints of particular historical moments have held a strong personal appeal to some of its key critics. Recognizing these biohistorical contexts for canonical definitions of Romantic lyricism does not discredit them, for of course the broader lesson is that all such explanatory models are historically contingent. Yet in the case of Romantic lyricism, the relations between critical paradigms and their historical contexts are particularly instructive, since there are crucial intersections between the historical exigencies that inform these definitions and the claims these models make about lyric poetry's relations to history.

In the case of Romantic lyricism, this phenomenon extends back to Mill, who influenced Abrams's definitions. Mill reports first reading Wordsworth's poems in the autumn of 1828, after a psychological breakdown and depression. He describes the crisis as a loss of faith in his earlier determination "to be a reformer of the world." By age nineteen, Mill's activities included writing for and editing the *Westminster Review* (established by his father James Mill in order to counter what he deemed the too-complacent Whig politics of the *Edinburgh Review*); organizing and participating in debating societies engaged with social issues; and compiling and editing Jeremy Bentham's monumental *Rationale of Judicial Evidence*. He recalls: "This did very well for several years, during which the general improvement going on in the world and the idea of myself as engaged with others in struggling to promote it, seemed to fill up an interesting and animated existence." He says that in 1826, when he was twenty years old, "I awakened from this as from a dream." In the wake of his collapse he developed a new concern with "the internal culture of the individual." Wordsworth's poems "seemed to be the very culture of the feelings, which I was in quest of":

> In them I seemed to draw from a source of inward joy, of sympathetic and imaginative pleasure, which could be shared in by all human beings; which had no connexion with struggle or imperfection, but would be made richer by every improvement in the physical or social condition of mankind. . . I needed to be made to feel that there was real, permanent happiness in tranquil contemplation. Wordsworth taught me this, not only without turning away from, but with a greatly increased interest[,] in the common feelings and common destiny of human beings.[10]

In reading the 1815 *Poems*, Mill discovered a new, less public and less engaged relationship to contemporary sociopolitical events. He was able to remain aloof from "struggle or imperfection" while retaining a humanitarian interest in the "physical or social condition." Mill models this new stance on the poet, exemplified by Wordsworth.

The humanist politics that Mill's Wordsworth embodies drew fire on canonical paradigms of Romantic lyricism from critics disturbed by Mill's premium on disinterestedness. To glean lessons about his "poetry," we need not take entirely at face value Mill's account of his sudden disaffection from radical politics and conversion to a culture of feeling. His retrospective narrative surely simplifies an ambiguous and traumatic transition in his career, and his critics and biographers have speculated variously upon its causes and its psychological content. Yet Mill's rehearsal of a turn away from activism to a humanist aesthetics directly informs his definition of poetry as comprised of sensory and emotional experience, and as such divorced from the austere Utilitarian politics in which he had participated. Poetry and politics seem antithetical at a moment of personal crisis for Mill, the moment at which he defines poetry as the opposite of an irony he had lived: Utilitarianism with passionate designs on the social world. Poetry, in contrast, derives power from emotion yet may remain disinterested.

Before turning to feminist and new historical critiques of this familiar model of Romantic lyricism, I want to consider the cost of giving up its persuasive account of the relations between poetics and politics. The persistence of Mill's precepts—whether in the form of their absorption into later definitions or as the catalyst for counterparadigms—indicates not only how high the critical stakes have been in defining the mode, but also something of the rhetorical power of the mode itself. The mode's conventional association with a transcendence of historical catastrophe has made it available to a surprising variety of aesthetic and political uses. For instance, Sharon Cameron finds in lyricism's drive to divorce itself from quotidian temporality a powerful poetic response to the inevitability of mortality.[11] Theodor Adorno launches a very different defense. He confirms that lyricism is the genre of the individual apart from society, but he claims this detachment as the site of political resistance. Adorno praises "[t]he lyric spirit's idiosyncratic opposition to the superior power of material things," an opposition that is "a form of reaction to the reification of the world," and, more particularly, to capitalism's conforming pressures on the individual. He exploits a suggestion implicit in canonical definitions: that the mode is "pure" because untainted by social interaction. Adorno evokes a familiar definition of the "poetic work" as "something opposed to society, something wholly individual," in order to argue that "the more heavily the situation weighs upon it, the more firmly the work resists it by refusing to submit to anything heteronomous and constituting itself solely in accordance with its own laws." The poet's detachment—"*sein Abstand*"—is necessary in order to imagine another world "*in der es anders wäre*" (in which things would be different). Here the utopianism associated with lyricism has an explicitly political valence. Adorno's notion that the most private language offers the greatest power of resistance enables him to turn Frye's poet into a man of the people: Baudelaire, Adorno claims, was "truer to the masses toward whom he turned his tragic, arrogant mask than any poor-people's poetry."[12]

Adorno's eloquent defense of the lyric demonstrates the advantage of retaining canonical models: the critic who adopts them gleans some of the auratic power with which the mode itself has been invested. Even critiques of Romantic lyricism have profited from the emphatic tone of canonical definitions: by exposing the ideological content of this talismanic poetics, the critic claims a role in what has been a high-profile agon, from William Wordsworth to the present. The Romantic lyric has long been a desirable critical object, in part, because a significance has attached to the task of treating it, as one of the field's key terms. Defining the mode once meant, in effect, defining Romanticism, and perhaps under this weight, criticism of the Romantic lyric has frequently displayed an impassioned tenor which is often said to characterize the mode itself. I advocate instead a less "eloquent," but more variegated account of Romantic lyricism that recognizes its vagaries, its vexed aims, and its mixed impulses.

One of my main questions in this chapter is how to use the critical history I have begun to sketch in order better to understand the period's vast output of lyric poetry, including its canonical poems.

My first concern is how a consensus—albeit fraught and contentious—developed about Romantic lyricism. I am interested in how the critical history of Romantic lyricism has preserved the mode's aura—the vestiges of certain extraformal qualities that are culturally constructed, yet apparently natural. Walter Benjamin describes the "aura" of the work of art in the age of mechanical reproduction as a quality that adhered to the work of art despite the development of technological processes that could reproduce that work and thus diminish what gave it aesthetic power: a sense of uniqueness, authenticity, and the artist's presence.[13] These qualities have long been associated with Romantic lyricism, and like the work of art before mechanical reproduction, the mode has been associated with a transcendence of immediate contexts. This aura is derived not from any actual belief in transcendence by poets or by critics, but rather from a sense that the lyric poet is aloof from quotidian concerns, a detachment necessary for the understandings, resolutions, and consolations that are the products of reflection and recollection. The history of Romantic lyricism has largely been the history of that aura. The narrowness of this definition long helped to keep the Romantic canon small and also produced a prescriptive and teleological reading of the mode's tropes. Solitariness, introspection, and remembrance seemed to add up to a transcendence of material concerns and local contexts. As a result, poets whose works do not fit this paradigm continue to face the question of whether or not they are "Romantic."

Since an enormous amount has been written about Romantic lyricism, I want to specify the strains of this critical history relevant to my argument. I am concerned with how the quality of inwardness became paramount, how the mode came to be defined by what might be called a poetics of privacy. One of my main concerns is how definitions of Romantic lyricism resound, either explicitly or implicitly, in broader critical debates about the construction of the Romantic poet and poetry: these models have been central to feminist critiques of the gendered construction of the poet, and to new historical investigations of the ideological impulses of Romanticism.[14] I begin with Mill's 1833 definitions, which persuasively describe an ideal poetry, devoid of precisely the kind of rhetorical impetus that characterizes his own critical prose.

Mill's great rhetorical maneuver is to make the qualities he assigns to poetry inherent or, to use Clifford Siskin's term, "essential."[15] According to Mill, that which distinguishes poetry from "what is not poetry" is "felt to be fundamental." It is an irrefutable argument because it is not an argument; emotion delineates the parameters of poetry. Mill's circular logic seeks to establish what it claims is already in place—poetry's detachment from the quotidian. He proposes:

> Let us then attempt, in the way of modest inquiry, not to coerce and confine nature within the bounds of an arbitrary definition, but rather to find the boundaries which she herself has set, and erect a barrier round them; not calling mankind to account for having misapplied the word *poetry*, but attempting to clear up to them the conception which they already attach to it, and to bring before their minds as a distinct principle that which, as a vague feeling, has really guided them in their actual employment of the term.

With this sleight of hand, Mill generates a sense of critical discovery. His statement of purpose defines his own role as uncovering foundations rather than building definitions. The critic has only to locate nature's delineations, a task made simpler because his audience already instinctively senses the "boundaries" that nature has established. "Feeling" confirms what the critic need only translate into terms less "vague." The critic's role is minimal since poetry speaks for itself, and the receptive reader listens. Mill explains that

> the word "poetry" *does* import something quite peculiar in its nature, something which may exist in what is called prose as well as in verse, something which does not even require the instrument of words, but can speak through those other audible symbols called musical sounds, and even through the visible ones, which are the language of sculpture, painting, and architecture; all this, as we believe, is and must be felt, though perhaps indistinctly, by all upon whom poetry in any of its shapes produces any impression beyond that of tickling the ear.[16]

Wordsworth's influence is evident in Mill's claim that poetry can exist in prose; it is not a form, but a quality, almost an essence. Mill's

vocabulary renders poetry unique—there is "something quite peculiar," and inherent, in its "nature." His ventriloquizing of poetry lends
a sense of the mode as having an integrity of its own. Giving poetry
this independence is an important step in Mill's effort to remove it
from a delimiting engagement with its social contexts, while retaining its audience. The "peculiar quality" of poetry is that it can be
aloof and still "move" readers. Its tangential relationship to everyday existence is crucial to poetry's power to reach an audience without a compromising desire to influence it to any particular end. In
order to negotiate a position for poetry close enough to a quotidian
world to be relevant to its concerns and yet untainted by them, poetry must be disinterested. Poetry's integrity would be diminished by
ulterior motives, so Mill must distinguish poetry from another kind
of language that also "moves" readers, and that he terms "eloquence."

Mill's determination to divorce poetry and eloquence requires
characterizing the poet as removed from contemporary social concerns. To claim that a genre is disinterested is less difficult than to
claim that poets have no designs on their readers, so Mill must resort
almost to caricature to hold his point: "Great poets are often prover-
bially ignorant of life." This portrait has proven influential; it echoes
in the new historical critique of the poet's willful ignorance, or repression, of social contexts. The surviving denominator is the poet's
isolation: "All poetry is of the nature of soliloquy." The poet must
have no message to convey, no interest in convincing an audience of
anything: "[W]e should say that eloquence is *heard*, poetry is *over-*
heard." Mill follows his famous remark with the explanation of the
poet's relationship to an audience: "Eloquence supposes an audience;
the peculiarity of poetry appears to us to lie in the poet's utter unconsciousness of a listener." This is a difficult distinction to make, and
Mill spends a large portion of the essay attempting to secure it. Both
the orator and the poet have audiences, but the poet's mode is con-
fessional—it is private and self-reflexive—since feeling necessarily
confesses itself. Poetry "is the natural fruit of solitude and meditation; eloquence, of intercourse with the world." Yet despite the critical effort needed to distinguish the poet's and orator's relations to
their audiences, Mill is certain about what he is excluding from poetry: the poet does not use language to influence others' sympathies,
beliefs, passions, or actions. Poetry is nonpartisan.

Still, in Mill's scheme, poetry must remain close enough to daily experience to speak to it. He does not want to sever poetry from a social world, but rather strictly to define poetry's position in that world. The objects of the poet's attention become catalysts for "emotion" rather than figures of interest in themselves:

If a poet is to describe a lion, he will not set about describing him as a naturalist would, nor even as a traveller would, who was intent upon stating the truth, the whole truth, and nothing but the truth. He will describe him by *imagery*, that is, by suggesting the most striking likenesses and contrasts which might occur to a mind contemplating the lion, in the state of awe, wonder, or terror, which the spectacle naturally excites, or is, on the occasion, supposed to excite. Now this is describing the lion professedly, but the state of excitement of the spectator really. The lion may be described falsely or in exaggerated colors, and the poetry be all the better; but if the human emotion be not painted with the most scrupulous truth, the poetry is bad poetry; i.e. is not poetry at all, but a failure.[17]

In short, we learn more about the poet than the lion; in Mill's model, the lion not only recedes into the background, but is also metamorphosed in the process. The lion's ferocity shrinks in the shadow of the poet's responses to it. Similarly, an audience does not disappear in Mill's account; it is simply irrelevant to the "human emotion" that retains center stage. In this manner, poetry reimagines the world according to a standard of pure feeling, a truth that can move readers because it is of their world and yet innocent of desires to change it. Although this argument has been made, in some variation, for almost all of "Literature," nevertheless the Romantic lyric has often been considered exemplary of the aloofness of the aesthetic from the mundane and the partisan.[18]

Mill's definitions have been reified via restatement, albeit often with new emphases. The adoption of his distinctions by other critics provides an ironic demonstration of Mill's own eloquence. Mill's differentiation of poetry and oratory was augmented, although often with different emphases, by influential successors. Like Mill, Matthew

Arnold was interested in defining Wordsworthian lyricism as exemplary of poetic truth. Arnold's "truth" is, however, not that of the poet's emotional responses, but rather that of nature, which he claims seems almost to write itself in Wordsworth's poems. In his preface to his 1879 edition of *The Poems of Wordsworth*, Arnold characterizes his own valued Wordsworth by defending the poet who "has not had a fair chance before the world." Arnold's answer to what he perceives as a history of underappreciation of Wordsworth is to present to the reading public the lyric poet, for "[h]is best work is in his shorter pieces." In the Wordsworth of the shorter lyrics, Arnold finds "*poetic* truth," which is "as inevitable as Nature herself." Arnold places an emphasis upon the poet's sincerity that would inform Abrams's interest in that quality and in an accompanying characteristic of Romantic lyric poetry, its "expressivity." Arnold proclaims on Wordsworth's behalf, "Nature herself seems, I say, to take the pen out of his hand, and to write for him with her own bare, sheer, penetrating power." He explains that "[t]his arises from two causes: from the profound sincereness with which Wordsworth feels his subject, and also from the profoundly sincere and natural character of his subject itself."[19] Poetry's difference from the orator's eloquence is confirmed to quite different ends in a 1953 lecture delivered by T. S. Eliot and subsequently published as "The Three Voices of Poetry." Eliot, writing not from an admiration of Wordsworth but from a deep suspicion of Romanticism, nevertheless contributes to a familiar portrait of the Romantic poet by separating the "first voice" of poetry, which is "the voice of the poet talking to himself—or to nobody," from the "second," which is "the voice of the poet addressing an audience, whether large or small."[20]

As Mill's tenets were adopted by critics such as Frye and Abrams, they were also tied to formal features of lyricism in general, and to Romantic lyricism in particular. (Although Mill cites Wordsworth in this essay, he uses him as a model for poetry in general.) Frye's definitions of lyricism in his 1957 study, *The Anatomy of Criticism*, are important to a history of Romantic lyricism, primarily because his sketch of the poet is so memorable. There is something almost incongruous about Frye's studied portrait of disinterestedness. His rhetoric surrounding a supposedly antirhetorical form is telling. In a famous instance, Frye augments Mill's portrait of the isolated poet.

Frye defines the lyric as "preeminently the utterance that is overheard," but he goes further than Mill in theatricalizing the poet's
detachment from listeners: "The lyric is the genre in which the poet,
like the ironic writer, turns his back on his audience."[21] An audience
is still present, and the poet aware of it, until the moment of introspection. Frye's theatrical metaphor might seem to compromise the
poet's disinterestedness, since it attributes a performative aspect to
the poet's role. Yet despite his acknowledgment of the auditor's role
in lyric poetry, Frye insists on the lyric's aura, which is rendered almost audible in his account: the mode has a kind of "verbal resonance."[22] While Frye enhances Mill's already "eloquent" definition,
it is Abrams who claims Mill's precepts as Romantic conventions,
and thus produces the field's most influential paradigm of Romantic
lyricism in his 1965 essay, "Structure and Style in the Greater Romantic Lyric."[23]

Eliot, Abrams, and Frye participate in the 1950s in the elaboration of an understanding of the lyric as nonrhetorical, an account
indebted to Mill. These critics do not devise precisely the same set of
qualities; they are in fact describing different things—Eliot's "poetry,"
Frye's "lyric," and Abrams's "greater Romantic lyric." As the precision of this terminology suggests, Abrams defines a poetic form with
a relatively small number of examples; even Keats's odes do not exactly fit its measurements. But the specificity of Abrams's definition is
precisely the quality that secures its importance to subsequent criticism. He gives Romantic lyricism "a local habitation and a name,"
tracing its antecedents to the eighteenth-century loco-descriptive poem,
William Lisle Bowles's sonnets, and seventeenth-century devotional
poems. Most importantly, Abrams links the more abstract qualities
that Mill assigns to poetry to thematic concerns associated with Romanticism. For instance, he associates the lyric's focus on the poet's
subjectivity with a Romantic attraction to natural solitudes: according to Abrams, the natural scene is central to a genre "in which mind
confronts nature and their interplay constitutes the poem."[24] Although
Abrams restricts his definitions to a small number of poems, he so
persuasively makes these local cases that other critics have appropriated his terms, and thus the characteristics he enumerates have been
extrapolated to Romantic lyricism, more broadly construed.

Thus Wordsworth is not the only figure to have been canonized and subsequently critiqued in debates about Romantic lyricism; as the primary architect of twentieth-century understandings of the mode, Abrams gained a similar centrality. His model became associated with a particular postwar moment in the academy and thus was invested with another kind of extraformal meaning: the traces of critical debates about the politics of Romantic poetry and literary criticism. Paradigms of Romantic lyricism were reified largely by being contested. Codified by Abrams in his essay on the "greater Romantic lyric," an understanding of the genre as disinterested has survived the field's recent debates about the Romantic canon and the Romantic ideology, although in the process the quality has become weighted quite differently. Abrams's elaboration of the shared features of a handful of poems proved paradigm-making; as the period's "poetic norm," the lyric has been associated with solitariness, introspection, and a desire for transcendence—the antithesis of the social and the quotidian.[25] It has also been implicitly gendered masculine. Romantic lyricism became equated with an "ideology of self," and as such it became the focus of critiques of the gender and social politics of canonical Romanticism.[26] Thus Abrams's model gained an odd afterlife as the object of critique itself, still referred to and contested, yet rendered increasingly inflexible in the process.

Because Abrams's description of his "variety of the longer Romantic lyric" has been incorporated into subsequent debates about Romantic lyricism's politics, his opening description sets the scene for this stage in my inquiry:

Some of the poems are called odes, while the others approach the ode in having lyric magnitude and a serious subject, feelingfully meditated. They present a determinate speaker in a particularized, and usually a localized, outdoor setting, whom we overhear as he carries on, in a fluent vernacular which arises easily to a more formal speech, a sustained colloquy, sometimes with himself or with the outer scene, but more frequently with a silent human auditor, present or absent. The speaker begins with a description of the landscape; an aspect or change of aspect in the landscape evokes a varied but integral process of memory, thought, anticipation, and feeling which remains closely intervolved with the outer scene. In the course of this meditation the lyric speaker achieves an insight, faces up to a tragic loss, comes to a moral decision, or resolves an emotional problem. Often the poem rounds upon itself to end where it began, at the outer scene, but with an altered mood and deepened understanding which is the result of the intervening meditation.[27]

Abrams anchors Mill's quality of detachment by linking it to formal features; it becomes a phase in a structured progression, and central to the work of the "greater Romantic lyric." The landscape prompts the inward turn to meditation, but the external scene is less important than the memories and thoughts evoked, and a hierarchy between poet-subject and natural object is established: "[T]he description is structurally subordinate to the meditation."[28] Abrams is not as concerned as Mill to sever the poet from social interaction (as differentiated by Abrams from overt political action); the poet often sustains a "colloquy" with "a silent human auditor, present or absent." But the remove from "intercourse with the world" that Mill describes is recognizable in Abrams's period of introspection from which the poet emerges "altered." Abrams recasts the detachment from banal concerns, which Mill specifies as "fundamental" to poetry, both as a psychological state and as part of the formal structure of the greater Romantic lyric.

The most influential aspect of Abrams's specialization of the mode has proven to be his psychologizing of it. His effort to codify its apparent formlessness naturalizes the Romantic lyric by basing it on a model of consciousness. The poem ends "when the lyric speaker achieves an insight, faces up to a tragic loss, comes to a moral decision, or resolves an emotional problem." Abrams reinforces Mill's "identification of the lyric with personal, subjective feeling" by establishing what Siskin calls "an ideology of generic essentialism that features the emotive, expressive, and creative lyric."[29] Abrams aligns Romantic lyricism and subjectivity, so that the mode comes to be defined less by formal features than by the formlessness of effusion, the expression of Mill's "feeling."[30] Romantic lyricism is rendered the poetic vehicle for psychological processes: the digressions of recollection and the associative mechanisms of reflection. Eliot provides Abrams with an important precedent by suggesting that "the 'psychic material' tends to create its own form." The result is the lyric's aura, which is related to its association with individuality; according to Eliot, "the eventual form will be to a greater or less degree the form for that one poem and for no other."[31] By implication, the poem will also be peculiar to the individual consciousness that composes it.

The effect on subsequent Romantic criticism of Abrams's equation of lyricism with subjectivity cannot be overestimated. It has particular relevance for new historicism, because Abrams's psychologizing of the form also renders it explicitly humanist. He states his position straightforwardly: "Romantic writers, though nature poets, were humanists above all, for they dealt with the non-human only insofar as it is the occasion for the activity which defines man: thought, the process of intellection."[32] There is certainly a political impetus to Mill's division of poetry from oration, and therefore from a desire to move auditors to action. But Abrams's association of Romantic lyricism with a particular historical moment invests the paradigm with more specific political meaning: he grounds the "greater Romantic lyric" in the aftermath in England of the French Revolution. The "outer scene" obscured by the poet's meditations in Abrams's model is a landscape, but the poet's loss of contact with his surroundings at the moment of reflection is easily politicized, especially when the essay is paired, as it often is, with another published two years earlier, "English Romanticism: The Spirit of the Age" (1963, in a volume edited by Frye). Although Abrams defends the canonical poets from charges of "escapism," his thesis severs poetry from political action: "The great Romantic poems were written not in the mood of revolutionary exaltation but in the later mood of revolutionary disillusionment or despair." Once again, Wordsworth proves exemplary for definitions of Romantic lyricism: Abrams argues that around 1797, the poet "came to see his destiny to lie in spiritual rather than in overt action and adventure."[33]

Abrams is key to the integration of a generic definition into broader critical debates. In *Natural Supernaturalism,* he incorporates the formal properties of the lyric so thoroughly into his larger paradigm of Romanticism that the "greater Romantic lyric" came to be associated with his version of the field. Challenges to Abrams's account of Romanticism—including feminist discussions of the canon and new historical critiques of the Romantic ideology—have typically

accepted his interpretation of the "greater Romantic lyric" in order
to interrogate Romanticism's gender and social politics. The focus of
both debates has been a portrait of the poet as independent of his
surroundings, whether a feminized nature or the French Revolution
and its aftermath. Romantic lyricism has been equated in these discussions with an emphasis on transcendence and a detachment from
local environments. Yet the cost of a strategy of appropriating
Abrams's terms in order to challenge his version of Romanticism has
been the necessity of taking him at his word that the primary impulse
of Romantic lyricism is a withdrawal from political engagement.

Each critical generation since Abrams has built—directly or indirectly—on his suppositions.[34] Levinson addresses the importance of
Abrams to new historical concerns in her landmark essay on the "Intimations Ode." She begins by reading together his essays on the
"greater Romantic lyric" and on the "Spirit of the Age," arguing
that he defines the former as "apolitical":

> The greater lyric—a private meditation born of the speaker's
> nonspecific, existential malaise—reaches articulation through
> his response to a present, particular, and precisely located
> natural scene. The meditation concludes with the production
> of a consolation which is valorized by the private and disin-
> terested character of its motivation and development.[35]

Levinson accepts Abrams's terms so that she may read against the
grain of his definitions. She even emphasizes the qualities he "valo-
rizes"—a premium on privacy and disinterestedness—in order to bring
out the political content of his paradigm. In Levinson's account, the
Romantic lyric formally embodies the Romantic ideology, "one of
whose chief illusions is the triumph of the inner life over the outer
world."[36] In the dialectic between subject and object, the former wins
out by lyricism's processes of internalization. Thus the relationship
between poet and environment is not only hierarchical, as in Abrams's
model, it is actually antagonistic. The lyric dissociates the poet from

history by assimilating events in the public realm into private experience; autobiography subsumes the events of history. For the poet, a certain detachment is both cost and profit. According to McGann, whose reading of "Tintern Abbey" exemplifies this critical narrative, "between 1793 and 1798 Wordsworth lost the world merely to gain his own immortal soul."[37] Alan Liu makes the mechanisms of this process explicitly psychogeneric. In his account of Wordsworth's career, the poet begins with the historically responsive genres of loco-descriptive and georgic poetry and then, in the wake of the French Revolution, breaks these forms in order to absorb social history into lyric autobiography. These new historical critiques continue a critical tradition of attributing abstract qualities to poetic form, a critical practice that effectively circumscribes the reading of individual poems by approaching them with a set of expectations about the implications of specific poetic features.

McGann, Levinson, and Liu are likewise faithful to Abrams's model in that they, too, psychologize the mode by describing the processes of reflection and recollection as part of lyricism's ideological machinery. Take, for instance, McGann's view of the lyric poet's acts of reflection: he claims that Wordsworth realizes that "his insight into the life of things" means the "loss of the concrete and particular."[38] In other words, the cost of private insight—the boon in Abrams's model—is in McGann's terms blindness to social surroundings. Levinson and Liu, in particular, adhere to Abrams's conventions in that their treatments of Romantic lyricism are concerned with genre. Both turn the psychogeneric processes he describes into ideological mechanisms for releasing the poet from social commitments. Thus, a new historical vocabulary of repression and denial is deeply indebted to Abrams.

New historical critics of Abrams's Romanticism have also remained true to him in keeping Wordsworth as a central object of critique. Levinson and Liu acknowledge their engagement with Abrams's models, and it is plausible that their efforts to historicize his account of Romanticism require at least a partial acceptance of his terms. Yet historicizing Romanticism and its formal models requires broadening critical attention beyond the exemplary figure of Wordsworth. Canonicity is, after all, part of the Romantic ideology. His centrality has been a formidable obstacle to critics who have wanted to include women and other marginalized writers in Romantic studies, as has the continued persistence of Abrams's model of lyricism as the formal standard against which to measure Wordsworth's contemporaries. As Tilottama Rajan argues, "the New Historicism has so far tended to perpetuate the lyricization of Wordsworth and the consequent attenuation of the canon."[39]

Early feminist treatments of Romanticism explicated the gender ideology of canonical poems and definitions of Romantic lyricism in order to clear a space for women writers. Margaret Homans's foundational critique of Romanticism describes a pervasive paradigm: a male poet whose sense of self is defined in relation to a feminized nature. According to Homans, conventional paradigms establish a sexual poetics and politics by relegating the natural world to the role of catalyst to the poet's meditations. Both new historicist and feminist critics have questioned the nature of the poet's detachment, which requires independence from immediate environments, whether a historical context or a feminized nature. In both critiques, lyricism is characterized by the poet's drive toward transcendence, an impulse that involves disengagement from an "other" associated with mortality, either the traumatic social scenes of the French Revolution and the Terror, or the natural environment. In a conventional view of lyric economy, both social and natural surroundings represent the confines of materiality.

Feminist critics have proposed several solutions to the dilemma posed by paradigms drawn from William Wordsworth and his canonical contemporaries. Homans has a rich history of treating this issue: her argument's progression is evident in her two accounts of Dorothy Wordsworth (which I discuss more fully in chapter 4). Her first response was to preserve for women poets the benefits of Romantic lyricism, as defined by critics such as Abrams. That approach required defending transcendence as a Romantic desire, since "if it is an evasion, it is a splendid one."[40] Meena Alexander similarly confirms a familiar model of Romantic lyricism, but to different ends, in order to privilege women's writing that diverges from it (a position toward which Homans moves in rethinking Dorothy Wordsworth's career).[41] Despite their differing conclusions as to whether women poets should be praised for appropriating or for disavowing masculinist paradigms of Romantic lyricism, both Homans and Alexander continue to define the mode by its transcendence of material contexts; Homans's definition of "the Romantic ideal" is that "the poetical character transcends time and place."[42] Although Alexander reverses the value of such "visionary" poetics from positive to negative, Romantic lyricism remains equated with privatization.

Another feminist approach to the predominance of a model of Wordsworthian lyricism has been to define competing, gendered models of the mode. This strategy recognizes different lyric poetics operative in the period, defined along masculine and feminine lines, determined not by the poet's sex but by the poems' gendered characteristics. Anne Mellor has most thoroughly theorized what a number of critics have suggested: that the period's lyric poems by women writers manifest a number of qualities antithetical to disinterestedness, including an emphasis on the quotidian and on community.[43] Thus, a new category of Romantic lyricism emerges, one that focuses less exclusively on the poet's subjectivity and more on that figure's relations to a social world. This strategy has the heuristic advantage of throwing into sharp relief examples of poems with qualities that have generally disqualified them from sustained critical attention. Moreover, such feminist projects have drawn the contours of a tradition of women's writing built on lines of influence (both between women writers, and between men and women writers) obscured in conventional views of the period.

This kind of work must be supplemented, however, by an inquiry into how well predominant paradigms account for canonical poems; this kind of thoroughgoing reassessment produces critical insights such as that which Susan Wolfson offers about Wordsworth: a critical awareness that "he is not the sure, secure figure of logocentric performance and egocentric confidence ascribed to him in some feminist (and older masculinist) readings of Romanticism."[44] An effort to break down a canonical category of Romantic lyricism in order to recognize other, more frankly engaged lyric poets and poems must be supplemented by a challenge to tenacious assumptions about a lyric mode that does not address its social contexts explicitly.

One of the most significant obstacles to this task is a still-operative standard of mimesis for determining a poem's political valences. The emphasis on subjectivity in canonical lyrics has long been cited as prime evidence of their resistance to sociohistorical engagement.

This latter assumption can only be challenged by reconceiving the terms by which poems are deemed responsive to their contexts, specifically a persistent, narrow definition of referentiality. Mimesis has been the standard for engagement. Mill's influence survives here, in his distinction between the novel and poetry:

> [T]he one is derived from *incident*, the other from the representation of *feeling*. In one, the source of the emotion excited is the exhibition of a state or states of human sensibility; in the other, of a series of states of mere outward circumstances.[45]

The novel represents social reality; lyric poetry refers only to "feeling." "Incident" and "outward circumstances" remain the prerogatives of the novel. Liu puts it emphatically: lyricism is "antimimetic."[46] According to this generic logic, material reality is altered in lyric poetry, and in the process divested of its significance as distinct from the poet's perceptions. According to Mill, the lion's presence in the poem is eclipsed by the poet's reactions to it: "[T]his is describing the lion professedly, but the state of excitement of the spectator really." Referentiality is compromised by lyricism's "transformational grammar," according to which the objects of the poet's attention are, in effect, translated into the poem's aesthetic arena.[47] The mode's intense focus on subjectivity transforms the "ordinary universe" according to the poet's "vision." Liu articulates the implications of lyricism's "antimimeticism" for its relationship to historical contexts: social history appears in lyric poetry "only" as it has been transformed from its actual, "narrative" state. For Liu, lyric and social realms are not separate so much as overlaid: the latter is repressed or "denied" in the former.

The critical tradition that I have outlined assigns Romantic lyricism a political content, but locates that meaning solely in the mode's rejection of sociohistorical specificity. This account of Romantic lyricism as not just nonmimetic but actually "antimimetic" has been ably challenged by a number of critics, and I will not rehearse here the entire case against the standard of mimesis.[48] Yet these challenges to what Claudia Brodsky Lacour calls a "law of determination by negation" are an important prelude to considering the varied, nonmimetic ways in which Romantic lyrics responded to their contemporary contexts. Critics have argued against the assumption that the omission of a relevant event or circumstance identifies it as the poem's suppressed social content.[49] Peter Manning makes a cogent argument against reducing referentiality to a language that is "transparent to a given ideology or 'social fact.'" To make lyricism accountable to a standard of mimesis is to ignore how poetic language operates—by indirection. I turn now to the practical implications of Manning's contention that "the historical situation of the text can only be reached along the treacherous, badly signposted byways of representation, and taking the circuitous route such recognition implies."[50]

If lyric poems' responsiveness to their historical contexts is not measurable by a standard of mimesis, then how we are to gauge poems' relations to their social environments? One answer to this question has been provided by critics in a variety of disciplines who have complicated models of subjectivity in ways that illuminate how lyric poems may respond to their historical contexts indirectly. An emphasis on subjectivity present in many of the period's lyric poems has long been viewed as contributing to the mode's privatizing tendencies. A sufficiently skeptical account of Romantic lyricism would be facilitated by a far more active sense of subjectivity as "not a thing made and finished," as David Simpson puts it, nor "a bold front for or against things as they were, but a medium constantly open to patterns of deconstruction and reconstruction."[51] Memory and sympathetic identification are categories long deemed crucial to Romantic lyricism's introspective impulses. The poet's act of recollection has often been viewed as redirecting that figure's attention from immediate surroundings to private landscapes, while a convention of focusing on the poet's exercise of the sympathetic imagination has encouraged a critical focus on that figure, to the exclusion of the reader's own acts of sympathetic identification with the poet.

The category of memory has been especially important to models of Romantic lyricism: recollection has often been viewed as the poetic practice that may rescue a Romantic subject always in danger of falling away from itself, in that remembrance may foster the subject's sense of coherence and self-sufficiency despite change and loss. Once again, Abrams has been influential, both in his arguments and in a history of responses to them. In his account, memory's restorative capacities are a means of countering an emerging modern alienation. New historicism has followed suit by accepting Abrams's terms while pointing out their ideological underpinnings. In Abrams's account, memory is a powerful resource for the construction and sustenance of a sense of identity; in new historical accounts, memory is similarly efficacious, but to different ends: it is a primary psychic defense against the incursions of social history into what Liu calls "the empire of the Imagination." Remembrance involves a turn away from the immediacy of historical events to a timeless past; the invocation of memory blocks out a social world. Levinson views Wordsworthian memory "as a barricade to resist the violence of historical change and contradiction." In Liu's account, memory is "a divinity arising unbidden and uncontrolled from within *cogito* itself to conserve identity" from the catastrophic pressures of history.[52] This consensus is built upon a notion of memory as fundamentally conservative: for Abrams, a sense of a self is preserved in the face of traumatic experience; in these early new historical accounts, memory provides a buffer to the destabilizations of social history.

Certainly memory may be efficacious; it can revise social as well as personal history in order to write the most advantageous story of a life. Yet the processes of memory exceed the subject's control. It is never certain that memory will protect the subject from past experience, since the act of remembrance always threatens a reencounter with traumatic material. A fuller recognition of the vagaries of memory in Romantic lyricism would view it as not only a resource for consolation, but also as a vital interface with sociohistorical experience. Benjamin describes memory's waywardness in his discussion of Proust's *mémoire involuntaire*. He defines this faculty in contrast to *mémoire voluntaire*—a faculty more fully in the service of the individual will—but for Benjamin it is impossible to separate these modes of recollection. The implications of this imbrication are significant: Benjamin construes a model of the subject's development as thoroughly embedded in social experience, rather than constituted in opposition to its pressures and demands:

Where there is experience in the strict sense of the word, certain contents of the individual past combine with material of the collective past. The rituals with their ceremonies, their festivals (quite probably nowhere recalled in Proust's work) kept producing the amalgamation of these two elements of memory over and over again. They triggered recollection at certain times and remained handles of memory for a lifetime. In this way, voluntary and involuntary recollection lose their mutual exclusiveness.[53]

Recollection requires encountering not only a "former" self, as "Tintern Abbey" proposes, but also that self's social milieux. Remembrance involves risks, since for Benjamin, "experience" is "less the product of facts firmly anchored in memory than of a convergence in memory of accumulated and frequently unconscious data."[54] Benjamin shows that the exchange between self and environment that informs Romantic lyricism may actually be more traumatic return than recuperative exchange. Thus the poet's struggle in "Tintern Abbey" with the loss of a former self may be read as an uneasy dialogue with his 1793 self, a radical poet still immersed in his recent life in France and haunted by his responsibility to it (as I argue in chapter 3).

Benjamin provides his own examples of the unpredictability of remembrance in an autobiographical essay of his childhood, *A Berlin Chronicle*. In recalling his school days in Berlin, he theorizes memory's workings:

Here, as in several other places, I find in my memory rigidly fixed words, expressions, verses that, like a malleable mass that has later cooled and hardened, preserve in me the imprint of the collision between a larger collective and myself. Just as a certain kind of significant dream survives awakening in the form of words when all the rest of the dream content has vanished, here isolated words have remained in place as marks of catastrophic encounters.[55]

Memory's involuntary aspect is manifest in the way that certain words can evoke the scenes and experiences with which they are associated, without—or even against—the writer's will. Moments that crystallize verbally can facilitate a "collision" between the subject and a "larger collective": traumatic social experiences produce vivid memories, which attain a life of their own, much like Wordsworth's "spots of time," with their familiar quotient of fear. Forgetting or misremembering certain events might be desirable, but memory does not always function according to desire, nor, by extension, is subjectivity autonomous. It is "imprinted" with social experience even as the subject tries to imagine itself independent. From Benjamin's perspective, one of the key mechanisms of Romantic lyricism is far from a "barricade" to social experience; it is rather one of the most powerful and unpredictable media for the intersection of the self and its social environments.

Benjamin's account of memory is part of a broader treatment of the relations of the historical past to the present that is instructive for rethinking Romantic lyricism, partly because his historical materialism is informed by an underlying generic contrast between narrative and lyric modes. Benjamin challenges a familiar equation of narrative with history, providing a sustained, if decidedly secondary, theoretical consideration of lyricism's potential as a social mode. In his treatment of Wordsworth, Liu bluntly outlines a familiar generic distinction that has defined canonical understandings of Romantic lyricism: that "history is quintessentially narrative," while the lyric is a mode for escaping history, because it is "antinarrativistic and antimimetic."[56] Liu makes this distinction strategically, in order to account for Wordsworth's major shifts between genres in his career. Yet this confident assessment of different modes' relations to history precludes a sufficient recognition of the various capacities of both modes.[57] Benjamin, in contrast, is suspicious of a story too well told, one that easily registers cause and effect in recounting historical events.

Benjamin is, in fact, profoundly skeptical about narrative's relationship to history. In the 1940 *Theses on the Philosophy of History*, he considers the various forms that an historical awareness might take and defines his project of historical materialism against what he calls "historicism," a view of the past that belongs to its victors. According to Benjamin, those who have profited from the events of the past have a vital interest in rehearsing those events as leading inevitably to the present moment of their power. Benjamin associates narrative with a totalizing and potentially totalitarian impulse to write the past in order to guard that power in the present. The historical material-ist, in contrast, "regards it as his task to brush history against the grain" in order to register the costs to those who have either been neglected in prevailing accounts of history or who have paid the price of the present's victories. Benjamin thus opposes to historicism's fully elaborated narratives an account of the past that might be described as lyric, in that it is comprised of fragments gleaned by individual acts of attention on the part of the historical materialist. That figure has an immediate and vital engagement with a past that "can be seized only as an image which flashes up at the instant when it can be recognized and is never seen again." Benjamin's metaphorical account of significant images and flashes of historical insight is juxtaposed to historicism's predilection for "a causal connection between various moments in history."[58] His argument in the "Theses" thus echoes in Adorno's 1957 description of the lyric's potential for political resis-tance. Adorno explicitly, and Benjamin implicitly, credits the mode with a significant capacity for social activism based on individual relationships to an historical moment.

I have elaborated Benjamin's treatment of the relationship be-tween literary genre and social history in some detail in order to counter a recent new historicist confidence in narrative as the mode of social history, yet I would not advance the counterclaim: that lyri-cism is inherently a social mode. A historical practice that depends upon the historian's personal encounter with the social past and with listening to its individual voices may relinquish the argumentative force of broader theoretical claims that may be necessary to activist arguments.[59] There is a risk, in other words, in locating a political argument too firmly in the realm of the local and the individual. I am arguing, instead, against limiting definitional oppositions between lyric and narrative capacities for historical engagement.

Like the faculty of memory, the capacity for sympathetic identifi-cation has long been associated with the Romantic poet's introspec-tiveness. This should initially seem a surprising association, since the gesture of sympathetic identification involves a going-out-of-oneself, toward other persons or a beloved, usually natural, place. But para-digms of Romantic lyricism traditionally have trained attention on the poet, whose keen responsiveness to other persons and to natural surroundings has been considered one of that figure's great strengths. An eighteenth-century category of ethics and moral philosophy, sympathy was appropriated by critics such as Coleridge and William Hazlitt to describe the ideal imagination. Both critics deem Shakespeare exemplary, in that his genius was his ability to identify with his characters. Coleridge champions "[t]he sympathy of the poet with the subjects of his poetry," and Hazlitt admiringly suggests that Shakespeare "had only to think of any thing to become that thing, with all the circumstances belonging to it."[60] Although Coleridge and Hazlitt refer specifically to Shakespeare's ability to identify with his characters, sympathy is relevant to Romantic lyricism because it becomes an ideal for the imagination. According to Wordsworth, "it will be the wish of the Poet to bring his feelings near to those of the persons whose feelings he describes, nay, for short spaces of time, perhaps, to let himself slip into an entire delusion, and even confound and identify his own feelings with theirs."[61] Coleridge makes it clear that the processes of sympathetic identification are also operative in the poet's relations to natural scenes; in discussing Shakespeare, he explains that natural images "become proofs of original genius only as far as they are modified by a predominant passion; or by associated thoughts or images awakened by that passion; or when they have the effect of reducing multitude to unity, or succession to an instant; or lastly, when a human and intellectual life is transferred to them from the poet's own spirit."[62] The sympathetic imagination facilitates the "coalescence" of poet-subject and natural object at the heart of Abrams's "greater Romantic lyric."[63]

A conventional emphasis on the Romantic poet's remove from social scenes has obscured how the workings of sympathy jeopardize any implicit claims of disinterestedness or self-sufficiency. Sympathy may be viewed as extending the boundaries of the self to incorporate an "other," in which case it becomes a mechanism for the commodifying, appropriating, colonizing subject that early feminist and new historicist critics have described. Like the processes of recollection, however, the exercise of the sympathetic imagination is never entirely within the subject's control. David Marshall's elaboration of the "problem" of sympathy illuminates its complexity: the "effects" of sympathy prove "surprising." Drawing on Adam Smith's *Theory of Moral Sentiments*, Marshall discusses how sympathy requires "a self-forgetting that threatens the concept of a stable identity and blurs the boundaries that define and differentiate both self and other." Sympathy involves a going out of oneself that carries with it the possibility of a loss of autonomy, and certainly of disinterestedness. Marshall explains that

> For moral philosophers, aestheticians, novelists, and proto-psychologists in the eighteenth century, sympathy was an act of identification in which one left one's own place, part, and person and took the place and part of someone else; while representing to oneself the other's feelings, one was transported outside of the self: placed beyond or beside the self in a moment of self-forgetting.

The risk is prompted by "the collapse of difference between the self and other that occurs in the 'too much sameness' of sympathy."[64] To identify with another means to become involved with that person, thing, or event. This more skeptical account of subjectivity does justice to the vagaries and risks of the subject's self-constitution through acts of identification.

Not only does the Romantic poet's traditional capacity for sympathetic identification jeopardize that figure's autonomy; its exercise is one of the mode's primary means of engagement with reading audiences. An acknowledgment of the sympathetic imagination's debts to the cultural tradition of sensibility makes plain how that capacity may foster an involvement with readers and social scenes. Although Coleridge and Hazlitt look back to Shakespeare for a model of sympathetic identification, the Romantic poet's practice of sympathy owes more immediate debts to a late-eighteenth-century interest in sensibility. The 1797 third edition of the *Encyclopædia Britannica* defines it as "a nice and delicate perception of pleasure or pain, beauty or deformity," which, "as far as it is natural, seems to depend upon the organization of the nervous system." Persistent distinctions between sensibility and Romanticism hinge in part on the reader's role: that figure's obscurity in traditional definitions of Romantic lyricism has served to emphasize the poet's introspectiveness. Frye makes the hierarchical distinction between Romanticism and sensibility clear: in Romanticism, "[w]here there is a strong sense of literature as aesthetic product," there is "a sense of its detachment from the spectator." In sensibility, in contrast, there is an emphasis on "moods which are common to the work of art and the reader, and which bind them together psychologically instead of separating them aesthetically."[65]

Whereas paradigms of Romantic lyricism have focused on the poet's capacity for sympathizing with others or with the natural scene, the cult of sensibility stresses the reader's sympathetic imagination. Works of sensibility are often frank in their desire to captivate and move readers, sometimes on social topics. Henry Mackenzie's *The Man of Feeling* and Charlotte Smith's *Elegiac Sonnets*, both of which express antiwar sentiments, make especially plain sensibility's interest in social events as sources of sorrow and lamentation, expressions that could sometimes serve as protest. Marilyn Butler describes how this capacity was turned to social ends in late-eighteenth-century literature, "a period when the cast of villains was drawn from proud men representing authority, downwards from the House of Lords, the bench of bishops, judges, local magistrates, attorneys, to the stern father; when readers were invited to empathize with life's victims, especially poor but true-hearted lovers, and even to shed a tear with Burns for a cowering field-mouse, or with Sterne for a trapped fly or a dead ass."[66] Moreover, sensibility "demands an emotional, even physical response" from readers: tears wept by Samuel Richardson's Clarissa and by Mackenzie's Harley are to be imitated by reading audiences.[67] Charlotte Smith very clearly models for her readers the sympathetic response that she desires for herself, as her poet expresses her keen and attentive understanding of the various plights of the exiles, captives, abandoned mothers, and beggars who populate her three collections of poetry.[68] Recognizing the continuities between the periods traditionally defined as ages of sensibility and Romanticism demonstrates another way in which the Romantic lyric's aura of disinterestedness is compromised: the spectacle of the poet absorbed in others' concerns or her own may paradoxically comprise the mode's best persuasive possibilities.

The Romantic lyric was thus an ideal vehicle for writers facing the rhetorical challenge of a widening distance between themselves and expanding reading audiences, because two of the mode's qualities—a sense of immediacy and of intimacy—combined to create a poetics of presence. The lyric mode foregrounds the poet's emotions and reflections and thereby invites readers of sensibility to respond in kind, since sympathy "is often an imitative faculty, sometimes voluntary, frequently without consciousness." In defining sympathy, the *Encyclopædia Britannica* (3d ed.) illuminates how the Romantic lyric might attract readers by arousing their sympathetic imaginations: the poet's expressions of feeling could elicit those same responses in readers, since sympathy is "the quality of being affected by the affection of another."

If a primary obstacle to theorizing Romantic lyricism's relations to its historical contexts has been a strong focus on the poet's subjectivity, then a related problem emerges: the audience disappears. That audience is necessary to an understanding of the mode's potential for responding to its contemporary environments. Jon Klancher points out that, in the wake of Abrams's models, critics have often imagined ideal auditors rather than seeking historically researched audiences.[69] An attention to the reactions of contemporary audiences encourages a broadening of the reader's role in definitions of Romantic lyricism. The prevailing view of the audience's importance in Romantic lyricism is articulated by W. R. Johnson, who argues that in the early nineteenth century, the audience becomes expendable: "At best, the audience is extraneous to this poetry[;] at worst, all sense of the audience has vanished."[70] Johnson makes a blunt case for the irrelevance of an audience for reading Romantic lyric poems; canonical models such as Frye's accord that figure scarcely more significance. Frye cites an anecdote from William Butler Yeats's *Autobiographies* to explain the lyric audience's role. Engaged in a discussion with the barrister and orator John F. Taylor, Yeats recalls, "I would say, quoting Mill, 'Oratory is heard, poetry is overheard.'" Taylor would then "answer, his voice full of contempt, that there was always an audience; and yet, in his moments of lofty speech, he himself was alone no matter what the crowd."[71] Although an auditor is acknowledged, that figure's presence must be inconsequential if the poet's disinterestedness is to be preserved. The moment the poet begins to address an audience, or even to be conscious of a listener, the poet becomes Mill's orator: poetry turns to eloquence; it becomes interested.

Like the relationship between poet and natural scene, the exchange between poet and reader is conventionally construed as hierarchical. The result is another reinforcement of the poet's independence from social contexts, including reading audiences.[72] But the poet's prominence in lyric poems is also an important site of the mode's rhetorical power, because the reader is tacitly invited to sympathize with the poet, as that figure articulates private thoughts, emotions, and memories. In this way, Romantic lyricism bears a relationship to soliloquy, another genre with silent listeners; it has a theatrical dimension that has been overlooked. The lyric mode is often defined by its sincerity, yet the premium on this quality has obscured its performative aspect: the mode's formlessness is said to accommodate the spontaneity of expressed emotion. The well-known hesitations and qualifications of Wordsworthian lyricism in "Tintern Abbey" and *The Prelude*, for instance, seem to confirm the unself-consciousness of the poet, who struggles with the task of articulation with no concern for his designated auditors, Dorothy Wordsworth and Coleridge, respectively. Thus another set of antithetical qualities emerges: between sincerity and theatricality, the latter of which alone would be associated with a desire to move an audience, like Mill's orator.[73]

Yet this familiar distinction between sincerity and theatricality fails to account for the effects of a speaker, lost in meditation, on readers. Frye's portrait of the poet turning his back on an audience ironically demonstrates a major source of this power: his description of the poet reveals a theatrical side to the mode that helps to explain its immense appeal. The poet's lack of attention to his or her surroundings leaves an audience free to observe—and perhaps to identify with—the solitary figure on stage. In Michael Fried's terms, a human figure absorbed in thought or in observation enables the audience to become engaged with that figure, precisely because he or she makes no demands. The lyric poet affects auditors because they have the pleasurable sensation of "*over*hearing" private thoughts and feelings. The key to this effect is that the poet seems to be "alone no matter what the crowd." As in a soliloquy, to lose sight of an audience does not mean to lose contact with it. The managed illusion of the poet's isolation is the means of captivating the spectator or reader. In her 1798 Introductory Discourse to *A Series of Plays* (which came be known as *Plays of the Passions*), Joanna Baillie explicates the theatrical possibilities of lyric poetry by analyzing the nature of the mode's appeal: "The highest pleasures we receive from poetry, as well as from the real objects which surround us in the world, are derived from the sympathetick interest we all take in beings like ourselves; and I will even venture to say, that were the grandest scenes which can enter into the imagination of man, presented to our view, and all reference to man completely shut out from our thoughts, the objects that composed it would convey to our minds little better than dry ideas of magnitude, colour, and form; and the remembrance of them would rest upon our minds like the measurement and distances of the planets."[74] She thus presents a contemporaneous argument for the persuasiveness of a lyric focus on the poet; this kind of appeal could interest reading audiences not only in the poet, but in "scenes" in which that figure appears.

Like the fashion for sensibility, the increasing popularity of biography in the eighteenth century enhanced an interest in poets' lives that complemented a taste for lyric poetry as the seeming expression of the poet's experience. Persuasive critical cases have been made for important parallels between a growing taste for biography and the rise of the novel in the eighteenth century, as genres which "profoundly express the modern discovery of the individual, of the autonomous subject."[75] I would argue that a readerly appetite for "lives" of poets also contributed to a keen interest in the apparently intimate and revelatory moments provided by the period's lyric poems. As both the subject of what is perhaps the most-studied biography in English and the author of *The Life of Mr. Richard Savage* and *The Lives of the Poets*, Samuel Johnson is a primary architect of literary biography. In the *Rambler*, no. 60, Johnson argues that value of biography depends upon its focus on the subject's private life, since "[t]here are many invisible circumstances which, whether we read as enquirers after natural and moral knowledge, whether we intend to enlarge our science, or increase our virtue, are more important than publick occurrences." The biographer's ability to delight and instruct depends upon enabling the reader to sympathize with a life well told. The detail of personal experience is necessary, since "[o]ur passions" are "more strongly moved, in proportion as we can more readily adopt the pains or pleasures proposed to our minds, by recognising them as once our own, or considering them as naturally incident to

our state of life." In contrast, "[h]istories of the downfall of king-
doms, and revolutions of empires, are read with great tranquillity."
Therefore, Johnson determines, "no species of writing seems more
worthy of cultivation than biography, since none can be more delightful or more useful, none can more certainly enchain the heart by
irresistible interest, or more widely diffuse instruction to every diver-
sity of condition."[76]
     The lyric mode offers readers a sense of personal knowledge of
the poet that Johnson deems crucial to biography. He provides an
even closer link between biography and lyricism when he distinguishes
the literary life as the subject best suited to effect biography's pleasure and instruction in the *Idler*, no. 102. He argues that "[n]othing
detains the reader's attention more powerfully than deep involutions
of distress or sudden vicissitudes of fortune." Ample material for this
kind of captivation may be found, he proposes, in "memoirs of the
sons of literature."[77] Johnson's influential emphasis on the private
rather than the public sides of poets' lives provides a contemporaneous recommendation for the (seemingly) intimate knowledge provided by an autobiographical lyric speaker's reflections and recollections. In Charlotte Smith's case, an interest in her life produced a
simultaneous demand for her lyric poems and for biographical treatments of her. Smith was featured in Richard Phillips's *British Public
Characters of 1800–1801*, and numerous biographical sketches of
her appeared during her lifetime and after her death. These included
an essay on Smith in *The Lady's Monthly Museum* (May 1799), a
"Literary Notice of the Late Charlotte Smith (With a Portrait)" in
the *European Magazine* (November 1806), a "memoir" of Smith as
an "eminent person" in the *Monthly Magazine* (April 1807), and
biographical treatments of Smith by Samuel Egerton Brydges in *Imaginative Biography* (1834), by her sister, Catherine Anne Dorset, in Sir
Walter Scott's *Biographical Memoirs of Eminent Novelists, and Other
Distinguished Persons* (1843), and by Anne K. Elwood in *Memoirs
of the Literary Ladies of England, from the Commencement of the
Last Century* (1843). In its review of the fifth edition of *Elegiac Sonnets*, the *European Magazine* reads the life in the works and praises
"the poetic ability as well as amiable private character of the fair but
unfortunate writer."[78] Smith herself was savvy enough to know that
her popularity depended upon her own work of autobiography, to

which she attended carefully in the many prefaces to her volumes of poetry and prose, in autobiographical characters sprinkled throughout her prose works, and in the sonnets themselves.

Poets such as Smith discovered that the often highly personal tones of the lyric might counter—or provide the illusion of countering—the widening distance between writers and expanding reading audiences. The familiar profile of the Romantic lyric poet removed from any particular time or place can thus be read as the product of a growing awareness of just how subject that figure was to a dense and unpredictable network of booksellers, publishers, critics, patrons, and readers. In fact, everything about the history of lyric poetry in this period seems to belie the possibility of the poet's autonomy and poetic transcendence. It is little wonder that even as lyric poems became increasingly available to more readers with advances in print technology, a fiction emerged (authored in part by Wordsworth and Coleridge) of solitary creation and an ideal of disinterestedness. Nor does it seem particularly ironic that the image of the lyric poet removed from those contexts was self-consciously bought and sold. The period's lyric poems were very much in dialogue with their particular historical moments, and not just in the sense that new historicism has advanced of denying or repressing an awareness of those contexts. Poets might eschew the novel's license of direct address, but lyric poems provided a supple medium of exchange understood by poets and readers alike, yet controlled by neither.

An understanding of the Romantic lyric as a popular cultural vehicle for exchanges between poets and readers, rather than as a form that resists such engagement, leaves practical questions about how we are to interpret poems' relations to their social contexts. Canonical definitions of the mode made interpretation easier by providing the equations with which this chapter began and against which I have been arguing: that solitary = asocial, sincere = antitheatrical and introspective = disengaged. If we approach the period's lyric poems without such guiding precepts, then our interpretations become more dependent upon the information provided by the specific contexts of poems' production and consumption. Paul Magnuson has argued that "a lyric's location determines its significance"; it requires, as he puts it, awareness of the poem's contemporaneous contexts, including the "public" poet and the "public location of the poem."[79]

This kind of critical attention is facilitated by a recent paradigm shift from a notion of poetic vocation, with its attendant categories of originality and inspiration, to an understanding of the poetic career as a series of complex and unpredictable negotiations in the literary marketplace. Whereas "[t]he teleology of the vocation is the promise, if not of worldly success, then of spiritual fulfillment," the "successful career" is a "social practice," and as such "can be planned but not fully controlled."[80] An analysis of the poetic career requires attention to the poet's public persona, as it is elaborated not only in the poems themselves, but also in the volumes in which they are housed. Poets communicated to reading audiences by framing their poems with advertisements, prefaces, introductions, engravings and glossaries. This was, after all, "an era when book production was and had been regarded for time out of mind as a set of rhetorical as well as technical and commercial practices."[81]

My next chapter turns to Charlotte Smith as a poet particularly well suited to the kind of analysis that I have described, because she so well understood the sonnet's possibilities. Wordsworth and Coleridge borrowed not only something of her poetics but also her keen sense of the popular potential of poems attractively framed. The entire volume of *Elegiac Sonnets* aims to introduce the poet appealingly and sympathetically to readers and critics who might question her entry into the literary marketplace as a woman writer; she makes ample use of memory's fascinations and of the captivating spectacle of an autobiographical speaker lost in meditation. The collection's success is attributable not only to her use of lyric form but also to the carefully worded prefaces to successive editions of the collection, to the engravings that accompanied some editions, including a frontispiece portrait of Smith, and to copious explanatory notes, in which the poet appears both as an avid reader and a natural historian. A wealth of critical and readerly responses to Smith's poet is available in the numerous periodicals that reviewed her works, in anthologies, and in her contemporaries' private and published writings. Smith thus provides excellent lessons on how to read an engaged lyric poetry that would influence her canonical and noncanonical successors before she faded into obscurity, as Wordsworth regretfully predicted she would.

TWO

"Dost thou not know my voice?":
Charlotte Smith and the Lyric's Audience

O! grief hath chang'd me since you saw me last,
And careful hours with time's deformed hand
Have written strange defeatures in my face:
But tell me yet, dost thou not know my voice?
                              —*The Comedy of Errors* (V.i.298–301)

No other grief that ever sighed has worn so much
crape and bombazine.
                              —Viscount St. Cyres on Smith (1903)

Two poems addressed to Charlotte Smith appear in the
August 1786 edition of the *European Magazine*, one submitted by
"W.P.," another by a "constant Reader." The poems respond to the
author of *Elegiac Sonnets*, a collection that had been "universally
admired" (in Anna Letitia Barbauld's words) when it appeared two
years earlier.[1] The poem by a "constant Reader," a sonnet, begins by
admitting that propriety recommends against the intensely autobiographical quality of Smith's lyric poems: "'Tis said, and I myself have
so believ'd / 'Fiction's the properest field for Poesy.'" Yet it is the
suspect quality that arouses a response: "For sure than thine more
sweet no strains can flow, / Than thine no tenderer plaints the heart
can move, / More rouse the soul to sympathetic love; / And yet—sad
source! they spring from REAL WOE."[2] Despite the reader's qualms,
it is Smith's "REAL WOE" that is engaging. Many critics proved no
more immune than this "constant Reader" to the spectacle of Smith's
autobiographical speaker lamenting her plight in natural settings. And
like this reader, they responded to the sonnets' forging of high emotion and believability. Readers and critics often reacted with "sympathy," their responses similarly personal in tone. According to Richard

39

Phillips's *British Public Characters of 1800–1801,* "an elevation of sentiment, a refinement of taste, a feeling, and a delicacy, breathe through her productions, which by moving the affections and engaging the sympathy of the reader, excite in him a lively and permanent interest."[3]

Smith had practical reasons for needing to generate an "interest" both "lively" and lasting. *Elegiac Sonnets* was published for her family's support after her husband's imprisonment at the King's Bench for debt in December 1783. Smith had been born into far different circumstances: her father owned estates in Sussex and Surrey, and a townhouse in London. She experienced a social fall into economic instability only after a marriage at age fifteen proved emotionally and financially disastrous. The second son of Richard Smith, a West Indian merchant and a director of the East India Company, Benjamin Smith plunged the family into debt. Richard Smith's death might have alleviated the family's precarious situation, but their circumstances were actually worsened by his intricate will, which was, ironically, meant to protect Charlotte and the children from Benjamin's unreliability. When her husband was sent to debtor's prison, Smith turned to publication as a way to maintain the family's social standing until the estate was settled and her children could be educated as she desired. But the will generated legal entanglements that remained unresolved throughout her career; the Chancery suit was not finally settled until after her death. As a result, Smith's temporary venture into the literary marketplace lasted twenty-two years.

Elegiac Sonnets succeeded—both in providing financial respite and in establishing Smith as a popular poet who would earn her family's primary income after the couple separated in 1787. What follows is an account of how she found her audience with an unlikely vehicle: quiet, reflective sonnets featuring a solitary speaker lost in private sorrow. Rather than reaching out directly to the readers she needed so urgently, Smith turned away from them, performing the gesture that Northrop Frye describes as characteristic of the lyric poet, who "turns his back on his audience."[4] Smith made an important discovery about the mode, which counters prevailing views of it: that a lyric speaker could win readers and hold their attention precisely by appearing to ignore them, by seeming absorbed in thought and oblivious to her surroundings. She became aware, in other words, of the impact that her poet could have on an audience on whom she turns her back in only the most literal sense. Smith's strong popular appeal illuminates the relationship between lyric poet and reading audiences as a dynamic exchange, a different account from predominant paradigms, which generally characterize the lyric's auditor as passive and silent. The availability of a wealth of contemporary responses to Smith's lyric poet by critics and readers illuminates a neglected aspect of the period's lyric poetry, for the mode's rhetorical capacities have been eclipsed by a conventional focus on psychological and emotional subtlety.

The discrepancy between Smith's immediate popularity and her virtual disappearance in the later arena of twentieth-century literary criticism recommends a return to her contemporaneous readers and critics. The contrast between their eager responses and her subsequent obscurity in literary history is telling. Qualities now generally deemed antithetical to the mode did not appear so to her readers: her sonnets combine self-consciousness with sincerity, introspection with rhetorical power. Popular success is not necessarily precluded in canonical models (although Byron's exclusion from M. H. Abrams's account of the "greater Romantic lyric" is suggestive), but a focus on the poet's subjectivity has discouraged consideration of readers' responses to lyric poems and lyric poems' responsiveness to their environments.[5] Smith's example suggests a method for reading the period's lyric poems—within the specific circumstances of their production and consumption, and within the trajectories of poets' careers. Smith's own readers included those who have defined canonical Romanticism—William Wordsworth, Samuel Taylor Coleridge, Byron, Leigh Hunt, and John Keats. Together, Smith and her reading audiences bring into focus the mode's potential for a more dynamic relationship to its social contexts than we have come to expect.

Smith's sonnets are an important measure of how the Romantic canon was shaped according to one particular version of Romantic lyricism, a model based largely on the poems and critical prose of two of her successors, Coleridge and Wordsworth. Wordsworth's debts to Smith are political and poetic: he visited her in Brighton on his way to France in 1791, and he was given letters of introduction to her acquaintances, including Helen Maria Williams (who had left Orléans by the time he arrived). His literary debts to her begin at

Hawkshead, where he read *Elegiac Sonnets,* and are formally acknowledged in a lavish 1835 explanatory note, expanded in 1837, to "Stanzas Suggested in a Steam-boat Off St. Bees' Heads."[6] Wordsworth describes Smith as "a lady to whom English verse is under greater obligations than are likely to be either acknowledged or remembered": "She wrote little, and that little unambitiously, but with true feeling for rural nature, at a time when nature was not much regarded by English Poets; for in point of time her earlier writings preceded, I believe, those of Cowper and Burns."[7] Coleridge's admiration of William Lisle Bowles has become a critical commonplace, and Bowles was, as Stuart Curran observes, one of Smith's "followers."[8] Yet the connection between Coleridge and Smith is even more direct: in his "Introduction to the Sonnets" (1796), Coleridge cites Smith and Bowles as the poets who "first made the Sonnet popular among the present English," and he feels "justified" in "deducing its laws" from their works. According to their examples, the sonnet is a "small poem, in which some lonely feeling is developed," preferably "deduced from, and associated with, the Scenery of Nature."[9]

The qualities responsible for Smith's appeal to Wordsworth and Coleridge— solitariness, an attraction to natural scenes, and an emphasis on feeling—are recognizable in foundational accounts of Romantic lyricism, including Abrams's influential definition of the "greater Romantic lyric." Abrams bases his paradigm largely on Coleridge's and Wordsworth's early poems, written in the period in which Smith's influence on them was keenest. It is not surprising, then, that the qualities that Coleridge and Wordsworth exclude in their laudatory portraits of Smith were also qualities subsequently deemed antithetical to canonical Romantic lyricism: a proven rhetorical ability that made her a popular poet. What was lost to canonical paradigms in Smith's example was an understanding of the mode's potential for engaging readers and responding to social concerns. Her poetry is especially provocative for the task of revising critical expectations of the period's lyric poems because her work resembles Wordsworthian poetics in important ways, and yet manifests marked differences, which cluster around the issue of her popular success. Thus, Smith helps to blur the lines between popular and canonical lyricism.

⤴

Smith's most important challenge to conventional assumptions about Romantic lyricism is her success in winning readers by seeming oblivious to them. Her example restores the significance of an overlooked corollary to Frye's famous description of the poet turning away from an audience: an acknowledgment that the audience, despite being ignored, remains on the scene. Smith knows that by seeming to forget her readers she gives them the pleasure of "overhearing." She employs the rhetorical allure of eavesdropping, making shrewd use of what is perhaps lyricism's most appealing quality, that of intimacy. Like Wordsworth, Smith finds in lyricism a vehicle for foregrounding the reflections and feelings of the poet. And like him, she drew charges of "egotism" for her intense introspection.[10] Yet Smith's sonnets disrupt an equation familiar to canonical accounts of the mode: that lyricism = disengagement. In her case, an intense autobiographical lyricism served a social function: it elicited responses that often matched her own in intensity.

Sir William Jones's comments on her sonnets exemplify the reaction that Smith desired. En route to India to assume a judgeship, Jones undertook a course of reading that included *Elegiac Sonnets.* In a letter, he thanks the friend who had given him "the tender strains of the unfortunate Charlotte, which have given us pleasure and pain." He reserves special praise for her most autobiographical poems: "[T]he sonnets which relate to herself are incomparably the best."[11] The *Gentleman's Magazine* concurs in its notice of the third edition (1786) of *Elegiac Sonnets,* judging that the "pieces . . . which are the genuine offspring of her own fancy, are by far the most interesting in her whole collection."[12] Although, from the first edition, the collection included both poems other than sonnets and translations of others' sonnets (Goethe, Petrarch, and Metastasio), the autobiographical sonnets that Jones admires established Smith's reputation.[13]

In her hands, an emphasis on interiority, which would also define the poetics of her canonical successors, turns a focus on the personal into a cult of personality. Smith's emphasis on the personal in *Elegiac Sonnets* is underlined by the collection's frontispiece portrait, which appeared in the first edition and in some subsequent editions (see figure 1). It is an engraving from a crayon drawing by George Romney, under which she places the first three lines cited in my epigraph, from *The Comedy of Errors* (lines that she slightly misquotes).[14] The lines from Shakespeare are printed in cursive, as if the poet had written them herself, and thereby taken personal possession of them. She omits the fourth line that I cite, but this is the line that, I would argue, underlies her poetic strategies: "But tell me yet, dost thou not know my voice?" Because Smith articulates private sorrows in the sonnets, readers came to feel as if they knew her, and so might respond to her as a familiar face in future volumes. A reviewer for the *British Critic,* quoting Smith, describes her appeal to readers: "So exquisite are the charms of Mrs. Smith's poetry, that it would indicate the utmost degree of insensibility not to be affected by her 'tale of tender woe, her sweet sorrow, her mournful melody.'"[15] Critics and readers not only associated the sonnet speaker with the poet herself, they also often addressed her as someone with whom they were personally acquainted, in reviews and in letters and poems submitted to periodicals (such as the sonnet by a "constant Reader").

The sonnets themselves aim to present the poet with the vividness of a portrait. In the poems, Smith allows readers ample opportunity to observe her, since she articulates her reflections and feelings while wandering through natural scenes. Readers respond because nothing, apparently, is demanded of them. "To the moon" (Sonnet IV) is an especially apt example because it is accompanied, in some editions, by an engraving featuring a solitary female figure, one hand on her heart, the other extended before her as she gazes on the moon (see figure 2). The engraving visualizes, in the upward tilt of her head and the expressive position of her arms, the stylized verbal gestures of Smith's poetry, an unsurprising congruence given that she was closely involved with the production of her volumes and provided instructions for the plates commissioned for *Elegiac Sonnets.*[16] The first half of line one appears underneath the engraving:

> Queen of the silver bow!—by thy pale beam,
> Alone and pensive, I delight to stray,
> And watch thy shadow trembling in the stream,
> Or mark the floating clouds that cross thy way.
> And while I gaze, thy mild and placid light

P. Conde sculp.

Oh! Time has Changed me since you saw me last,
And heavy Hours with Time's deforming Hand,
Have written strange Defeatures in my Face.

Figure 1

Plate.2.   Sonnet.4.

Corbould del.   Milton sculp.

Publish'd Jan.ʸ 1.1789. by T. Cadell, Strand.

Queen of the Silver Bow, &c.

Figure 2

Sheds a soft calm upon my troubled breast;
And oft I think—fair planet of the night,
That in thy orb, the wretched may have rest:
The sufferers of the earth perhaps may go,
Released by death—to thy benignant sphere;
And the sad children of Despair and Woe
Forget, in thee, their cup of sorrow here.
Oh! that I soon may reach thy world serene,
Poor wearied pilgrim—in this toiling scene!

Smith's speaker is characteristically occupied in observing her natural surroundings and pursuing the thoughts they prompt, leaving the reader free to observe her. In poem and engraving, she looks away from an audience (in the portrait by Romney, Smith's gaze is also averted). Addressing her thoughts not to the reader, but to the moon, the speaker turns to the "fair planet" and imagines transcendence. Not only does she fail to notice auditors, she also envisions leaving the quotidian arena that she shares with them for another "benignant sphere." She wants to "forget," and she succeeds in losing sight of an audience and her environment. In the final couplet, the intensely personal nature of her meditations becomes apparent, with her confession that she is one of the "wretched" of whom she has spoken. The poem ends with a sharp focus on the speaker herself, as a "[p]oor wearied pilgrim."

Yet how do we account for the voyeuristic pleasure that Smith's sonnets provided a popular audience? What is the mechanism of this appeal? Michael Fried makes a relevant argument in his treatment of French painting in the second half of the eighteenth century. He describes the powerful effect on the viewer of watching a human figure who is absorbed, either in thought or in an event taking place. This air of distraction can create a "supreme fiction": that of the beholder's absence. The illusion of being ignored has an unexpected side effect—the beholder may experience the sensation of entering the picture, precisely because he or she is not made self-conscious in the act of watching, an awareness that can produce resistance. Smith's sonnets achieve a similar effect, via the poet's apparent obliviousness to an audience. What seems to be a desire on her part to turn away from social scenes as she wanders, "alone and pensive," proves captivating. Fried describes a "paradoxical relationship between painting and beholder": the painter seeks "to neutralize or negate the beholder's presence, to establish the fiction that no one is standing before the canvas." Yet "only if this is done can the beholder be stopped and held precisely there."[17] Fried's paradigm helps make explicit what is implicit in *Elegiac Sonnets:* just as on the stage, the social world is not excluded by the gesture of turning one's back to an audience. Like a member of a theater audience or the beholder of a painting, the reader of a lyric poem must lose the self-consciousness of spectatorship, must feel forgotten in order to forget himself or herself and make the necessary leap of identification.

Fried's argument is particularly relevant to Smith's sonnets because the poems resemble small tableaux in the collection's layout. There is one poem per page in most editions, and their intensely autobiographical quality renders them miniature, verbal self-portraits. Thus the reader is also a viewer, or spectator. The sonnets' copious natural images emphasize their pictorial quality, and the engravings that accompany several sonnets visualize the scenes that the poems describe, sometimes elaborately framing those scenes. An ornate border for the oval engraving of "To the moon" features thick foliage and an owl—presumably Athena's—atop a book. The speaker addresses Diana, whose unstrung bow and quiver frame the bird, as if the god has turned aside from the hunt to other topics. These emblems develop the portrait of the poet, who is thus associated with wisdom, purity, and female strength. The engraving significantly supplements the act of reading the poems, for readers can "see" the poet as they read her words. They can also "hear" her: working within the conventions of sensibility, Smith's liberal use of exclamations, sighs, and pauses strives to approximate the cadences of spoken language.

The emphasis on the visual in *Elegiac Sonnets* contributes to a theatrical dynamic that structures the poet's relationship to her audiences. It might seem that the dramatic cast of Smith's sorrows could alienate potentially distrustful readers. Early in her career, before she had made explicit the biographical sources of her elegiac tenor, a critic ventured to hope that her sorrows were fictitious: The *Gentleman's Magazine* reviewer cannot "forbear expressing a hope that the misfortunes she so often hints at, are all imaginary," since "[w]e must have perused her very tender and exquisite effusions with diminished pleasure, could we have supposed her sorrows to be real."[18] Yet as David Marshall explains, presenting oneself sympathetically, as Smith urgently needed to do, demands a measure of theatricality. Drawing on Adam Smith, Marshall argues that "since we cannot know the experience or sentiments of another person, we must represent in our imagination copies of the sentiments that we ourselves feel as we imagine ourselves in someone else's place and person." This means that "acts of sympathy are structured by theatrical dynamics that . . . depend on people's ability to represent themselves as tableaux, spectacles, and texts before others."

Smith uses all available verbal and visual means to represent vividly to readers the emotions her poet experiences. Her efforts to create a fullness of presence which might captivate readers are rendered explicit in the frontispiece portrait, which depicts Smith as a Shakespearean character. The sonnets demonstrate a theatrical dynamic in the lyric's often overlooked relationship between poet and auditor: her poems make clearer the implications of Frye's representation of the poet turning his back to an audience. What seems to be pure unself-consciousness on the poet's part, and passive reception by the reader, actually operates more dynamically: the poet presents herself in a particularly revealing way by expressing her reflections and emotions as in a soliloquy. The reader's ideal response is the going-out-of-oneself that Coleridge describes as readerly or sympathetic identification. Smith learned what Marshall, quoting Diderot, claims that good actors know: that it is "more important for the spectator to feel forgotten rather than literally be forgotten."[19]

In his account of the sonnet's "laws" derived from Smith and Bowles, Coleridge suggests that the reader's role involves an act of identification. He describes a mode of consumption which encourages a sense of intimacy: "Easily remembered from their briefness, and interesting alike to the eye and the affections, these are the poems which we can 'lay up in our heart and our soul,' and repeat them 'when we walk by the way, and when we lie down, and when we rise up.'" The reader identifies so strongly with the poet's "moral Sentiments, Affections, or Feelings" that they seem to be his or her own, and "hence they domesticate with the heart, and become, as it were, a part of our identity."[20] In a letter to Smith, William Cowper exemplifies the kind of response that Coleridge describes:

I was much struck by an expression in your letter to Hayley, where you say that 'you will endeavor to take an interest in green leaves again.' This seems the sound of my own voice reflected to me from a distance, I have so often had the same thought and desire.[21]

Smith's poems and her letter to Hayley operate similarly: she succeeds in convincing others that they can understand her sorrows. In reading her words, Cowper mistakes her voice for his own and equates his thoughts and desires with hers. In Cowper's case, Smith wins not just sympathy but the practical assistance it inspires: he allowed her to dedicate *The Emigrants* (1793), her first long poem, to him. According to Marshall, when an act of sympathy is successful, the viewer may be moved to respond not just emotionally, but materially. He describes "the more specific response to a scene of tragedy, danger, or suffering that not only leaves one *affligé* but calls upon one to come to the assistance of someone in distress."[22] Thus Cowper reacts appropriately when he writes to William Hayley, who had himself aided Smith by accepting the dedication of *Elegiac Sonnets:* "I never want riches except when I hear of such distress."[23]

Accounts of Romantic lyricism have traditionally emphasized the poet's capacity for sympathetic identification with other persons or with beloved natural places; Smith's sonnets highlight another, less noticed structure of identification—between reader and poet. It is not that the reader has been entirely forgotten in paradigms of Romantic lyricism, but that figure is generally considered either tangential to the mode's main concerns—the identifications and understandings of the poet—or subordinate to them.[24] The intense identificatory relationship between reader and poet is, however, a primary site of the mode's rhetorical salience. The theatrical dynamic that informs Smith's lyric poems recommends a revision of paradigms that emphasize a standard of sincerity, without an attention to how this quality operates rhetorically. As the period's "poetic norm," the lyric has seemingly embodied its premium on sincerity, a quality traditionally associated with a naturalness of emotion and an emphasis on expressivity.[25] As a result, the theatrical dynamic established by the lyric scenario of "overhearing" articulated emotion has been neglected. Smith's sonnets foreground one of the mode's key complexities: the unexpected complementarity of sincerity and theatricality for contemporaneous readers, an issue to which I will return.

First, however, I want to address more specifically how *Elegiac Sonnets* won a popular audience. Smith's shrewd attention to the framing of her sonnets in the collection recommends a strategy for analyzing the rhetorical capacity of lyric poems: by reading them in the context of the volumes in which they appear. Smith is an excellent candidate for this kind of analysis because she reinforced the appealing self-portrait of the sonnets by carefully surrounding these poems with prefaces, explanatory notes, and engravings. The publication history of *Elegiac Sonnets* suggests that Smith keenly understood the nature of her readers' receptivity to her solitary poet. She took an active role in what Judith Phillips Stanton calls, quoting the poet, her "literary business," and this effort included crafting the collection to capitalize on the popularity of her melancholy speaker.[26] From the first edition, the collection's prose sections contributed to its success by enhancing the poems' portrait of the poet. In successive editions, Smith added new prefaces and expanded a section of explanatory notes that identifies literary allusions and the flowers, animals, and places mentioned in the poems. The prefaces and notes, with their conversational, quotidian prose, throw into bolder relief the poems' emphases on solitude, introspection, and a desire for transcendence. In a "memoir" published after Smith's death, the *Monthly Magazine* testifies to a contemporaneous association of her sonnets with an impulse toward transcendence. The critic speculates that Smith pursued her career after the sonnets' initial success because doing so "contributed to divert her thoughts, and to lead her mind into the visionary regions of fancy, rendering the sad realities she was suffering under, in some measure less poignant."[27]

In the sonnets themselves, Smith provides her audience with the pleasure of watching a poet removed from all that is mundane by the very language in which she spoke. Despite some experimentation with English and Italian forms, the poems follow strict rhyme schemes and use formal diction, a strategy that enhances a sense of the poet's detachment from daily experience. Thus, in addition to their strong focus on subjectivity, Smith's sonnets conform to another of the main ways in which lyricism is often assumed to distance itself from social contexts: a specialization of language that removes the poem from "the ordinary circuit of communication," in Jonathan Culler's terms.[28] In "Written at the close of spring" (Sonnet II), an explanatory note establishes the poem's linguistic difference from "ordinary" speech. The sonnet begins by describing how "[t]he garlands fade that Spring so lately wove, / Each simple flower which she had nursed in dew, / Anemonies, that spangled every grove, / The primrose wan, and hare-bell mildly blue." A brief explanatory note consists of two alternate names for the anemone: "*Anemony Nemeroso*" and "[t]he wood Anemony." Smith's gloss of "anemone" seems to translate from the rarefied language of poetry into the language of scientific classification and the vernacular. In the process the flower is transformed from poetic prop into an object from the reader's environment. In the poem, the anemone is significant only as a natural detail, which reminds the poet of her own lack of rejuvenation. In the explanatory note, the focus shifts to the flower as a natural object in the reader's environment, and the effect is to distinguish between poet's and readers' worlds.

A sense of the poet's remove from the ordinary is augmented by the establishment of a different temporality in the sonnets. Within the volume, the poet is held in a moment of perpetual sorrow that contrasts with a world of process in the prefaces and notes. "Written at the close of spring" thematizes the atemporality of the poet's world by juxtaposing the progress of the seasons with her unchanging state. The closing couplet asks, "Another May new buds and flowers shall bring; / Ah! why has happiness—no second Spring?" Thus the lyric, frequently associated with a desire for immortality and transcendence, seeks to wrest itself out of the cause and effect of social history, an impulse which prompted a new historical critique of the Romantic ideology. "Written in the church-yard at Middleton in Sussex" (Sonnet XLIV) and its accompanying note exemplify how Smith's sonnets seem to register fleeting moments detached from their narrative contexts:

> Press'd by the Moon, mute arbitress of tides,
> While the loud equinox its power combines,

The sea no more its swelling surge confines,
But o'er the shrinking land sublimely rides.
The wild blast, rising from the Western cave,
Drives the huge billows from their heaving bed;
Tears from their grassy tombs the village dead,
And breaks the silent sabbath of the grave!
With shells and sea-weed mingled, on the shore
Lo! their bones whiten in the frequent wave;
But vain to them the winds and waters rave;
They hear the warring elements no more:
While I am doom'd—by life's long storm opprest,
To gaze with envy on their gloomy rest.

The sonnet records an almost gothic moment: the sea, driven by the moon, washes on shore in a wave that removes dirt from the village cemetery, uncovering the dead. By using the present tense, Smith emphasizes the transitoriness both of the poet's view of the white bones and of her flash of recognition that unlike herself, the dead can no longer be "opprest" by "life's long storm." Natural event and psychological revelation occur instantaneously. The reader who turns to the back of the volume to read the accompanying note finds, in contrast, a world of gradual but inexorable change:

Middleton is a village on the margin of the sea, in Sussex, containing only two or three houses. There were formerly several acres of ground between its small church and the sea, which now, by its continual encroachments, approaches within a few feet of this half-ruined and humble edifice. The wall, which once surrounded the church-yard, is entirely swept away, many of the graves broken up, and the remains of bodies interred washed into the sea; whence human bones are found among the sand and shingles on the shore.

The note contains the prehistory and the aftermath of the sonnet's moment—its context. It reads as if the viewer has pulled back to a place from which the human and natural consequences of a transformative lyric instant could be surveyed. Smith's explanatory notes document a world of myriad change, embodied here in the erosion altering the landscape and the villagers' lives, while the speaker remains in an unalterable state of melancholy.

The sonnets' sense of timelessness is so pronounced that Smith eventually found it necessary publicly to defend her lingering sorrow. She addresses the issue in the preface to the sixth edition (1792) by reporting an exchange with a friend who had recommended that she try "'a more cheerful style of composition.'" The person who made what St. Cyres describes as this "highly unfortunate suggestion" receives in response a pointed justification: an account of continued misery. Recalling her early sonnets, she explains, "I wrote mournfully because I was unhappy—And I have unfortunately no reason yet, though nine years have since elapsed, to *change my tone*" (5). Smith's poet continues to hold her melancholy pose: it is as if she has been caught in one repeated moment of intense sorrow. Her sonnets seem to epitomize Sharon Cameron's description of how lyric poems "fight temporality with a vengeance," although Smith claims that her stasis is involuntary.[29] Yet St. Cyres cannily points to the rhetorical effect of this sense of lyric timelessness: "Having chosen to come forward as a Laureate of the Lachrymose, she thought herself bound in honour to live consistently up to her part, and treat whatever subject happened to engross her pen in terms of undiluted lachrymosity." Variety, she intuited, was not what her readers wanted. St. Cyres speculates that "quite an appreciable proportion of her tears was due to purely literary requirements," reminding us that she "was the servant of the public, and her many-headed master called for a melancholy tune."[30] His ironic commentary on Smith's career recognizes the rhetorical salience of a turn away from quotidian temporality and into an interior realm of the emotions, which have a chronology of their own.

I have been arguing that Smith's sonnets won readers by demonstrating her obliviousness to their presence, a pose enhanced by her formal language and what Cameron calls "lyric time." Yet her success depended equally upon her believability: the reader must have the sensation of witnessing "real woe" in order to respond with the sympathy and loyalty she required, publishing on average one work per year. The sonnets' success required both extreme emotions and a perception of their authenticity, a combination of exaggeration and actuality, theatricality and sincerity, which contemporary readers did not find contradictory. Leigh Hunt confirms her success at combining these qualities in her sonnets, testifying that several of them "are popular for their truth alone": "[E]verybody likes the sonnets because nobody doubts their being in earnest, and because they furnish a gentle voice to feelings that are universal."[31]

That most of Smith's readers seemed persuaded of the sonnets' truthfulness is especially remarkable given their self-consciously theatrical tenor. Moreover, as Adela Pinch points out, Smith's habitual use of literary allusions raises epistemological questions about the sources of her sorrow, since she borrows so many phrases to express it. How are her readers, or even the poet herself, to be sure that the despair she voices is hers?[32] Yet by the time that the first edition of the sonnets appeared in 1784, Smith's potential readers were well schooled in the conventions of sensibility, a tradition that collapsed the ostensible boundaries between life and art by presenting codes of behavior to be followed by poets, novel characters, and readers alike. As Janet Todd explains, "[i]n all forms of sentimental literature, there is an assumption that life and literature are directly linked, not through any notion of a mimetic depiction of reality but through the belief that the literary experience can intimately affect the living one."[33] Thus, Smith's readers would not necessarily question the authenticity of her poet's lamentations, even though her responses to loss were modeled on literary figures who had experienced a similar despair. The symbiotic relationship between art and life that sensibility prescribed would have encouraged Smith to borrow from other poets, even as her readers would feel encouraged to model their own expressions of grief on her poet—as contemporaneous sonnets addressed to or about Smith in periodicals suggest that many did.

In the preface to the first edition, Smith stakes her claim to the poems' sincerity by explaining their compositional origins: "Some very melancholy moments have been beguiled by expressing in verse the sensations those moments brought" (3). The explanatory notes support this claim to autobiographical veracity by grounding the poems in Smith's extensive reading and in her very public biography. A note to the poem, "Written in Farm Wood, South Downs, in May 1784" (Sonnet XXXI), glosses a reference to "Alpine flowers": "An infinite variety of plants are found on these hills, particularly about this spot: many sorts of Orchis and Cistus of singular beauty, with

several others." The note contextualizes the poem autobiographi-
cally: the sonnet was written on walks in Smith's native Sussex, where
"Alpine flowers" grew. Sir Walter Scott, who preferred her novels to
her poetry, comments: "It may be remarked, that Mrs. Smith not
only preserves in her landscapes the truth and precision of a painter,
but that they sometimes evince marks of her own favourite pursuits
and studies."[34] The notes' attention to natural historical detail lends
an authenticity to the volume that in turn lends credence to her emotional claims: her poet's extreme sorrow is more believable because
Smith situates her in a carefully documented environment. Thus, although Smith sets up a contrast between the self-consciously poetic
natural imagery of the sonnets and the empirical and vernacular vocabulary of the notes, the notes serve to confirm the poems' truthfulness by showing that her descriptions—of her environment and, by
implication, her emotions—are accurate.

John Clare testifies to the effectiveness of what might be termed a
rhetoric of empirical evidence in the notes. In Clare's description of
"[t]he Fern Owl or Goatsucker or Nightjar or nighthawk" in one of
his unpublished Natural History Letters, he alludes to Smith's poem,
"Composed during a walk on the Downs, in November 1787" (Sonnet XLII). He says of her poems, "I felt much pleasd with them because she wrote more from what she had seen of nature then from
what she had read of it there fore those that read her poems find new
images which they had not read of before tho they have often felt
them & from those assosiations poetry derives the power of pleasing
in the happiest manner."[35] Clare echoes Cowper's sense that reading
Smith's sonnets is like finding one's own reactions recorded in them.
For Clare, it is not emotions, but responses to natural scenes, that
seem familiar, yet "new." He testifies to the pleasure of this experience as a reader and incorporates her example into his own poetics,
especially his early, richly descriptive sonnets. What Clare learns from
Smith is that a sense of the sincerity of the poet's responses to a natural environment could be compelling, a lesson he proves himself with
his initial success in *Poems Descriptive of Rural Life and Scenery.*
Thus the notes both verify the poet's sentiments and confirm the timelessness of her plight. They remove the poet from her readers' quotidian experience even as they render her more accessible to their
understanding.

ℒ

In the sonnets, Smith learns to exercise the rhetorical potential of the often overlooked relationship between the lyric poet and an audience; in her longer poems, *The Emigrants* and *Beachy Head,* she most fully demonstrates that understanding, employing the capacity of lyricism for social ends. By turning her pen to specific causes, including but extending beyond her own financial relief, Smith pursues the implications of her discovery of the considerable appeal of an autobiographical lyric speaker lost in sorrowful reflections. In these poems, the implications of Smith's poetics for revisions of canonical models of Romantic lyricism are most fully evident.

These long poems represent not a departure from the sonnets but an extension of their poetic strategies. In *The Emigrants,* Smith makes a case for the émigrés arriving on British shores in 1793. Her rhetorical strategy remains lyric: she simply expands the sonnets' sharp focus on her autobiographical poet to include others whom she perceived as like her. Smith associates the émigrés with her already popular cultural figure, and thus attempts to lend to them some of the sympathy she had generated for herself. Stuart Curran describes the poem's "underlying metaphorical strategy," which is "to connect Charlotte Smith as center of perception to the exiles from France's Terror."[36] A strong sense of the poet's presence remains in the poem, even though the title figures are usually in the foreground. As the *European Magazine* observes, "we can discover" the poet "almost at the bottom of every page, as we may the portrait of some of the most renowned painters in the corner of their most favourite pictures." The critic recognizes the poem's lyric impetus by noting that "[t]he whole Poem may be considered as a soliloquy pronounced by the authoress."[37] Although much of the poem is devoted to describing the émigrés' circumstances, the speaker remains at its center, the filtering consciousness through which we view their wandering forms; their plight is seen through her melancholy lens.

Smith identifies herself with the émigrés by recalling her own experience of exile in Normandy, where the family fled from her husband's creditors, from fall 1784 to spring 1785. Smith seems to have accompanied her husband, with their children, because he could not speak French; she immediately returned to England in an effort to appease his creditors, but her failure prompted her return for the winter. She explains in the poem's dedication to Cowper that she was drawn to represent the plight of the émigrés because their figures "pressed upon an heart, that has learned, perhaps from its own sufferings, to feel with acute, though unavailing compassion, the calamity of others" (132). The émigrés were also attractive to Smith because their circumstances could easily be drawn into parallel with her own. Stanton points out that Smith emphasized her genteel origins in her works; she identified herself by her father's family estate in the first edition of *Elegiac Sonnets* by calling herself "Charlotte Smith, of Bignor Park, Sussex." In *The Emigrants*, she associates herself with French aristocrats, particularly a mother who sits disconsolate, surrounded by her children, on the Sussex shore. Smith features the clergy and nobility, whose falls from privilege made their histories resonate with her very public biography, although estimates of the social status of the émigrés have suggested that 25 percent were clergy, 17 percent nobility, and 51 percent from the Third Estate.[38]

Following Edmund Burke's *Reflections on the Revolution in France* and Thomas Paine's rebuttal in *The Rights of Man,* Smith enters the revolution debate with a poetics of sympathy pitched at middle- and upper-class readers. In the poem, she models for readers the kind of sympathetic response toward the émigrés that she wants them to imitate. *The Emigrants* is important to an understanding of the rhetorical salience of Smith's lyricism because it tests how successfully it could respond to social topics. Two facets of Smith's lyricism come into focus in *The Emigrants:* its potential for moving readers about others' causes, and the liabilities of this strategy for the poet. With *The Emigrants,* she learned that the strength of her poet's appeal could be turned against her, in that many critiques of the poem were highly personal in tone. Yet the negative responses that Smith received also testify to a contemporary understanding that lyric poetry could be an effective vehicle for addressing social events.

The poem appears in the same year as *The Old Manor House,* Smith's fifth novel, and after the sixth edition of *Elegiac Sonnets* (1792). It was published early in the summer of 1793, in the wake of the September massacres, the trial and execution of Louis XVI on 21 January 1793, and the outbreak, ten days later, of war between France and England. Smith's positive representation of revolution in

France and reform in England in *Desmond* (1792) was followed by *The Emigrants* and *The Banished Man* (1794), a poem that promotes sympathy for the émigrés and a novel that features an émigré protagonist. These works are part of what Florence Hilbish calls Smith's "French period," which included works published from 1791 to 1793, written "out of the author's sympathy for those oppressed, whether politically, socially, or economically."[39] The publication of Smith's "French" works follows a trajectory similar to the autobiographical narrative that Wordsworth provides in *The Prelude,* detailing his change of heart after the declaration of war and the increasing violence of the revolution's aftermath. Smith intimates a similar conversion in the poem's dedication to Cowper. Yet although she laments the excesses of the revolution, she does not renounce radical ideals, as does Coleridge in "France: An Ode." In fact, Smith circumspectly defends her radical ideals in the dedication, arguing that "by confounding the original cause with the wretched catastrophes that have followed its ill management," the revolution itself has unfairly become tainted, and "the very name of Liberty" has "lost the charm it used to have in British ears." But Smith publicly distances herself from radical politics in defending the exiles of the ancien régime.

She joins instead a popular middle-class cause, promoted by conservative figures such as Hannah More, who published two pamphlets to raise money for the émigrés' support, one titled *An Elegant and Pathetic Address for the Ladies of Great Britain on behalf of the French Emigrants.* More's profits were contributed to a "Fund for the Relief of the Suffering Clergy of France in the British Dominions," begun by John Eardley Wilmot, son of the lord chief justice, in September 1792. Wilmot had advertised for a meeting to organize relief, one prominent enough to be reported in the *Gentleman's Magazine,* which had a solidly middle-class audience.[40] The meeting was attended by such prominent figures as Edmund Burke, William Wilberforce, and the bishops of London and Durham. Other groups were simultaneously being formed for similar purposes. In 1795 the duchess of York organized a committee specifically for "'female emigrants who were ill or *en couches.*'"[41] Thus when Smith represents an émigrée surrounded by her children in *The Emigrants,* she features a figure already prominent in the popular imagination.

The poem opens with an expansive description of the poet's view of the Sussex coast, a scene that prompts reflections on the contrast between its tranquility and human suffering. We recognize Smith's autobiographical poet "on the Cliffs to the Eastward of the Town of Brighthelmstone in Sussex" on "a Morning in November, 1792." She watches a group of exiles: several members of the Catholic clergy, a mother with children, and a nobleman who speaks to the woman. They are "Fortune's worthless favourites" (I.315) and, as such, Smith can align their circumstances with hers. Solitary sorrow gives way to shared misery as she exclaims, "Alas! how few the morning wakes to joy!" In the sonnets, the poet is usually the sole unhappy figure in the scenes she surveys, yet the emigrants are easily incorporated into the poet's contemplations. They are linked with the poet formally by repeated turns in thought, which join their plight with hers. After describing several members of the clergy wandering along the Sussex cliffs, the poet's reflections shift to her own sorrows:

> . . .—Still, as Men misled
> By early prejudice (so hard to break),
> I mourn your sorrows; for I too have known
> Involuntary exile; and while yet
> England had charms for me, have felt how sad
> It is to look across the dim cold sea,
> That melancholy rolls its refluent tides
> Between us and the dear regretted land
> We call our own—as now ye pensive wait
> On this bleak morning, gazing on the waves
> That seem to leave your shore . . .
>   (I.153–63)

The passage begins with the poet observing "men misled" from a distance, but she quickly recognizes her affinity with them, practicing the sympathetic identification that she models for readers, as "I" becomes "us" and "we." She literally puts herself in their position: she recalls gazing "across the dim cold sea" toward home during her self-exile in France. In fact, meditation upon her own circumstances encourages the poet to detect signs of distress in others. She is drawn to the exiles because they resemble her; there is clearly a narcissistic impulse in her response to them. Yet that impulse also serves to keep her attention on their circumstances, and as a result she incorporates them into her meditations.

Like the poet of the sonnets, she observes her surroundings and then reflects upon what she sees. This turn inward is often assumed to mark the eclipse of the external world, yet here an internalizing impulse actually projects the poet into social scenes:

> Long wintry months are past; the Moon that now
> Lights her pale crescent even at noon, has made
> Four times her revolution; since with step,
> Mournful and slow, along the wave-worn cliff,
> Pensive I took my solitary way,
> Lost in despondence, while contemplating
> Not my own wayward destiny alone,
> (Hard as it is, and difficult to bear!)
> But in beholding the unhappy lot
> Of the lorn Exiles; who, amid the storms
> Of wild disastrous Anarchy, are thrown,
> Like shipwreck'd sufferers, on England's coast,
> To see, perhaps, no more their native land,
> Where Desolation riots: They, like me,
> From fairer hopes and happier prospects driven,
> Shrink from the future, and regret the past.
> (II.1–16)

The poet begins the passage "solitary" and "lost in despondence," but in the act of "contemplating" her "own wayward destiny," she begins to consider the "lorn Exiles." She demonstrates that the lyric's progress toward interiority need not lead to disengagement. The poem suggests that introspection should not be equated with solipsism, that a desire for transcendence can coexist with social feeling.

Moreover, the poem thematizes the poet's decision not to look away from what she sees. Near its opening, she confesses a desire for retreat, for the kind of detachment we expect of the lyric poet:

> How often do I half abjure Society,
> And sigh for some lone Cottage, deep embower'd
> In the green woods, that these steep chalky Hills

Guard from the strong South West; where round their base
The Beach wide flourishes, and the light Ash
With slender leaf half hides the thymy turf!—
There do I wish to hide me . . .

(I.42–48)

The poet longs to be "embower'd" and alone, and thus seems to exemplify a desire that has characterized Romantic lyricism in canonical paradigms. She does not want to "witness" the suffering she describes, and imagines that turning away from it might bring relief of her own unhappiness: she "might better learn to bear" the "woes" that "injustice, and duplicity / And faithlessness and folly, fix on me" (I.57-60). She feels an impulse to forget "human woes," one she ignores only because she understands that no bower "Can shut out for an hour the spectre Care" (I.90). In Smith's account, the sharp self-consciousness of the lyric poet results in an inability to "shut out" others' sorrows, rather than the protection of a strictly interior realm.

In Smith's poem, memory exceeds the categories with which it is associated in canonical models of Romantic lyricism: it is not reduced to private consolation, nor does it serve the ideological work of obscuring traumatic historical scenes. In Abrams's account of the "greater Romantic lyric," recollection marks the moment in which the speaker turns away from a world of daily events to a personal past and to private emotions; much new historicist work concurs.[42] In *The Emigrants,* in contrast, the poet's memory becomes the vehicle for the émigrés' recollections. She "remembers" their social scenes: "Shuddering, I view the pictures they have drawn / Of desolated countries, where the ground, / Stripp'd of its unripe produce, was thick strewn / With various Death" (II.216-19). In Smith's poetry, the act of recollection need not distance the poet from others, nor is it inherently an isolating practice. The poet connects her own recollections of happier times with similar reflections by the exiles, whose thoughts she seems to overhear like the omniscient narrator of a novel.

Memory here is double-edged: it restores images of a blissful childhood even as it resuscitates a traumatic past. After rehearsing the emigrants' recollections, Smith turns to another set of memories for consolation. As Wordsworth will do in "Tintern Abbey," she reverts

to childhood scenes for recovery from loss. But in *The Emigrants,*
that loss is explicitly social:

> . . . Memory come!
> And from distracting cares, that now deprive
> Such scenes of all their beauty, kindly bear
> My fancy to those hours of simple joy,
> When, on the banks of Arun, which I see
> Makes its irriguous course thro' younder meads,
> I play'd; unconscious then of future ill!
>   (II.328–34)

The "future ill" she refers to is the "chicane and fraud" that have
prolonged the Chancery suit and necessitated her "never-ending toil"
(II.355, 350). In an echo of Gray's "Eton Ode," the remembrance of
former happiness involves reflection upon its dissolution. For Smith's
poet, recollection provides both reassuring images of youthful vitality and a reliving of sorrows that, in *The Emigrants,* are decidedly
social. Far from being the vehicle of her individual history alone, her
memory cannot be distinguished from historical consciousness. Her
memory does not excavate an isolated past, but rather brings with it
traces of social history in the form of the contingent details associated with specific events.

Memory is social in Smith's poetry in another way—it strengthens the identificatory bond between poet and readers, and by extension, she hopes, between readers and émigrés. The faculty of memory
is an intimate one, and it furthers Smith's efforts to make readers feel
that they know her well enough to pity her and her subjects. As Walter
Benjamin puts it, the "two elements of memory" are personal and
social history: "Where there is experience in the strict sense of the
word, certain contents of the individual past combine with material
of the collective past."[43] Smith's poet shares with readers both her
past and the émigrés' former lives. Memory plays a role in the sonnets—underlying their mournful tone is a quintessential phrase from
Beachy Head—"I once was happy" (line 282). But in *The Emigrants,*
her memories are allowed to develop. The effect is an enhancement
of the intimacy between poet and readers fostered by the theatrical
dynamic of "overhearing" private thoughts. The poet's disclosure of

events in her past strengthens lyricism's autobiographical quality and lends emotional weight to the cult of personality generated by *Elegiac Sonnets*.

In considering how Smith develops the rhetorical uses of memory, I want to turn briefly to *Beachy Head,* unfinished at the time of her death, because in this poem she expands her repertoire of the historical uses to which her poet's memory may be put. *Beachy Head* features an antiquary who is Smith's alter ego in the poem, a figure who collects artifacts such as the "enormous bones" of the "huge unwieldy Elephant" (lines 412, 417), as the poet recalls the natural historical events such evidence indicates. Like *The Emigrants,* the poem opens with an embodiment of the lyric speaker's characteristic stance: she sits with her back toward us, on the "projecting headland" of Beachy Head, where she commands a vast perspective literally and figuratively. She begins, as in the sonnets and *The Emigrants,* by observing her natural surroundings: in the opening section, she follows a single day's passage, until she can see only a skiff "crossing on the moonbright line" before being "lost in shadow" (lines 115–17). After sweeping paragraphs of natural description comes the expected turn inward. The speaker compares herself to the familiar figure of "Contemplation," and the other primary figure associated with Romantic lyricism, "Memory." But here, the processes of reflection and recollection are the vehicles of both personal and social history. Repeated turns in thought link the Norman Conquest, the use of slave labor, theories of evolution, and her own past. As in *The Emigrants,* "Contemplation" raises social questions, and the evocation of "Memory" is followed by historical scenes:

> . . . Contemplation here,
> High on her throne of rock, aloof may sit,
> And bid recording Memory unfold
> Her scroll voluminous—bid her retrace
> The period, when from Neustria's hostile shore
> The Norman launch'd his galleys, and the bay
> O'er which that mass of ruin frowns even now
> In vain and sullen menace, then received
> The new invaders . . .
>
> (lines 117–25)

The speaker recalls, alternately, her own childhood and England's settlement; memory constructs a history of the ground on which she stands. The Sussex coast is both the site of her childhood and the setting for historical events. Memory's scroll is a historical record that documents the "growth," not only of a "poet's mind" but also of a nation. In *Beachy Head,* Smith aligns the lyric poet's practice of recollection with the historian's recovery of a social past.

In the poem, "Contemplation" and "Memory" facilitate social consciousness. The speaker begins her meditations by describing the scenes before her, the human and natural activity on the Channel, including "fishing vessels" and a "ship of commerce." Speculating on the ship's cargo leads the poet to reflect upon a political topic, namely, the use of slave labor for gathering pearls. Drawing on Robert Percival's *Account of the Island of Ceylon,* she imagines "the round pearl[s]" that the slave

> With perilous and breathless toil, tears off
> From the rough sea-rock, deep beneath the waves.
> These are the toys of Nature; and her sport
> Of little estimate in Reason's eye:
> And they who reason, with abhorrence see
> Man, for such gaudes and baubles, violate
> The sacred freedom of his fellow man—
> Erroneous estimate! . . .
>
> (lines 53–60)

These contemplations are especially pointed in a poem written before the abolition of the slave trade in 1807. This commentary is thoroughly integrated into wide-ranging speculations upon events past and present, human and natural, social and private. From these thoughts, the speaker turns her attention to the fishing boats returning home at evening and then to the Norman invasion, a brief account of which is incorporated into a description of the place. After narrating a setback to the British and Dutch forces in a 1690 naval battle against the French fought off Beachy Head, the speaker's "reflecting mind returns / To simple scenes of peace and industry" (lines 168–69).

Smith's success in gaining her primary end in *The Emigrants* is confirmed by critics who manifest the sympathy that she advocates.[44] The *Analytical Review* reports: "[S]he draws several interesting and affecting pictures of their misfortunes, and applauds that generous sympathy, which ministers relief to a brother in distress, without listening to the chilling remonstrance of national or political prejudice."[45] The *Monthly Review* also credits Smith with arousing readers' sympathy for the emigrants:

> Whatever is capable of exciting the generous emotions of sympathy is a proper subject of poetry, whose office is to afford pleasure by presenting interesting objects to the imagination. The sufferings of the French emigrants certainly furnish a subject of this kind; and poetry, like charity, will dwell only on such circumstances as are best fitted to excite its proper feelings. In the poem before us, Mrs. Smith has judiciously confined her attention to those particulars in the case of the emigrants, which have excited sympathy in the minds of the humane of all parties; and she describes their condition with that propriety and tenderness, which those who are acquainted with her former productions will be prepared to expect.[46]

Although Smith is praised here for choosing a "proper" subject and for treating it "with propriety and tenderness," these terms indicate the danger to Smith herself of her own poetic strategies: once she entered political debates, she submitted herself to critiques as a woman writer. In critical responses to *The Emigrants,* Smith discovered the risk to herself of turning her poet's personal appeal to political ends. Her poems' autobiographical focus made her particularly visible as a woman writer and thereby censurable along gendered lines.[47]

Smith's deft use of the lyric mode in *Elegiac Sonnets* made her a popular poet by drawing readers to her autobiographical lyric speaker. Yet Smith's prominence in her own works—in her poems' lyric speakers and her novels' autobiographical characters—had complex consequences for her career. In the early editions of the sonnets, Smith makes herself a sympathetic figure partly by presenting herself as reserved and solitary by nature. Adopting a familiar trope of modesty, she confides that she submits herself to public view only at others' urging: "Some of my friends, with partial indiscretion, have multiplied the copies they procured of several of these attempts, till they found their way into the prints of the day in a mutilated state; which, concurring with other circumstances, determined me to put them into their present form" (3). In the 1792 preface to the sixth edition, she assures readers, "I am well aware that for a woman— 'The Post of Honor is a Private Station'" (6). But in the course of her career, it became clear that she continued to appear in public willingly, if under financial duress.

Smith risked gendered critiques even more directly when she eventually explained the biographical sources of her poet's habitual elegiac tenor. The sixth edition of *Elegiac Sonnets* marks a turning point in the volume's history: for the first time, Smith assigns a material cause to her unhappiness by referring to her legal battle with the trustees of her father-in-law's estate. Critics have noted that in her novels, her anger emerges in her villainization of lawyers, the judicial system, and extravagant and abusive husbands. Her rage also surfaces in her poems and prefaces. In 1792, she elaborates her story in the context of the conversation with the friend who suggested she might venture "a more cheerful style of composition":

> The time is indeed arrived, when I have been promised by 'the Honourable Men' who, nine years ago, undertook to see that my family obtained the provision their grandfather designed for them,—that 'all should be well, all should be settled.' But still I am condemned to feel the 'hope delayed that maketh the heart sick.' (5)

I turn now to the implications of Smith's eventual attribution of a precise source of agency to sorrows that in early editions seemed almost existential. For in making a more explicit call for sympathy from readers, as she does in this preface, Smith relinquished some of the indirection that had constituted the sonnets' appeal, and in doing so she discovered the rhetorical limits of her lyricism for a woman writer. These restrictions were, however, not formal but social. An increasing ambivalence on the part of many of Smith's reviewers reflected not lyricism's rhetorical incapacity, but rather restrictions on what a woman poet with radical sympathies and a proven ability to move readers could say in a politically turbulent period. For Smith's new specificity about the sources of her sorrow gave her lamentations a political inflection that she increasingly employed not only to argue her own case in the court of public opinion but also to speak for others whom she considered fellow sufferers. Later editions of the *Sonnets* reflected this shift in Smith's public profile, when she added poems that alluded more explicitly both to the biographical sources of her poet's despair (such as "Written at Bignor Park in Sussex, in August, 1799" [Sonnet XCII]) and to social events (such as "The Sea View" [Sonnet LXXXIII], which expresses antiwar sentiments). More strikingly, in the same year that the preface to the sixth edition of the sonnets appeared, Smith published her fourth novel, *Desmond,* which features an English protagonist who travels to revolutionary France and is persuaded by its ideals.

Smith's increasing explicitness about the material conditions of her own melancholy was prompted by her frustration with the Chancery suit and the exhausting pace of her career. She established herself with the sonnets, but soon found it necessary to turn to a more remunerative genre, the novel. *Emmeline* appeared four years after the first edition of *Elegiac Sonnets,* which was then in its fourth edition. After the success of this novel, she published nine others between 1788 and 1798. She also entered the burgeoning marketplace for children's literature, beginning with *Rural Walks* (1795). Smith took several breaks from writing (in 1801, 1803, and 1805) in order to devote herself to her campaign to have Richard Smith's estate settled when it seemed that the Chancery suit might be resolved.[48] But persistent legal frustrations, and the continued financial needs of her family, kept her writing until her death in 1806; two works appeared posthumously: *Beachy Head, with Other Poems,* its title poem unfinished, and *The Natural History of Birds,* which also appeared in 1807. Smith also suffered the intermittent returns of her husband, who had legal rights to her earnings despite their separation. A book contract for *Desmond* named Benjamin, rather than Charlotte, as the legal party.[49]

In its notice of volume 2 of *Elegiac Sonnets* (1797), Joseph

Johnson's politically liberal *Analytical Review* exemplifies the ideal response to her growing frankness. The reviewer advances Smith's bid for sympathy, and thus attempts to lend her the practical assistance that Cowper also wanted to provide: "We have chosen to extract these passages from the preface of our author, for the purpose of contributing, so far as lies in our power, to the notoriety of her injuries, and of exciting the public attention to the peculiar circumstances of aggravation which attend them." The critic anticipates that, not only would publicizing Smith's cause fan the flames of popular support, but it might also shame her adversaries in the Chancery suit into greater benevolence: "As to her oppressors, however they may be dead to honesty and humanity, we can scarcely believe it possible that they should have outlived all sensibility to shame: no man is not gratified with the smiles of the world, or is any one so completely hardened, that he would not feel mortified at one universal frown of contempt and indignation." Thus the critic becomes Smith's advocate, publicizing her cause and using the periodical's influence to pressure her "oppressors."[50]

Yet critics from both ends of the political spectrum—including the *Analytical Review*—were alarmed when it became clear that Smith understood her influence as a popular cultural figure, and that she was willing to use it to address social issues. They recognized that even Smith's habitual practices of self-promotion and self-defense were political gestures, for as Curran notes, many of her works reflect "her recognition that the law is a social code written by men for a male preserve, and that the principal function of women within its boundaries can only be to suffer consequences over which they have no control."[51] Critics have identified different moments as inaugurating a decline in Smith's popularity, and have attributed this decline to various causes, including her prolific output. Yet there is a persuasive consensus among Smith's latter-day critics that this decline begins sometime in the years in which her public figure became politicized, with the publication of the sixth edition of *Elegiac Sonnets, Desmond, The Old Manor House* (1793), *The Emigrants* (1793), and *The Banished Man* (1794).[52] In the two latter works, Smith renders sympathetic French émigrés from the nobility, aristocracy, and clergy in works that some critics read as a retraction of her support of revolution abroad and reform at home in *Desmond.*

Critical responses to *The Banished Man* by the *British Critic* and the *Analytical Review* testify to a keen contemporaneous recognition of the influence that Smith could exert in treating political topics. The *British Critic,* delighted with Smith's seeming change of heart about the revolution, deems that "she makes full atonement by the virtues of the Banished Man, for the errors of Desmond," and closes its review by "congratulating the lovers of their king and the constitution, in the acquisition of an associate like Mrs. Charlotte Smith." The critic concludes by declaring with evident satisfaction that "[s]uch a convert, gained by fair conviction, is a valuable prize to the commonwealth." The legitimacy of this boast is supported by the simultaneous lamentation of the *Analytical Review* for its perceived loss of Smith as an ally: "As commonly happens to new converts, she is beyond all measure vehement in her exclamations against the late proceedings of the french."[53]

Although critics such as these often directly assailed Smith's politics, others employed a more ingenious strategy, by censuring Smith's conduct as a woman writer. She was assailed for the very quality that had initiated her success—her works' intense autobiographical focus—when critics charged her with "egotism," a critique particularly damning for a woman whose literary success was greatly facilitated by her personal appeal. The *European Magazine* focuses on the autobiographical impulse of Smith's works in its review of *The Banished Man.* The critic explains that "the apology she makes for her frequent recurrence to family distresses will have its full weight with us," yet "we would have her rail like a gentlewoman always." Smith is warned that the strong language she uses for her enemies in the legal battle over her father-in-law's estate is reserved for men: "terms of abuse," she is told, have been "appropriated" by the "male sex," and their rights to them are not to be "invaded" by women, with one significant exception, "those resistless nymphs who deal out the scaly treasures of the ocean from a certain part of this metropolis."[54] Smith is publicly warned that her writings are taking her out of the company of respectable women and placing her in the company of the fishwives who populated Billingsgate Fishmarket, and whose colorful and unusually inventive obscenities have earned them a place to this day in encyclopedias of English culture and language.

In the course of her career, Smith discovered that she could only act indirectly, winning readers who might become advocates by turning away from them and asking for nothing. In the lyric, she found a mode in which she could render herself sympathetic by expressing her sorrows, ostensibly to herself, her solitary stance proof against charges that she had designs upon readers. Smith's averted gaze in the sonnets was both effective and necessary. Readers, including patrons and critics, were often glad to act for her, and Smith received generous assistance from publishers (especially her first publisher, Thomas Cadell Sr.), and from various patrons throughout her career. But she discovered that she was reliant upon their continued sympathy, and upon the sustained interest of her readers. She similarly lacked the ability to act for herself in the Chancery suit: she could not prod its resolution directly because women could not act as legal agents. The necessity of enlisting the help of others, including Sir George O'Brien Wyndham, third earl of Egremont, and continually urging them to act eventually cost her patrons, including Egremont and Hayley. In the sonnet "To Dependence" (Sonnet LVII), Smith's poet laments: "Dependence! heavy, heavy are thy chains." In the poem, Smith alludes to the Chancery suit in declaring her determination to devote herself to "the Mountain Nymph," (Milton's Liberty in "L'Allegro") even "tho' Pride combine / With Fraud to crush me."

In its final review of her poetry, published after her death, the *British Critic* provides a clear assessment of Smith's predicament. The review opens by acknowledging, "[w]e could not, indeed, always accord with her in sentiment." The critic chastises her in gendered terms: "With respect to some subjects beyond her line of experience, reading, and indeed talent, she was unfortunately wayward and preposterous; but her poetic feeling and ability have rarely been surpassed by any individual of her sex." Yet this censure is qualified by the review's close: "We take our leave of this author with unfeigned regret and sympathy." The critic explains why:

Her life was embittered by sorrow and misfortune, [and] this gave an unavoidable tinge to her sentiments, which, from the gay and the vain, and the unfeeling, may excite a sneer of scorn and contempt; but in the bosoms of those who, like Charlotte Smith, with refined feelings, improved by thought and study, and reflection, have been compelled, like her, to

tread the thorny paths of adversity, will prompt the generous
wish, that fortune had favoured her with more complacency;
and will induce the disposition to extenuate such portions of
her productions, as sterner judgment is unable to approve.[55]

This eulogy of Smith, patronizing and "generous," censorious and
admiring, testifies to her precarious position throughout her career:
she could win sympathy but could not state her case bluntly without
risking her income and her gentlewomanly reputation.

In the lyric, Smith found a formal vehicle of indirection and complexity: by appearing to be lost in mournful reflections, she won a
popular audience; in presenting herself as a mother writing only to
support her children, she gained a public position from which to
pressure the trustees of her father-in-law's estate. Her career makes
plain that for a woman writer dependent upon her earnings, the lyric
offered the necessary guise of modesty, the proper stance of an averted
gaze. Smith's pragmatic view of the form is highly instructive. By
continuing to present her readers with more sonnets in the multiply-
ing editions of *Elegiac Sonnets,* she proved herself wise enough to
know that she had found in the sonnet's "small plot of ground" a
rare and viable, yet sharply circumscribed, forum for a woman to
make public the sorrows of dependence.

THREE

William Wordsworth and the Uses of Lyricism

Wordsworth's words always *mean* the whole of their possible Meaning.

—Samuel Taylor Coleridge (1803)

From the very first, no doubt, he had his believers and witnesses. But I have myself heard him declare that, for he knew not how many years, his poetry had never brought him in enough to buy his shoe-strings. The poetry-reading public was very slow to recognise him, and was very easily drawn away from him.

—Matthew Arnold on Wordsworth (1879)

Models of Romantic lyricism and Wordsworth's career have existed in a kind of palimpsest: beneath the tableau of the solitary poet turning his attention from his surroundings to private meditations is the career of a "representative" poet, who moved away from active political engagement toward the aesthetic realm of the imagination.[1] As the only canonical poet to have been in revolutionary France, Wordsworth's life has seemed to exemplify a historical shift on the part of English radicals from engagement in revolution and reform to retreat in the wake of the Terror, war, and governmental repression at home. Models of lyricism have played an important role in critical discussions of Wordsworth's political conversion. Given the scarcity of Wordsworth's own explanations of his radical associations and increasing conservatism, critics have analyzed his literary forms as one measure of political change. The emergence in 1798 of what has been deemed the mature lyricism of "Lines Written a Few Miles Above Tintern Abbey" has proved a helpful marker in murky psychological and historical terrain: Wordsworth's acts of reflection and recollection in that poem and in *The Prelude* have been interpreted as a withdrawal from political engagement. But there has been a cost in using a notion of lyric transcendence to elucidate psychological and historical complexity: a simplification of a key modal paradigm, a narrowing of its tendencies to a drive toward introspection. I am not suggesting that there is not an impulse in Wordsworthian lyricism toward transcendence, but rather that critics have made their cases for lyricism's formal enactment of a disengagement from political sympathies too successfully; that is, we have come to associate the form exclusively with one particular political trajectory. Neither am I arguing that Romantic lyricism is inherently radical, but rather that the mode's potential for social engagement has been obscured by influential critical models. I argue instead for an understanding of Wordsworthian lyricism as the frequent site of vexed personal and political impulses, a model that accords with Coleridge's notion that "Wordsworth's words always *mean* the whole of their possible meaning."[2]

Paradigms of Romantic lyricism are invested with a heavy, if invisible, weight of biographical and sociohistorical meaning in M. H. Abrams's two influential essays, "Structure and Style in the Greater Romantic Lyric" and "English Romanticism: The Spirit of the Age." In defining the "greater Romantic lyric," Abrams influentially links poetics and politics: "The great Romantic poems were written not in the mood of revolutionary exaltation but in the later mood of revolutionary disillusionment or despair."[3] The persistence of this paradigm is evident in Alan Liu's dissenting but parallel argument that *The Prelude*'s lyrical autobiography is Wordsworth's "crowning denial of history."[4] The bond between poetic form, biography, and social history has been so firmly forged that Marjorie Levinson takes it for granted in her new historicist revision of Romantic lyricism. She reads "Tintern Abbey" as a "conversion of public to private property, history to poetry."[5] These critics equate a mature Wordsworthian lyricism with an apolitical stance, whether they view that stance as aesthetically valuable or as ideologically suspect. I view the relationship as more dynamic than either Abrams's model of transcendence or these new historical models of repression, or denial, presume.

As I argued in chapter 1, political content was built into our definitions of Romantic lyricism by critics such as John Stuart Mill, precisely by his efforts to dissociate the two. Mill had to enforce a distinction between "poetry" and "eloquence" because it is so easily collapsed, and the relationship between poetics and politics so readily complicated. This is nowhere more evident than in Wordsworth's works, which provide Mill with many of his precepts. I have largely credited Mill with investing Romantic lyricism with an aura it has never shed, although the halo has been tarnished as transcendence gave way to ideological critiques by deconstructionist, feminist, and new historicist critics. But it is important to remember how significantly Mill was aided in the construction of Romantic lyricism by the poet who provided one of his primary examples. If one of the difficulties of Wordsworth's early career was his failure at *"creating the taste by which he is to be enjoyed,"* he has made up for it in the long critical wake of his success.[6] Before Mill looked to Wordsworth's example in answering "What is Poetry?" the poet provided his own answer in terms that laid the foundations for paradigms of Romantic lyricism. The poet published influential explanations of his poetic project in 1814-15: the Prospectus to *The Excursion* and the 1815 *Poems*, including its Preface and Essay, Supplementary to the Preface. Mill cites the 1815 *Poems* as his first important encounter with Wordsworth's poetry; Abrams describes the Prospectus as "the manifesto of a central Romantic enterprise."[7]

Originally meant to appear together, these two works were part of Wordsworth's major effort to define his career, both retrospectively and prospectively. One of my main concerns is how, in the process, Wordsworth protectively revises an earlier self and more engaged lyricism that he had presented to the public in *Lyrical Ballads*. By absorbing that collection, with its Preface, into the 1815 *Poems*, Wordsworth incorporates a more politically active poet into a conservative account of his poetics. In light of the 1814–15 definitions, "Tintern Abbey" especially has seemed to usher in a mature Wordsworthian lyricism. But reading the poem as part of a collection of experiments in the uses of lyricism discovers, at the heart of canonical Romantic lyricism, a strong counterimpulse to the poem's introspective pull. It also opens to question the relationship between poetics and politics in the poem, and proposes that it is less clearly defined than our critical paradigms, drawn mostly from Wordsworth's 1814–15 accounts, presume.

In what follows, I argue that Wordsworth investigates the uses of lyricism in *Lyrical Ballads*, including its potential for social engagement.[8]

Wordsworth's lyric poems manifest, in varying degrees across his career, a conservative withdrawal from social arenas, including the literary marketplace, and conversely, a rhetorical awareness of the reader and a desire to involve that reader not only in the poet's thoughts and feelings, but, especially in *Lyrical Ballads*, in shared social concerns. By the time of the 1815 Essay, he has declared his allegiance to a poetry of "transcendence," but his own earlier lyric poems demonstrate a complexity that cannot be reduced to a poetics of privacy. The contradictory impulses of Romantic lyricism—its impetus toward introspection, on the one hand, and engagement with a natural and social environment, on the other—are evident even in *the* canonical Romantic lyric, "Tintern Abbey." By reading this poem through the lens of the 1814–15 definitions, critics have followed Wordsworth's lead in equating poetic maturity with political withdrawal, and thereby obscured the ambivalences about engagement and introspection that the poem's lyricism accommodates. I focus on two sites at which the poem seems particularly permeable by history: first, in the often downplayed role of its audiences; second, in its key practices of reflection and recollection. Before turning to *Lyrical Ballads*, however, I want to consider how Wordsworth's prescriptive 1814–15 definitions developed within the context of his career, a first step in distinguishing his tenets from his varied lyric practices.

The 1815 Essay, Supplementary to the Preface is one of the main documents in the critical construction of a Romantic lyricism associated with the aesthetic and defined against the social. But a closer look at its rhetorical context raises questions about how fully Wordsworth himself accounts for his earlier poetics. Its portrait of the detached lyrical poet must be considered as part of a polemic aimed at critics, especially Francis Jeffrey, and toward the readership he had failed to win with *Lyrical Ballads* and the 1807 *Poems*. The 1815 Essay was written between two periods in his career when he was more open toward audiences: after the general disappointment of *Lyrical Ballads* and before he eventually won an audience for *The Excursion*. In response to those who had critiqued or ignored him,

Wordsworth presents a stoic figure, steady in his faith in his poetic creeds. Yet those creeds were less fixed and more responsive to readerly response than he concedes. The 1815 portrait required a revision of an earlier self, the poet of *Lyrical Ballads*, who still wore openly his hopes of revolutionizing public opinion about the subjects and forms of poetry. In 1815, Wordsworth describes himself as indifferent to a popular audience, a solitary poet with his gaze directed beyond the literary marketplace. Jon Klancher credits the Essay with establishing "the view that has dominated Romantic scholarship for at least the last forty years: rejecting the social and historical audiences of his own time, Wordsworth imagined the distant prospect of an ideal audience."[9]

At the Essay's close, Wordsworth distinguishes the "Public" from his ideal readership, the "People," a familiar contemporaneous dichotomy that became firmly attached to definitions of Wordsworthian lyricism. Placed as it is, as a kind of final word, the distinction assumes an almost antagonistic tenor. It is part of a "defensive formulation," as Peter Murphy terms it, an effort to resolve Wordsworth's inability to find popular success by inserting himself into a long line of poets he describes as similarly unrecognized in their day, including Spenser, Shakespeare, and Milton.[10] Wordsworth's argument is strained, and the Essay betrays his struggle to assume a posture of disinterestedness, independent of readers' disdain or neglect. They must be sublimated into "the People, philosophically characterised." He addresses himself only to "the embodied spirit of their knowledge, so far as it exists and moves, at the present, faithfully supported by its two wings, the past and the future." Reduced to an "embodied spirit" and temporally dispersed, his readers are in effect stripped of their influence in criticizing his work. Abrams's comment indicates the implications for subsequent criticism: "There is, in fact, something singularly fatal to the audience in the Romantic point of view."[11]

Although Wordsworth seems to turn his back on readers in the Essay, this too was a rhetorical gesture aimed at the "Public" he claimed not to notice.[12] Wordsworth's pronouncements in the 1815 Essay would eventually define many of the terms by which he would be read, but his tone reflects an inability to internalize the disinterest that his definitions assert, especially when he elaborates his strategy for coping with a lack of popular success:

The love, the admiration, the indifference, the slight, the aversion, and even the contempt, with which these Poems have
been received, knowing, as I do, the source within my own
mind, from which they have proceeded, and the labour and
pains, which, when labour and pains appeared needful, have
been bestowed upon them, must all, if I think consistently, be
received as pledges and tokens, bearing the same general impression, though widely different in value;—they are all proofs
that for the present time I have not laboured in vain; and
afford assurances, more or less authentic, that the products
of my industry will endure. (*Prose*, 3:80)

This rather tortured line of reasoning attempts to translate "indifference," "slight[s]," "aversion," and "contempt" into "pledges and
tokens" and "proofs" of endurance. This is difficult alchemy, and the
only way that Wordsworth can sustain his faith in its process is to
remove himself from the immediacy of negative and positive responses
alike, making himself immune even to "love" and "admiration." I
use the term "faith" advisedly, for there is in this passage a straining
toward confidence in something lasting beyond the moment that requires a power greater than the poet's. Deciding to consider the mixed
responses to his poems as "tokens," or promises of "'something ev-
ermore about to be,'" he turns to a visionary mode to secure this
pledge, confirming that his poems "evince something of the 'Vision
and the Faculty divine.'"

Putting the essay into the context of a career that thus far had
generated more "indifference" and "contempt" than "admiration,"
we recognize a desire to protect his fragile investment. Wordsworth's
poems will "endure"; they will outlast their contemporary setting
and its ambivalent audiences. He defines poetry not only as a solitary
endeavor but also as one corruptible by the marketplace that he had
failed to enter successfully: "Grand thoughts . . . as they are most
naturally and most fitly conceived in solitude, so can they not be
brought forth in the midst of plaudits, without some violation of
their sanctity" (*Prose*, 3:83). He resolves instead to stay focused on
"the sources within my own mind," and thus establishes a rhetoric
of interiority which has been translated in formal terms into a model
of Romantic lyricism's turn away from social scenes.

These descriptions of the poet and his audience have assumed prominence partly because of their textual setting: Wordsworth's first collected edition represents an effort to establish a public account of his career. It is a retrospective act in which he reorganizes his oeuvre in order to reimagine it, dividing his works into a new system of descriptive categories. This broader desire for consolidation was supplemented by a more immediate need to respond to a serious professional disappointment, the apparent failure of *The Excursion*, memorably announced by Jeffrey's famous review, with its opening salvo, "This will never do."[13] In response to Jeffrey's attack, Wordsworth held up the publication of the *Poems* in order to write the Essay (the collection already contained a preface). Kenneth Johnston argues, "Wordsworth's period of retrenchment and consolidation of his reputation begins here; it was time to save the poet, not the world."[14]

The model self that he invents in the Essay represents a response not only to Jeffrey's disapprobation but also to a series of more personal recuperations. He presents a self-possessed poet (to borrow Marlon Ross's term), in an effort to recover from a period of personal, professional, and economic instability.[15] The 1810 breach with Coleridge had been partially bridged after their relationship came to a crisis in 1812, but the tenuous rapprochement of late spring could not return the pair to the productive interaction of the Alfoxden period. The collapse of this collaboration left Wordsworth vulnerable; he was now without the support of the theorist and advocate of *The Recluse*, a work he was announcing for the first time in the collection's Preface as the culmination of his career. Sorrow was succeeded by tragedy. While in London attempting to ease the estrangement from Coleridge, Wordsworth learned of the death of his three-year-old daughter, Catherine. Then, in December, six-year-old Thomas died of measles. Following the deeply felt loss of his brother John in 1805, this was an era of dissolution, especially in comparison to the brief tenure of community that had been inaugurated at Alfoxden, which was the setting for both a family reunion with Dorothy and John, and a productive partnership with Coleridge.

Given these personal losses, it is clear why the stoic remove Wordsworth describes in the 1815 Essay was desirable. It was also newly affordable. The family's persistent financial anxieties had added economic pressure to Wordsworth's frustration at not finding a broad reader-ship. His recent assumption, in 1813, of the post of distributor of stamps alleviated immediate financial concerns and urgency in finding a "Public." Supported by a waning system of patronage at various moments in his career (including the Raisley Calvert legacy, much of it loaned to friends), Wordsworth still needed the remuneration of popular success, yet was released from more extensive reliance upon readers. Newly in possession of a steady income, Wordsworth in 1815 was in a position to harbor resentment about his previous need for a supportive readership and yet to be elated at the prospect of writing with greater financial independence.

I have described various factors that made the disinterested stance of the 1814–15 documents desirable. But it is important to recognize that this period's impulse to withdraw from social arenas, including the literary marketplace, is manifested throughout his career, in vary-ing degrees. The conflict between an outward-looking, engaged rheto-ric and an impulse toward withdrawal and disengagement was fre-quently operative. The composition history of the Prospectus illus-trates the persistence of Wordsworth's ambivalence about his audi-ences. Two cardinal points in the Prospectus are the poet's attention to inner realms ("the Mind of Man") and the definition of his reader-ship borrowed from Milton ("'fit audience let me find though few'"). The Prospectus elaborates these features into a fuller portrait of the ideal Wordsworthian poet. Abrams's reliance on the Prospectus in *Natural Supernaturalism* makes this figure immediately recognizable. He is meditative and solitary: "Musing in solitude, I oft perceive / Fair trains of imagery before me rise, / Accompanied by feelings of delight / Pure, or with no unpleasing sadness mixed."[16] His is a po-etry of expressivity; there is something "pure" about the emotion given "utterance in numerous verse" (line 71). Memory is important to this work; he is "conscious of affecting thoughts / And dear re-membrances" (lines 64–65). Yet as ideal as he is imagined in the Prospectus, the poet retains the tangential relationship to a social world necessary to a humanist poetics subsequently championed by Mill and Abrams: "the individual Mind" is solitary in that she "keeps her own / Inviolate retirement" (lines 75–76), but his subject is how "exquisitely" that mind is "fitted" to the "external World" and how "[t]he external World is fitted to the Mind" (lines 121–26).

The life span of the Prospectus testifies to long-standing conflicts in Wordsworthian lyricism. The Prospectus was drafted as early as 1800–1806, and thus belongs as much to the period of *Lyrical Ballads* as to more conservative era of *The Excursion* and the 1815 *Poems*. Moreover, important lines from it were written at Alfoxden in 1798: his promise of looking "[i]nto our Minds, into the Mind of Man— / My haunt, and the main region of my song" (lines 98-99). The grandeur of his aspirations in the Prospectus has made it difficult to recognize the variety of lyrical practices that Wordsworth's oeuvre displays; this ambivalence is overwhelmed by the intensified rhetoric of the Prospectus and the 1815 Essay. Moreover, Wordsworth often seems averse to the heterodoxy of his own work and seeks to obscure it; the Preface to *The Excursion* presents us with an architectural model that seeks to unify the varied impulses of his career. He streamlines epic desires and lyrical effusions toward one grand aim in his model of the "gothic church." He integrates his previously published "minor Pieces" into the whole, asserting that when "properly arranged," they "will be found by the attentive Reader to have such connection with the main Work as may give them claim to be likened to the little cells, oratories, and sepulchral recesses, ordinarily included in those edifices" (*Prose*, 3:5–6). What disappears in 1814–15 in the loftiness of Miltonic aspirations is a clear view of *Lyrical Ballads* and its projected audience. Murphy describes the results for critical history: "[E]ven though recent writing on Wordsworth has taken some notice of his interest in his readers, we still remember the 'fit audience' of 1815 better than the anxiously solicitous Wordsworth of the Preface to *Lyrical Ballads*."[17]

But ironically, the real obstacle to recognizing a heterodox Wordsworthian lyricism is his willingness to keep his more radical self in partial view. His poet's habitual practice of reflecting upon younger selves enables Wordsworth to construct an autobiographical narrative that equates political disengagement with poetic maturity. Although Wordsworth obscured his political past in works published during his lifetime, he provides a public record of his change of heart in *The Prelude*. In recollecting his strong sympathies with revolutionary France during the 1790 tour with Robert Jones, Wordsworth incorporates youthful political enthusiasm in his portrait of a self matured.[18] His radical self's political edges are honed down for the lasting portrait of personal and poetic development presented in *The Prelude*. As Richard Onorato points out, Wordsworth is candid in allowing the poem to "remain very suggestive and revealing of his younger self while taking on the supervisory and judgmental presence of his older self."[19] What Wordsworth discovers in lyricism, and what draws him to it repeatedly, despite epic ambitions, is its capacity to accommodate both his radical and conservative selves, and not just consecutively, but simultaneously, as ambivalence.

Coleridge is an important author of canonical definitions of Romantic lyricism not only in the "conversation poems" but also in his prose writings about poetry and politics. In an 1818 lecture on Shakespeare, Coleridge praises "the Lyrical" as "that which in its very essence is poetical."[20] He is crucial to Abrams's model partly because, in comparison to Wordsworth's, his public repudiation of radical politics and simultaneous turn to nature and the aesthetic was decisive. Because Coleridge played an important role in encouraging Wordsworth to assume the disinterested stance that becomes preeminent in the 1815 Essay, and because he is central to Abrams's model, I turn briefly to his role in constructing canonical paradigms of Romantic lyricism. We discover that once again, a poetics is sponsored by material circumstances. Coleridge's imprint on definitions of Romantic lyricism is evident both in his influence on Wordsworth and in his own later, retrospective accounts, in which he performs what David Simpson has called "revisionary magic" in reconstructing the 1797–98 experiments and his own career.[21] In 1798, Coleridge began to receive an annuity of £150 from Tom and Josiah Wedgwood. Eager to justify his worthiness, Coleridge announces his withdrawal from politics in terms that resonate with critical constructions of Romantic lyricism. Writing to his brother George in March 1798 from Nether Stowey, he explains, "I have for some time past withdrawn myself almost totally from consideration of *immediate* causes, which are infinitely complex & uncertain, to muse on fundamental & general causes—the 'causae causarum.'" He continues, juxtaposing political arenas with rural scenes,

> I love fields & woods & mounta[ins] with almost a visionary fondness—and because I have found benevolence & quietness growing within me as that fondness [has] increased, therefore I should wish to be the means of implanting it in others—

&'to destroy the bad passions not by combating them, but by keeping them in inaction.

The combat to which Coleridge refers is presumably that of radical politics, for he declares, "I have snapped my squeaking baby-trumpet of Sedition & the fragments lie scattered in the lumber-room of Penitence"; he continues, "I wish to be a good man & a Christian— but I am no Whig, no Reformist, no Republican."[22] The poet-philosopher is to arrive at understandings that will benefit humanity, yet his relationship to contemporary social scenes is tangential; he has acquired the geographic and psychological remove that will be necessary to Mill's disinterested poet and humanist poetics.

Wordsworth's career demonstrates the impossibility for him of such a divide between politics and poetics, "eloquence" and lyricism. Although we find a far more explicitly social poetics in *Lyrical Ballads* than in the Prospectus, the Advertisement makes clear a divided attitude toward readers. While Wordsworth's anxiety about readers' waywardness is manifest, the document also displays a confidence, greatly diminished in the 1815 Essay, in his ability to correct readers' tendency to stray. Once again, the circumstances of Wordsworth's career illuminate his rhetorical gestures, for Wordsworth had already experienced professional disappointments that made him suspicious of popular tastes. Dorothy Wordsworth reports in a February 1793 letter to her childhood friend Jane Pollard that William regretted having published *An Evening Walk* and *Descriptive Sketches* before submitting them to the judgment of a "friend" who might have helped him to correct their "Blemishes."[23] Less than a year before *Lyrical Ballads* appeared, Wordsworth endured the rejection of *The Borderers* by Thomas Harris, manager of Covent Garden, and learned from Coleridge of the success of "Monk" Lewis's *Castle Spectre*. Wordsworth would himself witness the enthusiastic response to the play in Bristol in May 1798. In a March 1798 letter to James Tobin, Wordsworth concedes that "if I had no other method of employing myself Mr. Lewis's success would have thrown me into despair." He assures Tobin, "There is little need to advise me against publishing; it is a thing which I dread as much as death itself." Instead of entering the literary marketplace, "privacy and quiet are my delight."[24] We can hear in Wordsworth's self-protective reactions to Lewis's success the familiar distinction between popularity and a poetics of privacy that has informed canonical models of Romantic lyricism.

These events help explain the somewhat defensive stance of the Advertisement, his suspicion that readers "will perhaps frequently have to struggle with feelings of strangeness and aukwardness: they will look round for poetry, and will be induced to enquire by what species of courtesy these attempts can be permitted to assume that title." His preemptive response is to prepare his readers for disorientation and to guide their faltering steps in developing "[a]n accurate taste in poetry" (*Prose*, 1:116). Wordsworth's eventual abandonment of this explicitly pedagogical stance later prompted him to claim that he had written the Preface only at Coleridge's urging, but the dramatic expansion of the brief Advertisement into the 1800 and 1802 Prefaces indicates not only sustained but increasing determination to explain the nature of his literary experiments.[25]

These experiments largely concerned the uses of lyricism. The range of lyrical practices in *Lyrical Ballads* has, however, been understated because of the preeminence of "Tintern Abbey" as the quintessential Romantic lyric. Even the issue of which poems are "lyrical ballads" and which are the "other poems" of the 1798 edition's full title remains unresolved. John Jordon declares the question of what the title means in terms of generic categorization "one of the interesting and probably finally unanswerable questions of literary history."[26] This issue emerged early in the collection's history: in a February 1801 review of the second edition, the *British Critic* comments that "[t]he title of the Poems is, in some degree, objectionable; for what Ballads are not *Lyrical?*"[27] In the absence of explanations by Wordsworth or Coleridge, critics have more frequently asked to what the term refers rather than how variously lyricism operates in *Lyrical Ballads*.[28] In what follows, I locate in two poems from the first edition a complexity that registers an actively ambivalent relationship both to audiences and to social scenes.

In his abrupt halting of narrative progress for a moment of "emotion recollected in tranquillity," the poet of "Simon Lee" fails as a ballad speaker and becomes almost a proleptic parody of the Romantic lyric poet. The poem falls apart formally at a moment of emotional and social crisis, as the narrator abandons his rehearsal of Simon Lee's decline and turns to the reader to explain why he does not provide the expected "tale." Stuart Curran describes the generic clash that results: "Simon Lee's inability to uproot a tree stump transforms the traditional objectivity of the ballad into a lyrical—which is to say, psychological—confrontation."[29] The poem's generic collapse exemplifies a central preoccupation of *Lyrical Ballads:* what is at stake in formal choices, and specifically, what is at stake in choosing between narrative and lyric modes.[30]

The poem may seem to confirm the familiar dichotomy between narrative as the mode of sociohistorical temporality and lyric as the disruption of quotidian temporality for moments of introspection. According to Sharon Cameron, "the contradiction between social and personal time is the lyric's generating impulse."[31] The poet interrupts his rehearsal of the history of Simon Lee in order to take stock of the psychological and emotional import of his encounter with the man. Moreover, lyricism is often associated with a breakdown of generic form.[32] In "Simon Lee," lyricism lapses from the ballad's narrative discipline by gesturing toward thoughts and feelings that resist generic constraints, in this case the necessity of a "tale." In addressing the poem's explicit contrasting of narrative and lyric modes, I am interested in the implications of each for the poet, the reader, and the objects of their attention.

The poem's investigation of lyricism's uses hinges on the poet's role, which changes with the shift of tone that occurs at the moment of formal rupture. The poet embodies the poem's heterodoxy. Critics have often assumed that he is an autobiographical figure, yet initially he is one of Wordsworth's ballad personae, less inept than the speaker of "The Idiot Boy," yet still wed to generic conventions. He acknowledges an understanding of what is expected of him when he declines his obligation to produce a "tale." The poet is not exclusively a ballad speaker, nor does he fully qualify for Abrams's definition of the "greater Romantic lyric," which requires "the free flow of consciousness, the interweaving of thought, feeling, and perceptual detail, and the easy naturalness of the speaking voice." Yet there are important parallels with a quintessential Romantic lyric, the "Ode: Intimations

of Immortality from Recollections of Early Childhood." Both poems
end with a gesture toward ineffable emotion. Both poets are silenced
by thought, and both poems leave them moved by loss and suffering,
an experience that characterizes Abrams's lyric poet: it is "a profound sadness, sometimes bordering on the anguish of terror or despair, at the sense of loss, dereliction, isolation, or inner death, which
is presented as inherent in the conditions of the speaker's existence."[33]
Finally, both poets engage in reflections that produce new understanding, in accordance with the teleology of the "greater Romantic lyric."
But there is a crucial difference in the nature of what they learn. The
poet of "Simon Lee" does not provide readers with the ballad's expected moral, yet he and the poet of the "Intimations Ode" alike
offer models of emotional response to an understanding of loss.

The difference comes in the objects of their attention and the
kinds of loss considered. "Simon Lee" demonstrates lyricism's uses
in addressing social scenes. As a natural emblem, the flower at the
poet's feet in the "Intimations Ode" generates a reflection upon the
diminishment of the poet's own vital relationship to nature. The poet
of "Simon Lee," in contrast, is moved by the sight of someone's suffering; reflection produces social understanding, rather than a "moral
decision" or the resolution of an "emotional problem." The moment
of generic rupture in "Simon Lee" distinguishes between two different kinds of involvement—one narrative, one lyrical—with Simon
Lee and his circumstances. The poem asks which mode is more effective in engaging readers with the "rural life and scenes" Wordsworth
takes as his subject, the ballad "tale" or the lyric's "emotion recollected in tranquillity"?

Wordsworth's answer hinges in large part upon the reader's role,
and it is important to my argument that Simon Lee's circumstances
would be recognizable to contemporary readers as a familiar account
of rural poverty. In chapter 1, I argued that an adequate understanding of the complexities of the period's lyric poems requires greater
attention to the reader's role, and an acknowledgment of a range of
possible responses broader than the silent, passive stance generally
imagined. In the case of "Simon Lee," this analysis includes considering what Wordsworth's middle- and upper-middle-class readers knew
about contemporary contexts of rural poverty. Explaining that "[a]
scrap of land they have, but they / Are poorest of the poor" (lines 59-

60), the poet provides a brief history of their economic decline that would have been highly resonant in a period of social unrest over similarly destitute figures:

> This scrap of land he from the heath
> Enclosed when he was stronger;
> But what avails the land to them,
> Which they can till no longer?
> (lines 61–64)

The poet relates a fall from economic stability and strength to financial and physical vulnerability. These two kinds of debility are related:

> And though you with your utmost skill
> From labour could not wean them,
> Alas! 'tis very little, all
> That they can do between them.
> . . . .
> Few months of life has he in store,
> As he to you will tell,
> For still, the more he works, the more
> His poor old ancles swell.
> (lines 52–55, 65–68)

In the poet's account, physical and economic failures reinforce each other's deleterious effects: agricultural labor makes Simon Lee increasingly unfit to make a living.

The couple's plight finds a contemporary analogue in the biography of Parker Clare (1765–1846), John Clare's father. Unlike Parker Clare, Simon Lee and Ruth have managed to acquire a "scrap of land." They have thus avoided the worst that could befall a rural laborer in this period: reliance on public relief or the necessity of emigrating to a more prosperous area, an untenable alternative given their physical limitations. Parker Clare's circumstances were similar to Simon Lee's but eventually became more desperate; his experience demonstrates the fate that might await Simon Lee and Ruth, a possibility that Wordsworth's readers would be able to anticipate. A day laborer, Parker Clare developed rheumatoid arthritis by the time he was 40, a condition Simon Lee may share, making the cultivation of even a small plot of land difficult. Parker Clare's debility eventually left the family dependent on their son's erratic income. Clare recalls his father's resistance to applying to the parish for relief (the period he describes is roughly 1811 to 1812):

> [M]y father, who had been often crippled for months together with the rumatics for 10 or 12 years past, was now tottaly drove from hard labour by them and forced to the last shifts of standing out against poverty—My fathers Spirit was strongly knitted with independence and the thoughts of being forced to bend before the frowns of a Parish to him was the greatest despair, so he stubbornly strove with his infirmitys and potterd about the roads putting stones in the ruts for his 5 shillings a week, fancying he was not so much beholden to their forced generosity as if he had taken it for nothing.[34]

This is the threat that Simon Lee and Ruth face; the speaker encounters a similar resistance in the man's determination to uproot a tree stump that frustrates his efforts. Critics have been disturbed by the poem's emphasis on Simon Lee's "gratitude," for Wordsworth seems to emphasize the humility of the destitute. But there is a counterimpulse in Simon Lee's response that Clare's account of his father clarifies: an emphasis on what Clare calls "independence" and stubborn refusal.

Like Clare's father, Simon Lee is caught between a vestigial paternalistic feudal system and an industrialized exchange economy. When Lord Fitzwilliam, for whom the Clares sometimes worked as day labourers, discovered Parker Clare's increasing debility, he sent him to the Sea-bathing Infirmary at Scarborough. Although his condition improved, Parker Clare's decision to return home on foot, to save travel expenses, undid what progress he had made. His decline necessitated an eventual turn to parish relief. Like Parker Clare, Simon Lee straddles two social and economic systems; the death of the "master" of Ivor-hall leaves his former huntsman without economic protection, while his age and physical infirmity disqualify him from competition in a changing agricultural market. He and Ruth are only barely managing subsistence farming when Wordsworth's narrator meets him.

Dorothy Wordsworth's *Alfoxden Journal* and *Grasmere Journals* provide another perspective on the case of Simon Lee and Ruth, one particularly relevant since the man on whom the poem is based "had been huntsman to the squires of Alfoxden."[35] The journals' slow-moving parade of the domestically and economically dislocated, many of whom begged at the Wordsworths' door or approached them on walks, testifies to the convergence of a number of pressures on the rural poor: accumulating national war debts, poor harvests in 1794–95, and the ongoing processes of enclosure. By raising rents on land, enclosure forced many smallholders into giving up their property or working it at a subsistence level. An impoverished rural class became increasingly visible as its members emigrated to urban areas and the demand for public relief escalated. E. P. Thompson observes that "[p]oor-rates had risen from under two million pounds per annum in the 1780s, to more than four millions in 1803, and over six millions after 1812."[36] A fierce public debate about solutions to these conditions resulted in parliamentary attempts to deal with the situation, including the controversial 1797 Bill for the Better Support and Maintenance of the Poor.

The question for critics of "Simon Lee" has been what Wordsworth's poet makes of that history, a question foregrounded in the address to the reader about how the old man's story is to be interpreted. According to Liu's generic model, the moment at which the narrator interrupts his account of Simon Lee's decline signals the "transformation" of this complex social history into autobiography, the sublimation of Simon Lee's history into feeling, the profit of the poet's contemplations:

> —I've heard of hearts unkind, kind deeds
> With coldness still returning.
> Alas! the gratitude of men
> Has oftener left me mourning.
> (lines 101–4)

The poet attempts to leave the reader in a state of reflection similar to his own. But the moment's ethical or didactic import is vexed:

> O reader! had you in your mind
> Such stores as silent thought can bring,

> O gentle reader! you would find
> A tale in every thing.
> (lines 73–76)

According to new historicism's interpretation of generic distinctions, this lyric turn into "silent thought" generates a profit from Simon Lee's suffering. The poet responds to Simon Lee as a Mackenzian man of feeling, who "transforms" displays of dignity in the face of adversity into a melancholy exclamation: "Alas! the gratitude of men / Has oftner left me mourning" (lines 103–4). The shift from narration to effusion is accompanied by a change in perspective, from the broader contours of a social narrative to the interiority of reflection and emotion or, in Curran's terms, from "objective" account to "subjective" experience. As readers, we are instructed to turn our thoughts from the quotidian particularities of Simon Lee's story to the abstract category of "the gratitude of men." In the process, specific empirical details, however eccentric ("And, though he has but one eye left, / His cheek is like a cherry"), are obscured. The human outline of Simon Lee seems to lose definition when he comes to represent, for Wordsworth, a kind of dignity that verges uncomfortably on grateful abjection.

The poem's focus on the poet's responses to Simon Lee risks exploiting the man for poetic gain. This is the social liability of Romantic lyricism's emphasis on the poet's subjectivity. Yet the poem is also an examination of lyricism's potential for facilitating a more direct encounter with Simon Lee and his socioeconomic situation than the ballad's narrative would allow. Wordsworth's rupturing of the ballad narrative makes possible the abruptness of the reader's encounter with Simon Lee. By staging a lyrical encounter with the man, Wordsworth provokes his readers' consideration of Simon Lee's material circumstances. His readers have already been informed of the cycle of physical and economic decline that followed youthful vitality and stability, so that when we witness the poet assisting Simon Lee with the tree root, readers have been prepared—or rather made—to recognize the personal and social history that lends the exchange its pathos. The "incident" only makes sense, in fact, in light of the broader social context evoked in the brief rehearsal of Simon Lee's biography. The poem makes an important case for reading the period's lyric poems within the specific contexts of their reception, since Wordsworth's contemporaries would have been far more immediately and powerfully aware of the implications of the scenes described than would his twentieth-century readers. The circumstances of rural poverty are not made resonant, to poet or to reader, until the generic rupture, which prompts thought and feeling rather than narrative cause and effect.

The poet's "mourning" is produced by an understanding, generated by reflection, of what Simon Lee's gratitude implies. It is, as Simpson points out, a moment of confusion for the poet, consisting in part of embarrassment about his own relative economic and physical strength. Simpson criticizes the poem's uses of sympathy, but he reads the encounter as a complicated exchange, an ambivalent exercise in sympathetic identification. On the one hand, the poet identifies with Simon Lee because of his own sense of disenfranchisement: "[H]e laments at once the plight of the old man and his own condition as a poet without a patron." But the poet's response to this recognition is confused, producing an "odd mixture of emotional release, honest sympathy, condescension and embarrassment," the result of "the conflicting aspiration and anxieties in the Wordsworthian psyche."[37] The poet's discomfort is passed on to the reader, who, via the poem's sudden generic shift, is put into the poet's position in encountering the old man and the social circumstances he reflects.

The reader's role is important to any claim for lyricism's rhetorical capacity. The poem presents the possibility that a lyric poem could bring poet and reader into a sharper confrontation with Simon Lee's destitution than the "tale" he chooses not to tell. It dramatizes the way in which the lyric speaker's acts of reflection and emotional reaction can facilitate an audience's engagement with a sociohistorical context. The poem stages an encounter between the reader and Simon Lee that is meant to convey to the reader the significance of the poet's own exchange with the man. The poet aims to position the reader in the "incident" he relates and accomplishes this rhetorical feat through lyrical means. "Simon Lee" first foregrounds the act of consuming poetry by disrupting readers' expectations; as Geoffrey Hartman speculates, "[T]he swift changes from teasing narrative to genuine emotion . . . must have been felt as a breach of style."[38] The poem's generic rupture makes the reader self-conscious about witnessing the scene that unfolds:

My gentle Reader, I perceive
How patiently you've waited,
And I'm afraid that you expect
Some tale will be related.
                    (lines 69–72)

The poet breaks his generic contract with readers in order to alter their relationship to him and to Simon Lee. The poet is no longer the purveyor of the entertainment that a popular audience has been trained to consume passively in ballads. Instead he requires his readers to participate in "making" a "tale" out of the "incident" that he of-fers.[39] In "Simon Lee," lyricism is central to soliciting that involve-ment. The poet shows readers how to derive the ballad's expected moral, produced here by lyrical means: the reader is brought by the abrupt halting of the narrative into what approximates a personal encounter with Simon Lee. The kind of response to Simon Lee that the poem attempts to provoke could be described as lyric: the reader is encouraged to follow the poet's example in laying up "stores" of "silent thought" that could be drawn on in similar future encoun-ters. Heather Glen finds the poem's lyric turn to reflection and "mourn-ing" a conservative move: unlike Blake's *Songs*, the poem does not "point directly into the world of human interaction," but inward, to emotion and thought.[40] Yet this reading assumes that introspection = privatization, that lyricism necessarily prompts disengagement. Be-cause Simon Lee is a member of an impoverished rural class whose circumstances are evident in the "incident" related, speculation on the reader's part could easily have political implications.[41]

In "Simon Lee," lyricism demands engagement, while narrative is equated with entertainment. The poet refuses to turn this social history into a ballad, which would be to make a profit on it. If the poem's lyricism threatens to capitalize on Simon Lee's abject state, the narrative with which the poem begins invites a different kind of exploitation. Before the poet abruptly abandons his rehearsal of Simon Lee's life, he narrates his history in preparation for a "tale." At the moment when he interrupts his narrative, he offers two possible ge-neric directions for proceeding. He could continue with a story ap-propriate to ballad tradition, but instead he derails the narrative and thereby foregrounds the consequences of turning Simon Lee's life into a story. This implicit generic critique is consistent with Wordsworth's stated aim in the Preface of providing a corrective to the sensationalism of popular literature, including "frantic novels, sickly and stupid German tragedies, and deluges of idle and extravagant stories in verse." The moment of generic collapse interrogates the relationship between himself, his readers, and the shared human object of their attention. The result is a realization that reader and poet are trafficking in the "tale" of Simon Lee's decline. In failing to perform his generic obligations, he balks at "transforming" the man's biography to fit ballad conventions, even as he has himself already cast it into the ballad's stanzaic form. The turn to lyricism encourages a more immediate engagement with a person about to be turned into a ballad character.

In disappointing audience expectations, he questions the nature of readerly desire. This is not to say that any one response can be legislated, by the poet or by the genres that he employs, nor even that the poet's own reactions to Simon Lee are as straightforward as he reports. Several outcomes of the reader's experience are possible; heterodoxy characterizes Wordsworthian lyricism, most visibly in these early experiments. Mary Jacobus argues that the poem "aims to extend our sympathies—much as the literature of sensibility had done—by revealing that the humblest episodes of everyday life have a bearing on the human condition."[42] Other critics have found the poem's promised humanist boon vampirish in the way it draws poetry out of the "incident" with Simon Lee.[43]

I have rehearsed two readings of the poem—one that makes use of Levinson's and Liu's new historical categories of genre, and then my counterreading—not in order to replace one generic paradigm with another, nor to suggest that there is anything inherently radical about Wordsworthian lyricism, even in *Lyrical Ballads*. Rather, both readings are possible if we do not view them as mutually exclusive, if we do not insist either that the poem's shift to lyricism reduces a social exchange to its personal relevance or that lyricism is radical in confronting the reader with the humiliations of rural impoverishment. Both accounts are viable, a critical proposition that relinquishes the polemical edge of arguing that the poem manifests either the bad faith of Romantic ideology or its disruption, but that allows something that I consider more valuable: a circumspect view of Wordsworthian

lyricism as the site of conflicting motivations and aims. It is possible
to read the poem, then, without fully accepting either Abrams's description of the "egalitarianism of a revolutionary poetics" or the
claim that, as Levinson says about "Tintern Abbey," "[t]he primary
poetic action is the suppression of the social."[44]

It could be argued that new historical models of lyricism, and
especially Liu's, acknowledge psychological complexity. The familiar
vocabulary of repression and denial makes clear new historicism's
debt to Freud (and to Richard Onorato).[45] Liu argues that "strong
denials of history are also the deepest realization of history."[46] Yet
the psychogeneric complexity he describes is unifaceted; it does not
allow for either a more ambivalent response to historical trauma nor
a more straightforward engagement with social events. Denial is, after all, only one kind of psychological complexity. The argument for
a more flexible and more variously conflicted lyricism is easier to
make in *Lyrical Ballads* than in Wordsworth's other collections because of its rhetoric of experimentation, but "Tintern Abbey" remains, at the end of the 1798 edition, as an apparent counterexample
to the experimental poetics of a poem such as "Simon Lee." In
"Tintern Abbey," Wordsworth is often considered to have found his
lyric voice, a compensation for his political ideals. Any argument for
a more various Wordsworthian lyricism must account for its seam-
less meditations.

"Tintern Abbey" has served as a paradigm of a mature Wordsworthian poetics, and thus of Romantic lyricism. Its exemplary status rests partly on its perceived difference from his earlier works,
including the other poems in *Lyrical Ballads*. Contemporaries created this distinction; critics were often "enthusiastic about the poem,
and used it as a stick to beat the 'lyrical ballads' proper," as John
Barrell observes.[47] A tradition of treating "Tintern Abbey" not only
separately from, but as heterodox to, the other poems has been justified partly by composition history. Added late to the collection and
placed at the end of the first edition, "Tintern Abbey" has seemed to
many a culmination or conclusion of the "experiments" that precede

it. Yet other critics have viewed the poem as more integral to the collection's social concerns: Johnston reads "Tintern Abbey" as bringing together its "'lyrics' of meditation upon natural beauty" and the poems of suffering, "roughly, his 'ballads.'"[48]

Despite a movement away from the directness of the encounter between poet, reader, and social environment in "Simon Lee," "Tintern Abbey" makes central the relationship between the speaker and an auditor. Moreover, in both poems contemplation and memory are the vehicles for an exchange that concerns not just personal, but also social, dissolution. In "Tintern Abbey," the poet meditates upon the loss of a "former" self, so that the poem's concerns seem more personal than in "Simon Lee." But the self mourned in "Tintern Abbey" is also a social figure: the poet with radical sympathies. The changes in political perspective that Wordsworth underwent between 1793 and 1798, when he returned to the Wye Valley, would have been experienced by many other English radicals who witnessed, in those five years, the escalation of war and the rise of French imperialism, dramatized by the invasion of Switzerland in spring 1798. For Wordsworth to recall his 1793 self was thus both private history and shared experience. He stages this self-encounter covertly: away from the more openly engaged poetics of "Simon Lee" and toward what would culminate in a rhetoric of transcendence in the 1815 Essay. But the persistence in "Tintern Abbey" of a social dynamic between poet and auditor, poet and social past, raises questions about equating the poem with Wordsworth's turn away from politics to poetry, and therefore about the studied disinterestedness of Wordsworthian lyricism.[49]

Why, then, does Wordsworth not address the questions raised by the spectre of his 1793 self directly? James Chandler points out that "[a]lthough 1793 marks the center of his revolutionary phase, the poem makes no mention of political affairs."[50] This is the question that Levinson proposes to answer: why is Wordsworth so specific about date and place in the title and so vague in representing the scene in the poem? Her answer is that the title is part of a strategy to "transform" a specific social context into personal history. But what Wordsworth accomplishes by providing readers with the present date and then referring to himself five years younger is actually the evocation of his 1793 self.[51] Why couldn't this be accomplished less evasively? Johnston provides another way of viewing the poem's indirect handling of historical events, one that suggests revision and "some retrenchment," rather than a more sweeping account of repression.[52] He makes a case for the poem's suppressed political meanings, arguing that Wordsworth does not deal directly with the disruptive material of the Industrial and French Revolutions in order to protect the poem's narrative of the development of consciousness. As I will argue more fully below, Wordsworth employs the lyric's indirection at an historical moment in which engaging his former political self more explicitly would have been difficult.

Instructions for reading the poem in this manner are provided in part by "Simon Lee," which alerts us to the importance of the role of readers in analyzing lyric poems' relationship to their historical contexts. Reading "Tintern Abbey" as part of *Lyrical Ballads*, rather than as a poem standing alone, fosters a sense of how the poem employs lyric strategies, and to what end. I want to discuss the two main ways in which the poem engages a contemporary social world—by indirectly addressing both reading audiences and Wordsworth's political past. The two poems share an urgent concern with the effects of lyric expression upon an audience, and in both cases the meaning conveyed involves loss, which is both personal and social. The "Reader" in "Simon Lee" retains a threatening independence that Dorothy Wordsworth possesses less fully. Yet although the poet of "Tintern Abbey" begins as an apparently solitary, supremely introspective lyric speaker, when he turns to his sister near the poem's end he is keenly interested in moving her as a reader of his poetic reflections. "Tintern Abbey" opens with what seems to be a soliloquy, but then makes the alleviation of its deepest fears dependent upon the responses of a silent auditor. The poet depends upon his sister for the sense of continuity that would compensate for the losses he has suffered.[53]

In both "Simon Lee" and "Tintern Abbey," a speaker is ambivalent about an audience whose responses to his lyrical effusions he wants to direct but cannot control. "Tintern Abbey" makes explicit its central poet-audience dynamic only after the poet seems to have come to a conclusion, and to have completed the contemplative process described by Abrams as necessary for internal renovation:

> . . . Therefore am I still
> A lover of the meadows and the woods,

And mountains; and of all that we behold
From this green earth; of all the mighty world
Of eye and ear, both what they half-create,
And what perceive; well pleased to recognize
In nature and the language of the sense,
The anchor of my purest thoughts, the nurse,
The guide, the guardian of my heart, and soul
Of all my moral being.

(lines 103–12)

A rhetoric of closure is operative in the poet's assertions of confidence in his lasting relationship to nature. His language encourages a sense of resolution: beginning "Therefore," he gathers "all that we behold" of "all the mighty world" in a grand gesture in which he seeks an "anchor" to secure the bond between "nature," the senses, and his "thoughts." Thus the poem seems to be concluding almost fifty lines before it ends, but it cannot close before his lyrical reflections are ratified by a social exchange. William needs Dorothy to secure the "chearful faith" he has devised. She is integral to the poem's will to transcendence of loss, the guarantor of the sustenance of vitality. According to "Tintern Abbey," his acts of reflection and emotional response are dependent upon being heard.

Dorothy Wordsworth's sudden appearance in the poem has always surprised readers: why don't we know earlier that she accompanies him? Her position in the poem resembles that of Frye's auditor of the lyric, whose presence is temporarily forgotten. But the poet cannot conclude before he locates an audience, and makes sure he has been understood. He must do more than be heard; he must try to engender an exchange in which she agrees to perform the acts of remembrance that he describes. William attempts to employ Dorothy's memory for his own ends in the "prayer" that closes the poem:

Therefore let the moon
Shine on thee in thy solitary walk;
And let the misty mountain winds be free
To blow against thee: and in after years,
When these wild ecstasies shall be matured
Into a sober pleasure, when thy mind

Shall be a mansion for all lovely forms,
Thy memory be as a dwelling-place
For all sweet sounds and harmonies; oh! then,
If solitude, or fear, or pain, or grief,
Should be thy portion, with what healing thoughts
Of tender joy wilt thou remember me,
And these my exhortations! Nor, perchance,
If I should be, where I no more can hear
Thy voice, nor catch from thy wild eyes these gleams
Of past existence, wilt thou then forget
That on the banks of this delightful stream
We stood together; and that I, so long
A worshipper of Nature, hither came,
Unwearied in that service; rather say
With warmer love, oh! with far deeper zeal
Of holier love. Nor wilt thou then forget,
That after many wanderings, many years
Of absence, these steep woods and lofty cliffs,
And this green pastoral landscape, were to me
More dear, both for themselves, and for thy sake!
                                        (lines 135–60)

Dorothy is imagined as exposing her body to the elements, and as willing to be acted upon by them. William's words are to operate with equal force, and she is to "let" them affect her mind and heart with the same acceptance she offers to moonlight and the wind. The poem enacts a turn from meditation to persuasion that recalls Charlotte Smith's repeated turns between childhood memories and exclamations over the émigrés' plight in *The Emigrants*. In order for his words to possess the same elemental strength, the poet must become more like Mill's orator than his poet, desiring to move an audience not only to feeling but also to action. William needs to impress upon Dorothy's understanding the necessity of the future acts of recollection that he describes: to that end he reiterates his main point—that she will not forget—like an orator repeating a key phrase.

William's rhetorical drive is evident not only in his need to affect Dorothy in the present moment but also in his desire to direct her future thoughts. He actually elaborates her memories for her. As in

"Simon Lee," the implicit relationship between poet and reader is one of identification: the poet's subjectivity is foregrounded in the poem, and the reader is expected to make the leap of sympathetic identification with that figure. The poet articulates private thoughts, memories, and reflections, which are "overheard" and create the emotional bond needed for the reader to identify with the poet. For William, Dorothy is a particularly apt choice for reader: familial resemblance facilitates the process of identification desired of the lyric's audience. She is prepared and presumably willing to perform the task he gives her. But her suitability for the role of reader raises questions about the extent to which she can then represent an audience, and hence a social arena, in the poem.

Can there be a social dynamic in "Tintern Abbey" when the audience is nearly a reflection of the poet himself? Does her incorporation collapse the poet-audience exchange? The poem makes clear his desire to close the distance between himself and Dorothy by reducing her physically to mirrorlike eyes and a voice that echoes his. Can we claim for the lyric audience a significant presence if she seems only a reflection of the speaker? Feminist critics have found Dorothy Wordsworth's silence troubling. For Margaret Homans, "Tintern Abbey" enacts the subordination of a female Other that defines Romantic lyricism as a masculinist mode. In her account, William acquires his subjectivity by distancing himself from nature, while Dorothy remains close to it, and thereby "represents a possibility for the self that he cannot consciously adopt for himself, a merging with nature that is at once desired and feared."[54] For Homans, Dorothy Wordsworth's role in the poem is no model of agency. The relationship between poet and auditor, as elder poet and younger sister, is firmly established as hierarchical.

Homans's doubts about the poem's representation of Dorothy Wordsworth's agency are justified. Nevertheless, William's efforts to control Dorothy's responses and to shape her memories are not guaranteed by the superior position he assumes. Although William is active while Dorothy is acted upon, his power in the poem is compromised because it is, to a large extent, implausible. Anne Mellor locates the fault in the poem's hierarchy: William's subordination of a listener does not spell success, because "the poem itself acknowledges the existence of an unbridgeable gap between the poet's forever-lost past subjectivity and his present self."[55] Critics have repeatedly pointed out the doubts and hesitations that define the poem's language. To claim that the poem is more revealing of his inadequacy than of her powerlessness (in which it is simply less interested) is not to deny that he enlists her in the protection of his fragile, even tyrannical, self. But the poem also threatens this hierarchy by making him dependent upon her future actions. Although Dorothy is silenced in the poem, his articulation of a "chearful faith" compromises him in a different way, by publicizing that faith's dependence upon her actions; he needs her to protect it if he is "where I no more can hear / Thy voice" (lines 148–49).

The poem's concern with an auditor's response recalls the speaker of "Simon Lee," who worries that readers will not react as he desires: he is "afraid" that by disappointing them, he will lose his audience. His admonition, that if readers had laid in "stores" of "silent thought" they would know what to make of his "incident," bears a resemblance to William's "exhortations" to Dorothy to remember him in "Tintern Abbey." In different moods and upon different subjects, both poets are concerned with being heard and receiving a needed response. In both poems, Wordsworth wants an auditor to confirm the poetic self he presents to them. But the significance of the audience's role in Wordsworthian lyricism is not fully evident until the poems are considered in the contexts of *Lyrical Ballads* and Wordsworth's career. If William is dependent upon Dorothy's preservation of his memory, then she possesses a power similar in kind, if not in degree, to his contemporary audiences and critics.[56] Toward his sister he assumes an admonitory tone similar to, if gentler than, that which he uses with the reader in the Advertisement to *Lyrical Ballads*.

The poem's position at the end of the collection is relevant: William closes the 1798 volume by presenting his audience with a model of ideal readership. Like Dorothy, the reader is to look to the poet for the guidance of an elder sibling. The didactic tone of the Advertisement, its advice to readers to trust his judgments rather than their own immediate impressions, is rendered as brotherly advice. In his interpretation of the uses of Dorothy and Coleridge in "Tintern Abbey" and *The Prelude*, Clifford Siskin speculates that "[w]hen represented as potential family, the influx of readers in the 1780s and 1790s became not a threat to poetry and community but an opportunity."[57] Yet the need to transform the unknown reader into a sister betrays a desire for known faces, and better yet, an ability to reduce the mass to one face, one that looked to him for direction. In this light, the sudden appearance of Dorothy Wordsworth makes more sense: as silent auditors, we are meant to identify with her. Thus, the construction of an audience in *Lyrical Ballads* is informed by both a juncture in a particular poetic career and a broader historical shift to a literary marketplace from a system of patronage. The anxious gestures toward readers throughout the collection—from the Advertisement to the final image in the 1798 edition of the poet's sister as ideal auditor—are legible in the light of personal ambition being tested at an historical moment when writers were under an increasing necessity of securing their own audiences.

The poem's internalization both of political loss and of an audience does indeed suggest a pulling away from the direct exchange between poet, reader, and social context in "Simon Lee," as critics have suggested.[58] But the poet-reader dynamic it retains also reflects a pronounced continuity with the rest of *Lyrical Ballads*. Read within the context of William's desire, however ambivalent, to gain an audience with the collection, Dorothy is not easily dismissed. She is situated in the poem at a moment of "cultural transformation," since "perhaps for the last time, it was still possible to conceive the writer's relation to an audience in terms of a personal compact."[59] The image of Dorothy as reader would certainly be more comforting than the unimaginable figures of a popular audience; but in either case the poet faced with an auditor had to confront his ultimate lack of control over how his words would be received and whether they would be acted upon as he hoped.

The social world enters "Tintern Abbey," not only in its gestures toward an audience but also in the substance of its concerns. The poem is autobiographical, but it also alludes to the broader social narrative of English radicals' involvement with France, for the self confronted in "Tintern Abbey" is Wordsworth shortly after his unwilling return to England at the end of 1792. Although the "former" self that William describes is himself on the pedestrian tour that took him through the Wye Valley in 1793, he was at that moment far from being simply a poet back at home in nature. To recall his 1793 self was to remember the immediate aftermath of his engagements in

France. I view "Tintern Abbey" as the site of a difficult encounter
with a former self and that self's lost political ideals, a loss the poem
wants to represent as cataclysmic, yet survivable. Hartman describes
Wordsworth in the poem as a "self-haunting" spirit, and the self who
lingers is the more political poet of 1793. Lyricism is the vehicle of
engagement with that younger poet.[60]

It does seem likely that in 1798 Wordsworth would want to rec-
oncile, or even to forget, what could not but appear on one level as
an abandonment of that earlier self, Annette Vallon, and France.
Chandler finds the poet's handling of his former self "an evasion of
what he had actually stood for in 1793" and critics have been fasci-
nated by the emergence of a sense of "betrayal" in the poem.[61] That
this motivation was pure, however, seems implausible, and his success at resolution unlikely. Nor was the meditative genre he chose
likely to perform the therapeutic renovation he desired. A note to the
poem in 1800 explains, "I have not ventured to call this Poem an
Ode; but it was written with a hope that in the transitions, and the
impassioned music of the versification would be found the principal
requisites of that species of composition" (*Lyrical Ballads*, 357). The
poem is constructed on two primary turns: the return to the scene of
his 1793 visit, and his earlier self, and the unexpected turn to Dorothy Wordsworth near the end of the poem. To evoke this period at
all, and then to treat it in a poetic form that encourages repeated
turns in thought is to invite a continued dialogue with his 1793 self.
The turns enact the poet's engagement with both a sociohistorical
past and with an audience. Lyricism may have offered Wordsworth
the possibility of transcendence, but it also involves the necessity of
facing memory's material, both personal and social, private and political. In this sense, the lyric is a perfect vehicle for dealing with a
troubling past whose social contents are still volatile in the present.

Moreover, in 1798 Wordsworth had practical reasons to borrow
the lyric's indirection in evoking his 1793 self. Thompson argues that
in assessing Wordsworth's actions in this period we have inadequately
recognized the contemporary volatility of rural England. He points
to John Thelwall's visit in summer 1797 as indicative of the political
tension that informed the retreat at Nether Stowey and Alfoxden.
Thelwall had recently given up his radical lectures because of threats
and actual acts of physical violence. Having in 1794 been acquitted

for high treason, along with other radicals including Horne Tooke, Thelwall was notable for his determination to continue his political lectures after the passage of the "Two Acts," which aimed to stifle radical agitation by outlawing "seditious meetings" and "treasonable practices." During his visit, the man who was "at this moment the most notorious public Jacobin in England" wrote "Lines, written at Bridgewater, in Somersetshire, on the 27th of July 1797."[62] Addressed to Coleridge, Thelwall's "Lines" imagine joining a fraternal solitude, "far from the strifeful scenes / Of public life!":

> Ah! let me, far in some sequester'd dell,
> Build my low cot; most happy might it prove,
> My Samuel! near to thine, that I might oft
> Share thy sweet converse, best-belov'd of friends!
> (lines 85–88)

But the community at Nether Stowey and Alfoxden remained too haunted by its recent political past and too anxious about the taint of radical politics, especially during the invasion alarm, to accommodate Thelwall's desires. Failed efforts to locate a place for Thelwall to rent were followed by a letter from Coleridge anticipating "even riots & dangerous riots" if he insisted on residing in the neighborhood.[63] Coleridge's fears proved prescient; Thelwall moved to Llyswen in South Wales but was forced to leave within several years. Thelwall's visit, reported to the government by the spy James Walsh, contributed to the rumors of political radicalism at Alfoxden and Nether Stowey, and the Wordsworths' own lease was not renewed at the end of their first year.

Thus Wordsworth would have plausible motives for failing to make clear exactly what recalling his 1793 self involved: his ties, both personal and political, to France. Wordsworth remembers himself shortly after his return to England, when his uncles' refusal to advance money necessitated his departure. Caroline, his daughter by Annette Vallon, was born in Orléans in the middle of December 1792, probably just after Wordsworth's departure from France. But letters exchanged in the spring suggest that there were plans for Annette, Dorothy, and William to share a cottage in England with Caroline.[64] Neither was his political involvement, nor its relationship to his poetry, over. William's decision to remain in London for seven months after

his return, rather than to join Dorothy at Forncett for a long-antici-
pated reunion, suggests a desire to remain close to news of develop-
ments in France and at home. He may also have continued his political activity in London by associating with organized abolitionists.[65]
Soon after returning to London, Wordsworth wrote the polemical
Letter to the Bishop of Llandaff, and although he did not publish it,
he arranged for Joseph Johnson to print *An Evening Walk* and *Descriptive Sketches*, both of which poems deal with social suffering.
As Chandler puts it, in early 1793 "England declared war on France
and Wordsworth declared war on the Bishop of Llandaff."[66]

During this period in London, Wordsworth accepted an invita-
tion to be William Calvert's guest on a tour in the west of England
and Wales. They set out at the end of June or the beginning of July,
although Wordsworth completed the tour alone and on foot after an
accident destroyed their carriage (Calvert proceeded by horse). This
biographical narrative—of a return from France and a turn to nature—has encouraged a reading of "Tintern Abbey" as ratifying a
shift from politics to nature, from social activity to solitude.[67] But it
is by no means clear that Wordsworth had given up his radical sympathies, in thought or even in action. By the end of August, he arrived at the house of Robert Jones's father at Plas-yn-Llan in Clwyd.
In the following months—from mid-September to early December—
Wordsworth is likely to have made a covert return to France. The
most conspicuous evidence for this trip consists of Thomas Carlyle's
Reminiscences, which report an 1840 conversation with Wordsworth
in London in which the poet claimed:

> He had been in France in the earlier or secondary stage of the
> Revolution; had witnessed the struggle of *Girondins* and
> *Mountain*, in particular the execution of Gorsas, 'the first
> *Deputy* sent to the Scaffold'; and testified strongly to the
> ominous feeling which that event produced in everybody, and
> of which he himself still seemed to retain something: 'Where
> will it *end*, when you have set an example in *this* kind?'[68]

Antoine Joseph Gorsas, a Girondin deputy and journalist, was guil-
lotined in Paris on 7 October 1793. Nicholas Roe gives as additional

evidence Wordsworth's marginalia to *The Works of Edmund Burke:* "Gorsas's name appears, marked with a cross and penciled note in Wordsworth's hand: 'I knew this man. W.W.'"[69] Citing various pieces of evidence, Mark Reed concludes that "[t]here seems little chance that W was not in Paris at the time of the death of Gorsas."[70]

But let us suppose first that Wordsworth did not return to France. Wordsworth's presence at Gorsas's execution would only have made considerably more traumatic what was already an extremely disturbing period. Gorsas's public murder is associated with an "ominous feeling" Wordsworth must have experienced in 1793 whether or not he returned to France. Witnessing the execution would only have made more horrifically clear the question that Carlyle remembers Wordsworth asking: what was his own culpability for his recent activities? Wordsworth's engagement with radical ideals and his affair with Annette Vallon presented the dilemma of his continued responsibility to this period. The self he remembers was one still enmeshed in the consequences of his sexual and political involvements. If he did witness Gorsas's execution, then memory in "Tintern Abbey" returns him to the period in which occurred a scene that would have embodied, in grotesque form, betrayal, guilt and danger. If Carlyle's account is correct, then the event raised for Wordsworth a sense of complicity in a cause formerly embraced, one that remained vivid enough that he "testified strongly" and "still" seemed affected by what he saw more than forty years later.

The traumatic nature of his experience of revolutionary France contributes to the disparity that exists between his 1798 and 1793 selves. Only five years have passed, yet William needs the mediation of Dorothy to come into contact with his former self: "May I behold in thee what I was once." His sense of estrangement seems excessive—"I cannot paint / What then I was"—as if the changes he has experienced have rendered him inarticulate. He cannot fully describe that time of confusion, of "aching joys" and "dizzy raptures." What he does recall is a strong responsiveness to his surroundings—"The sounding cataract / Haunted me like a passion." Wordsworth's recollection of his response to nature in 1793 is echoed in his description of what it was like to be in France, in book IX of the 1805 *Prelude*.[71] As he describes it,

The land all swarmed with passion, like a plain
Devoured by locusts—Carra, Gorsas—add
A hundred other names, forgotten now,
Nor to be heard of more; yet were they powers,
Like earthquakes, shocks repeated day by day,
And felt through every nook of town and field.
(IX.178–83)

Not only does Wordsworth describe both his response to nature and to political scenes in this period as "passionate," but his imagery also collapses the distinction between an attraction to nature and to revolution: the Girondin journalists Carra and Gorsas were like forces of nature. In prevailing accounts of Romantic lyricism, an attraction to natural scenes is deemed antithetical to an attraction to political scenes. Yet in Wordsworth's retrospective view of this period, a "passion" for each was experienced as complementary.

Although the poet claims that he does not "mourn," the elegiac tone that infuses "Tintern Abbey" suggests instead that mourning for his earlier self and the events with which it was associated was incomplete. In its elegiac tone and its muted expressions of doubt, "Tintern Abbey" casts the poet more as melancholic than as one who has successfully completed what Freud calls *Trauerarbeit*, or the work of mourning. The successful mourner grieves for something or someone recognized as other, and so is able, eventually, to withdraw emotional attachments to the dead in order to resume living.[72] In contrast, the melancholic is unable recover because he or she suffers a loss of self. For Hartman and Onorato, Wordsworth struggles in the poem with mortality. This argument may seem to confirm that the poet's concerns in the poem are private, that he mourns only himself. Yet even assuming that his own mortality is one of the poem's concerns, to recall 1793 is also to remember other deaths, the fatalities of counterrevolution and war, including the execution of Gorsas. Wordsworth could well be haunted by his former self if he had not successfully mourned the broader historical catastrophe associated with it. The mourning for revolutionary figures such as Gorsas would have been vexed by his lingering identification with their political ideals.

Moreover, in 1798, under surveillance by government agents,

Wordsworth would have had external reinforcement of an inability to forget his involvements in France. Thus I return to the metaphor of the palimpsest with which I began this chapter in order to describe a different kind of overlay in "Tintern Abbey," that of present and past selves. In the course of the poem, the poet's 1793 self and the socioeconomic circumstances in which that self was embedded are rendered palpable, though their specifics remain furtive. The poem bears traces of the poet's attempts to overwrite his younger self, efforts continually vexed by a self-imposed imperative to remember.

On his return to the Wye Valley in 1798, Wordsworth may in fact have wanted to remember only his return to nature after the months in London, rather than his recent life in France. Yet the poem indicates that any recollection of a period of confusion and recent trauma requires engagement with its contexts, especially given Wordsworth's impulse to revise rather than to renounce former selves. Thompson argues that, unlike Coleridge, who disavows his radical ideals in the March 1798 letter to his brother George, for Wordsworth "the moment of tension—of Jacobin affirmation and recoil—was far more protracted." One of the sources of sustained internal conflict was Wordsworth's investment in the processes of memory: "[H]e had that extraordinary faculty of recollecting earlier emotional states— of musing over them—that tenacity of truth toward them."[73] While Wordsworth may indeed desire memory's consolations, remembrance brings other consequences. Even when the conscious desire is to revise history by reconstructing painful events, recollection is never solely an introspective process, because personal and social history are necessarily imbricated. The recollection of a former self brings with it the various contexts of personal experience.[74]

I have described the poem's engagement with the past as far more covert and tenuous than Charlotte Smith's "Beachy Head," a poem that makes social history the explicit content of the poet's recollections. Wordsworth's lingering involvement with his radical past occurs via his poem's troubled odal turns and returns of memory. Another important site for Wordsworth's continued engagement with that past is his keen interest in Smith, to whom his former self bore a resemblance, in terms of both radical politics and lyric poetics. More specifically, Smith served for Wordsworth as an alternate self, whose radical past was a matter of public record. In Wordsworth's handling of Smith's public profile, a broader pattern of treating his past ambivalently is discernible, an impulse enacted poetically in "Tintern Abbey."

In witnessing Smith's long career, which began in 1784 with the publication of *Elegiac Sonnets* and extended even beyond her death in 1806 with her posthumous publications, Wordsworth could consider the consequences of publicly acknowledging political allegiances and of being economically dependent upon success in the literary marketplace. He could also contemplate the possible results, for the poet, of a lyric poetry that was more obviously inflected by a need to reach audiences: in her three volumes of poetry, Smith routinely employed lyric features to court the "Public" and to address contemporary events, including the uses of slave labor, the war with France, poverty in England, and the arrival of émigrés on English shores. From her example, Wordsworth gained perspective on the consequences for the poet of a more overtly engaged lyricism. Smith's career demonstrated the cost for the poet of exploiting the rhetorical capacity of lyricism to social ends, and her experience would have encouraged Wordsworth's own increasing rhetoric of disinterestedness. Smith, who began to write for a living after her husband's imprisonment for debt in December 1783, represented the necessity of submitting oneself to an audience that made demands, which one could not ignore, on what one wrote. Wordsworth may have turned away from an audience that he felt had rejected him, but Smith could—quite literally—not afford to ignore her "Public." Her career displayed a striking lack of "self-possession."

A member of her popular audience, Wordsworth had ample opportunity to form a complex identification with Smith, beginning with his first encounter with her sonnets at Hawkshead.[75] As I discuss in chapter 2, his numerous literary borrowings from her have been ably documented, and she had a salient connection with his radical years. Perhaps the most disturbing aspect of her career to Wordsworth would have been the spectacle of a poet prominent enough to be caught in the crossfire of England's shifting reactions to events in France. In contrast to Wordsworth, whose radical works remained unpublished, Smith represented revolution in France and reform at home sympathetically in *Desmond* (1792). The novel won Smith the gratitude of English radicals and a public profile as a political figure. Albert Goodwin describes a dinner given at White's Hotel in Paris on 18 November 1792 to celebrate recent French military victories. Wordsworth was in Paris at the time and may have been present. The group included some eighty British ex-patriots, and toasts were offered that were "chivalrous, egalitarian and treasonable—to the 'lady defenders of the Revolution, particularly Mrs Charlotte Smith, Miss Williams and Mrs Barbauld'; 'the speedy abolition of titles and feudal distinctions in England'; and 'the coming Convention of Great Britain and Ireland.'"[76] During what Florence Hilbish calls her "French period," Smith alienated influential friends and politically conservative critics.[77] In its 1806 obituary notice for Smith, the *Gentleman's Magazine* indicates that the association of her popular figure with politics was lasting. The critic alludes to another aspect of Smith's public profile—her long-term involvement in a Chancery case over her father-in-law's estate: "Ensnared and entangled as she was in the toils of Law, and suffering as she did under legal oppression, it is no wonder she should embrace those extravagant but fascinating sentiments of liberty which were promulgated in France, under pretense of founding a Republick, and that she should regard with disgust that union of Law and Liberty which forms the beauty of the British Constitution."[78]

This, then, is the figure that Wordsworth remembered and whose public memory he preserves, not only in his explanatory note to "Stanzas Suggested in a Steamboat Off St. Bees' Heads" but also in his efforts to keep Smith visible to the reading public, in letters to Alaric Watts and Alexander Dyce in the 1830s urging them to include her sonnets in their anthologies.[79] Wordsworth's recollections of a poet who resembled, and who in fact had personally known, his former radical self indicates his desire to preserve a memory of that younger poet. Yet Wordsworth's "remembrance" of Smith is highly, and tellingly, selective. His ambivalence about a political past they shared is registered not only in "Tintern Abbey" but also in his revision of Smith's public profile.

The explanatory note "acknowledges" only debts based on poetic form and a love of nature: Wordsworth reports borrowing Smith's stanzaic form and "something in the style of versification" from "St. Monica." He praises her because she wrote "with true feeling for rural nature, at a time when nature was not much regarded by English poets." But he strikingly misrepresents Smith's contemporary fame when he claims that "[s]he wrote little, and that little unambitiously." On the contrary, bewildered critics commented on the stream of writing that came from Smith's pen. In 1801 the *Antijacobin* complains that "she has almost wearied criticism in its attempts to keep pace with her."[80] Nor could her continual courting of audiences in prefaces to her works easily be construed as unambitious. Moreover, Wordsworth focuses exclusively on the poet of the sonnets, thus omitting from his record of her influence the popular cultural figure that she became. Although Smith made her name with *Elegiac Sonnets*, her three volumes of poetry are far outnumbered in her oeuvre by prose, including ten novels and six titles for children. While Smith was perhaps the most popular novelist of the 1790s, Wordsworth publicly identifies only with the lyric poet.

Wordsworth imagines Smith as an idealized solitary poet in his explanatory note, a portrait reinforced in his recommendation of one of her sonnets to Dyce for inclusion in a second edition of *Specimens of English Sonnets* (1833). In "To Night," the speaker expresses her affection for "mournful, sober-suited Night," a time when she wanders alone, confessing her "embosom'd grief" to "sullen surges and the viewless wind." She finds no listeners, no response in the "deaf cold elements." Yet she tells the night, "I still enjoy thee," and describes herself as "hopeless, yet resign'd." The reason for her contentment emerges only in the final couplet. She explains that "the exhausted heart / Is calm," because she believes that her sorrows "[m]ay reach—tho' lost on earth—the ear of Heaven!" Smith, in her effort to present herself winningly, ironically succeeds by providing the portrait of herself that Wordsworth adopts, one whose only desired—or required—audience is "the ear of Heaven." He thus recommends, as a representative poem, a sonnet that denies a desire for an earthly audience.

Although Wordsworth revised Smith's public profile, emphasizing the private lyric poet over the popular cultural figure, his ongoing identification with her indicates an ambivalence about his own decisions against an explicitly engaged lyricism by the time of the 1814–15 definitions. His sustained interest in her sonnets suggests a reluctance to abandon his former self. He is intent on preserving that figure publicly, but only in the persons of Dorothy or Smith. The tableau in "Tintern Abbey" of the mature poet as elder brother, admonishing his sister to stay as she is—that is, like he was once—is emblematic of the divided motives of Wordsworthian lyricism. The poem is exemplary of Romantic lyricism's capacity for contradictory impulses. If, however, "Tintern Abbey" demonstrates the potential in "mature" Wordsworthian lyricism for engagement with audiences and a social past, it is also typical in its obfuscation of the exact nature of his involvement.

FOUR

Dorothy Wordsworth and the Liabilities of Literary Production

Nothing detains the reader's attention more powerfully than deep involution of distress or sudden vicissitudes of fortune, and these might be abundantly afforded by memoirs of the sons of literature. They are entangled in contracts they know not how to fulfill, and obliged to write on subjects which they do not understand. Every publication is a new period of time from which some increase or declension of fame is to be reckoned. The gradations of a hero's life are from battle to battle, and of an author's from book to book.
　　　—Samuel Johnson, *The Idler*, no. 102

Her information various—her eye watchful in minutest observation of nature—and her taste a perfect electrometer—it bends, protrudes, and draws in, at subtlest beauties & most recondite faults.
　　　—Samuel Taylor Coleridge on Dorothy Wordsworth

Dorothy Wordsworth makes a cogent case for Romantic lyricism's responsiveness to its social environments precisely by declining the role of poet as she was helping to define it at Alfoxden and Grasmere in the collaborative literary enterprise with her brother William Wordsworth and Samuel Taylor Coleridge, 1797-1802. More prose writer than poet, Dorothy Wordsworth nevertheless offers some of the period's keenest insights into Romantic lyricism's rhetorical possibilities and liabilities, by weighing the cost to the poet of the mode's focus on an autobiographical speaker. She recognized that lyricism fosters that figure's exposure to reading audiences. Charlotte Smith's case would have served as a cautionary tale for both Dorothy and William Wordsworth, since Smith discovered that the lyric's focus on an autobiographical speaker subjected the poet herself to personally

113

inflected critiques that could be particularly damaging to a woman writer. I have been arguing for Romantic lyricism's potential for engaging reading audiences; Dorothy Wordsworth supports this case precisely by recognizing its potentially deleterious effects. In her prose works and in her refusals to publish them, she makes an important contemporaneous argument that, far from being the mode of aesthetic remove that William hoped it could be, and that literary history has largely suggested that it is, lyricism could not grant the disinterestedness that John Stuart Mill and others since have desired. Viewed from her perspective, the familiar portrait of the Romantic poet turned away from auditors, and therefore immune to the demands—or the adulation—of reading audiences, looks more like a tenuous myth constructed by William and Coleridge and by latter-day critics interested in the promise and consequences of such a protected state.

Dorothy Wordsworth's skeptical inquiry into the liabilities of the lyric stance for the poet has been easy to overlook because it unfolds not in the declamatory tones of prefaces or defenses of poetry, nor even in reflective musings, such as John Keats's letters provide. Rather, her critique emerges in her epistolary explanations of her decisions against publishing her works, and also in the works themselves, in her definition and refinement of a reticent autobiographical speaker. The claim that Dorothy Wordsworth provides a critique of Romantic lyricism is not in itself new; important feminist reassessments of her place in the field in the 1980s cast her as a subtle critic of the gendered ideology of the Romantic poet and poetry as William and Coleridge were defining these terms.[1] She is credited with emphasizing qualities conventionally excluded in those models—including a sense of community and an attention to the quotidian—and thereby challenging the masculinist orientation of her brother's and Coleridge's emerging poetics. Yet her critique is more expansive, in that it includes an astute assessment of how the poet and poetry were being defined and contested within the exchanges and negotiations between poets, publishers, critics, and readers.

My argument requires a revision of some early feminist interpretations of Dorothy Wordsworth's repeated refusals to publish her prose works, decisions that have often been understood as reflecting her internalization of contemporaneous strictures against women's authorship. Certainly, her reluctance reflects a diffidence about authorship that was felt in part as an incapacity. Although she allowed William to publish anonymously some of her poems in his volumes, she found not only the prospect of publication but even the act of poetic composition painful. Any argument for Dorothy Wordsworth as a critic of the poet's role must acknowledge her agonized explanations of her own struggles with authorship. In an 1806 letter to Lady Beaumont that encloses two poems, she tells her friend why she does not compose for adults: "I have no command of language, no power of expressing my ideas, and no one was ever more inapt at molding words into regular metre." She offers as evidence for her case a comparison of herself to William: "I have often tried when I have been walking alone (muttering to myself as is my Brother's custom) to express my feelings in verse; feelings, and *ideas* such as they were, I have never wanted at those times; but prose and rhyme and blank verse were jumbled together and nothing ever came of it."[2] I argue that her rejection of the role of poet reflects both this acute sense of inability and an informed assessment of the consequences of the kind of literary success that William sought. I therefore read her decision against publicly assuming the cultural role of poet as both a gendered anxiety of authorship and a shrewd and skeptical assessment of the costs of the poetic enterprise undertaken at Alfoxden and Grasmere.

A fuller sense of the range of Dorothy Wordsworth's misgivings about publication may be gleaned from her famous letter to her friend Catherine Clarkson, in which she states her aversion to "setting myself up as an Author." This claim has been cited as evidence of her acceptance of a pervasive disapprobation of female authorship, yet if her statement is read within the context of the entire letter, her case against publication becomes more complex. She writes in response to Clarkson's suggestion that Dorothy Wordsworth publish her *Narrative of George and Sarah Green*, an account of the orphaning of a local family's children that was written as part of a community effort to raise money for their support. Dorothy Wordsworth offers an extensive justification of her decision against publication, and in the process launches an argument about the exposure to reading audiences that publication involves. The letter provides valuable evidence of her perspective on authorship because she rarely articulates her critique in such explicit terms. She is candid here only because her subject is not so much her concern with her own exposure—her aversion to "setting myself up as an Author"—but rather her acute awareness that she would be submitting five children to the kind of public scrutiny that she herself wishes to avoid: "My reasons are entirely disconnected with myself, much as I should detest the idea of setting myself up as an Author." She could, as she acknowledges, publish the *Narrative* anonymously, but she is concerned with the effects of public visibility on the Green children. For her to publish an account of their loss that also detailed the family's poverty would, in her view, be to subject the children to a potentially damaging visibility. She worries that "by publishing this narrative of mine I should bring the children forward to notice as Individuals, and we know not what injurious effect this might have upon them." She declares that she would only consider publication "[t]hirty or forty years hence when the Characters of the children are formed and they can be no longer objects of curiosity."[3] Although she is vague about exactly how the children might be harmed, she imagines an almost physical transformation: such exposure could actually mold them in unpredictable and undesirable ways.

Dorothy Wordsworth investigates the nature and consequences of an exchange between the writer and reading audiences that significantly informs her works and *Lyrical Ballads*: she examines how the rural scenes these works feature are presented to and consumed by readers. Her exploration of these issues unfolds largely in her treatment of how the writer's sympathetic identification with local scenes involves her in them, generating a complex network of interdependence and responsibility which quickly becomes problematic in her myriad encounters with the rural poor. The misgivings and anxieties which also inflect William's account of his poet's encounter with "Simon Lee" become a substantial theme in Dorothy Wordsworth's writing project, especially in the *Grasmere Journals* and the *Narrative*.

Her investigation of these concerns unfolds not only in her arguments against publication, but also indirectly, as formal experiments in the works themselves. In the domestic journals, she adopts some of the key features that would come to define canonical models of Romantic lyricism: an autobiographical speaker who is often alone in nature, though sometimes accompanied by companions (as William is in "Tintern Abbey" and as Coleridge longs to be in "This Lime-

Tree Bower My Prison"). Like their poets, her speaker closely observes her rural surroundings and describes them in prose rich with natural images. Her journals are non-narrative in that, although anecdotes are occasionally related, an overarching story never develops. Her entries are not joined by transitions; there is a fragmentary quality to the *Journals* that is closer to lyric poetry than to conventional prose narrative. Her *Journals* also resist a narrative temporality by repeatedly describing present moments—the gathering of a storm, a view of the ocean—without ordering them, except by the dates provided with each entry and the seasonal calendar that accompanies such documentation. Unlike Romantic lyricism traditionally understood, she does not focus primarily on her own responses to natural scenes, yet a subjectivity less strictly defined certainly accommodates her speaker's autobiographical stance.

The *Alfoxden Journal* and *Grasmere Journals*, along with the *Narrative*, frame the early phase of Dorothy Wordsworth's writing career, 1798–1808, during which her collaboration with William was most intense. As Elizabeth Fay observes, Dorothy Wordsworth's journals "are not only viable sites for the location of her poetic productivity but the only work of any quantity besides her letters from the years when she and William created their Romantic version of artistic life together."[4] This era coincides with what Matthew Arnold designated William's "great decade," spanning the publication of *Lyrical Ballads* and the 1807 *Poems*.[5] The domestic journals situate Dorothy Wordsworth in the middle of conversations articulating the tenets that were largely to define canonical Romantic lyricism. In a Grasmere entry for 3 October 1800, Dorothy reports a walk with William to Ambleside during which "he talked much about the object of his Essay for the 2nd volume of LB." Despite the implication that she listened rather than talked, the entry makes clear that she was immersed in the ongoing conversation. Especially in the *Alfoxden Journal*, we can trace the convergence of Dorothy's emerging prose style and William's developing poetics, since the two, along with Coleridge, often share images and borrow words in this period.[6] The advent of settling at Alfoxden in order to be nearer to Coleridge, at Nether Stowey, closely associates her *Journals* with the project of *Lyrical Ballads*. Her *Alfoxden Journal* opens on 20 January 1798, roughly six months after she and William arrive from Racedown, and spans the period in which *Lyrical Ballads* comes together. It ends on 22 May 1798, a month before they leave for Bristol, where William oversees the volume's publication. The *Grasmere Journals* begins on 14 May 1800, after Dorothy and William settle into Dove Cottage in December. The second edition of *Lyrical Ballads* appears in January 1801 (dated 1800), and another edition, with an expanded Preface, appears in 1802. The final entry of the *Grasmere Journals* is dated 16 January 1803, several months after William's marriage, which marked at least a partial turn in Dorothy's attention from William and from her own writing.

Dorothy Wordsworth had ample reason for skepticism about the costs of authorship as a participant in William's long struggle to find the reading audiences he sought. But she experienced the marketplace not only by her involvement in William's career (as interlocutor, amanuensis, and collaborator) but also by considering publication herself. The twice disrupted plans for the publication of her 1803 *Recollections of a Tour in Scotland* were handled primarily by William, who unlike Dorothy could act as a legal agent. Yet she revised and prepared her manuscript for publication and was fully aware of the steps involved. Not only was she attentive to the practical aspects of a literary career, she was also indirectly dependent upon reading audiences. Dorothy Wordsworth experienced a double dependence on her brothers and on William's readers until his assumption in 1813 of the post of distributor of stamps for Westmorland. The anxiety this dependence induced is evident in her letters and becomes acute surrounding William's decision not to publish *The White Doe of Rylestone* in response to the hostile reviews and poor sales of the 1807 *Poems, in Two Volumes.*

In May 1807, Wordsworth assured his friend and advocate Lady Beaumont that he was unconcerned with the collection's reception: "It is impossible that any expectations can be lower than mine concerning the immediate effect of this little work upon what is called the Public."[7] Yet the negotiations for the publication of *The White Doe* belie this indifference. In the wake of negative reviews to the

1807 *Poems*, Wordsworth entered into the process of submitting his next work to the "Public" defensively and even antagonistically. Francis Jeffrey's response to the *Poems* in the *Edinburgh Review* issued an influential "verdict against this publication."[8] Wordsworth accurately understood the import of such proclamations upon sales of the *Poems* and of future volumes; his fears about the prospects of *The White Doe* were justified. Yet as Dorothy Wordsworth made clear to him and as William acknowledged, his family required his perseverance.[9] William traveled to London in February 1808 to see Coleridge and to negotiate with Thomas Longman about *The White Doe*. He returned without making the arrangements when the publisher did not agree to his stipulations.

Having learned that the negotiations were in peril, Dorothy Wordsworth wrote to Coleridge at the end of March in hopes of influencing William's decision. In a letter that arrived after William's departure for Grasmere, she makes especially plain that not only his poetic reputation but the family's resources were dependent upon his continued submission of himself as poet to critical and readerly responses:

We are exceedingly concerned to hear that you, William! have given up all thoughts of publishing your Poem. As to the Outcry against you, I would defy it—what matter, if you get your 100 guineas into your pocket? Besides it is like as if they had run you down, when it is known you have a poem ready for publishing, and keep it back. It is our belief, and that of all who have heard it read, that the *Tale* would bear it up— and without money what *can* we do? New House! new furniture! such a large family! two servants and little Sally! we *cannot* go on so another half-year; and as Sally will not be fit for another place, we must take her back again into the old one, and dismiss one of the Servants, and work the flesh *off our poor bones*. Do, dearest William! do pluck up your Courage—overcome your disgust to publishing—It is but a *little trouble*, and all will be over, and we shall be wealthy, and at our ease for one year, at least.[10]

William did not relent; the poem remained unpublished until 1815. The domestic pressures so evident in this letter were partly relieved in May when a larger house became available and the family moved across Grasmere to Allan Bank. At the time of this letter, Dove Cottage housed Dorothy, William and Mary and their three children, and Sara Hutchinson; the Wordsworths' fourth child, William, was expected. Dorothy Wordsworth's anxiety about financial stability and her desire for a measure of security had already been made plain in her request to her other brothers, at the time of William's marriage to Mary, that she be given a regular yearly income.[11] But as the episode of *The White Doe* indicates, Dorothy's economic security continued to be tied to William's, so his fortunes in the literary marketplace still affected her.

Dorothy Wordsworth's reluctance to enter that arena with her own works must be considered within this biographical context. Likewise, her sustained ambivalence about the publication of her poems and prose should be juxtaposed with William's views as she describes them at this low point, after the disappointments of *Lyrical Ballads* and the 1807 *Poems* and before the eventual success that followed the appearance of *The Excursion* in 1814. She reports to Jane Pollard Marshall in May 1808 that William "has no pleasure in publishing—he even detests it—and if it were not that he is *not* over wealthy, he would leave all his works to be published after his Death."[12]

By the time she wrote the famous letter eschewing authorship to Catherine Clarkson in 1810, she had considerable experience of her own to support her ambivalence, including the abandoned plans to publish her 1803 *Recollections of a Tour in Scotland*, which recalled a six-week excursion in Scotland with William and Coleridge. It was written not on the journey itself but after the party's return and was directed to particular readers. She recalls in June 1805, after Captain John Wordsworth's death at sea, "I had written it for the sake of Friends who could not [be] with us at the time, and my Brother John had been always in my thoughts, for we wished him to know every thing that befel us."[13] After John's death, Dorothy found solace in completing the *Recollections*. The party met the poet Samuel Rogers on the trip, and he was among the family and friends who read the work (probably in 1813). Upon meeting the Wordsworths again in 1820, he urged its publication and offered to help. In a January 1823 letter to Rogers thanking him for his advice and his willingness to help her publish the *Recollections*, Dorothy Wordsworth expresses her distaste for appearing publicly as an author and asks if a deal might be made with a bookseller whereby she would receive a certain sum of money—not less than two hundred pounds—in exchange for the rights to publish a limited number of copies. Since her aim was pecuniary, as William had explained to Rogers, this scheme would secure her goal with minimal public exposure. She tells Rogers, "I am apprehensive that, after having encountered the unpleasantness of coming before the public I might not be assisted in attaining my object." She prefers a "middle course" which limits her visibility on the literary horizon.[14] It is unclear why negotiations fell through, but fifteen years later the possibility of publication was again investigated. William once more contacted Rogers, who renewed his offer of assistance, but William ultimately decided against accepting it because of Dorothy's sharply deteriorating health.

The *Alfoxden Journal* and *Grasmere Journals* grant Dorothy Wordsworth in formal terms the less visible role that she defined for herself in the literary marketplace. Especially in the *Alfoxden Journal*, her speaker remains firmly in the background of many of the scenes that she describes. When juxtaposed to her brother's lyric poet, this stance, and its apparent construction of her speaker's subjectivity, has seemed to many feminist critics troublingly elusive. Feminist critics have noted what appears to be an excessive modesty on her part; her reluctance to appear publicly as a writer has seemed to translate, formally, into her speaker's reticence. Dorothy Wordsworth's resistance to authorship has been a central concern to critics who would introduce her into the Romantic canon, since to decline to be the writing subject has traditionally meant to disavow the period's privileged role. Critics have generally concluded that she does not follow the model of solitary production defined by canonical paradigms of Romantic lyricism, a circumstance either lamented or celebrated. The apparent evasiveness of Dorothy Wordsworth's speaker in the journals and the ambivalence she expresses about authorship have suggested to some critics a debilitating internalization of contemporary strictures on women's writing. In her pioneering study of the *Journals*, Margaret Homans considers Dorothy Wordsworth's choice of prose rather than poetry a refusal to adopt Romanticism's preeminent form—the lyric—and, by association, to assume a literary identity. She concludes that "[t]he result is not poetry, but it avoids conflicts."[15]

Other feminist critics have praised Dorothy Wordsworth's departure from Romantic norms. Homans herself subsequently revises her account of her as a failed poet who accepts the female "Romantic role" of "the object of representation," by contending that she discovers how to write "from the perspective of the literal." Homans argues that Dorothy Wordsworth finds a source of agency in an apparently subordinate position: "[S]he speaks for the literal nature that is most often silent within [William's] texts."[16] Meena Alexander also extols her "renunciation of male-identified power." She contends that by refusing a masculinist model of Romanticism, which betrays the natural world by using it merely as a "starting point" for "symbol" and "the visionary," Dorothy Wordsworth "exemplifies at its finest one possible female response to the call of Romanticism."[17] Homans and Alexander point out the implicitly gendered hierarchy of canonical paradigms of Romantic lyricism: a masculine subject's subordination of a feminized nature to his emotional and contemplative responses.

Dorothy Wordsworth's actual writing practices indicate a more ambivalent relationship to what would become a canonical lyric stance. She experiments with her speaker's position in the landscape in her early domestic journals, and in the process develops concerns that she pursues about the writer's role in the rural community and in the literary marketplace. Her visibility is at stake in both arenas, in the landscape and on the literary scene. The *Alfoxden Journals* and *Grasmere Journals* investigate the writer's role in the local environments she surveys. Her sustained inquiry into models of authorship begins with her experiments with the popular cultural traditions of natural history and travel writing, both of which foreground the natural scene rather than the observer. Coleridge produces almost a parody of this aloof stance in his description of her as a "perfect electrometer" in the letter quoted in my epigraph. Acknowledging Dorothy Wordsworth's uses of authorial models from natural history and travel writing does not explain why she chose genres that assigned her this less visible role. But an attention to those experiments demonstrates her active participation in the enterprise at Alfoxden and Grasmere. In the daily production of the *Alfoxden Journal* and *Grasmere Journals*, she elaborates her view of the writer-nature exchange as fraught with social meaning that imposes a responsibility for its literary products on the writer and that informs her decisions against publication.

The first entry of the *Grasmere Journals* provides an example of how her entries are constructed on a generic model derived from natural history writing, which reverses Romantic lyricism's traditional hierarchy between human observer and nature:

> The wood rich in flowers. A beautiful yellow, palish yellow flower, that looked thick round & double, & smelt very sweet—I supposed it was a ranunculus—Crowfoot, the grassy-leaved Rabbit-toothed white flower, strawberries, Geranium—scentless violet, anemones two kinds, orchises, primroses. The heckberry very beautiful as a low shrub. The crab coming out. (*GJ*, 14)

Her aim in the passage is to describe seasonal change, and thus her own preferences are subordinated to the demands of accuracy and thoroughness. Achieving a standard of expertise requires her to remain in the background. She employs both vernacular and empirical terms, demonstrating her familiarity with the practices of natural history writing. The *Journals* document her earnestness in developing her skills as an amateur natural historian. A May 1800 entry expresses a desire for "a book of botany" (*GJ*, 2), a request fulfilled the following March with the arrival of the third edition of William Withering's four-volume *Arrangement of British Plants according to the latest Improvements of the Linnaean System and an Introduction to the Study of Botany*. Evidence of her studies is found in a note penned on a flyleaf of the first volume of the *Grasmere Journals*: two days after observing a "pretty little waxy-looking Dial-like yellow flower" as she and William "sate in the orchard," she identifies it as "Lysimachia Nemorum, Yellow Pimpernell of the Woods Pimpernel Loosestrife May 30 1802."[18]

Considered within the context of travel writing, the reticence of Dorothy Wordsworth's speaker is neither anomalous nor unexpected, nor is the scarcity of personal responses. Although there was a shift toward more subjective travel accounts over the course of the eighteenth century, her reserve fits established paradigms.[19] Critics have suggested that the domestic journals should also be read in the context of the period's travel writing, since the Lake District was a popular destination by the late eighteenth century.[20] Dorothy Wordsworth reports to Lady Beaumont in an August 1805 letter that "the end of summer and the autumn" are "the season of bustle for we are, directly in the highway of the Tourists."[21] Their presence encouraged Dorothy and William to view their environment from a tourist's perspective. A June 1800 entry in the *Grasmere Journals* reports: "[A] coronetted Landau went by when we were sitting upon the sodded wall" and that "the ladies (evidently Tourists) turned an eye of interest upon our little garden & cottage" (*GJ*, 9). In this scene, Dorothy and William become the human figures in the landscape. By the time she and William began writing, their environs had been thoroughly chronicled, in Thomas Gray's *Journal in the Lakes*, Arthur Young's *Six Months Tour Through the North of England*, William Hutchinson's *Excursion to the Lakes*, William Gilpin's *Observations on the River Wye* and *Observations on the Several Parts of England*, James Clarke's *Survey of the Lakes of Cumberland, Westmorland, and Lancashire*, and Thomas West's *Guide to the Lakes*. Dorothy and William Wordsworth themselves were involved in promoting the Lake District as a scenic destination. The *Grasmere Journals* records a visit in March 1802 by Joseph Wilkinson, who published his drawings of the Lake District in 1810 as *Select Views in Cumberland, Westmoreland, and Lancashire*, a volume to which William anonymously contributed a descriptive text which he revised and published in 1820 as *Guide to the Lakes*. Dorothy Wordsworth's familiarity with the aesthetic conventions of travel writing, including the picturesque and the sublime, is evident in the *Journals*, which chronicle her experiments with these practices.[22]

It is, ironically, by adhering in the *Alfoxden Journal* to generic paradigms that require a discrete speaker that Dorothy Wordsworth launches an investigation of her relations as a writer to the rural surroundings that are her primary subject. The *Alfoxden Journal* experiments with conventional stances toward the landscape, a prelude to her inquiries into what it means to turn those scenes to account in literary production. This question is especially pointed in the case of the *Alfoxden Journal*, since the scenes she chronicles would provide much of the material for a contemporaneous literary enterprise with a pecuniary aim: *Lyrical Ballads* was meant to finance the trip to Germany that she, William, and Coleridge undertook after William oversaw the volume's production in Bristol.

The *Alfoxden Journal* initiates Dorothy Wordsworth's career of chronicling her environment by adopting a familiar cultural role: the picturesque observer. But in the very act of defining her speaker as removed from the scenes that she surveys, she discovers the complications and costs of such detachment. Picturesque conventions physically position the observer in the landscape by requiring adequate distance to view a scene as a tableau, like a painting. To attain a desirable vantage point, the picturesque observer often sought out an aerial perspective by climbing an eminence. One of the picturesque observer's props, the Claude glass, literalizes the necessary remove of observer from countryside: "With his back turned to the landscape, the viewer might raise an oval, tinted Claude glass, to see the view actually framed as a picture."[23] The observer should be situated outside of the scenes surveyed.

Dorothy Wordsworth's earliest journal employs picturesque conventions that require the observer's organization of the landscape. The first entry of the *Alfoxden Journal* is frequently cited for its accurate approximation of picturesque perspective, and as such it is a model of her speaker's authorial distance from the objects of her attention:

The green paths down the hillsides are channels for streams. The young wheat is streaked by silver lines of water running between the ridges, the sheep are gathered together on the slopes. After the wet dark days, the country seems more populous. It peoples itself in the sunbeams. The garden, mimic of spring, is gay with flowers. The purple-starred hepatica spreads itself in the sun, and the clustering snow-drops put forth their white heads, at first upright, ribbed with green, and like a rosebud; when completely opened, hanging their heads downwards, but slowly lengthening their slender stems.

The slanting woods of an unvarying brown, showing the light through the thin net-work of their upper boughs. Upon the highest ridge of that round hill covered with planted oaks, the shafts of the trees show in the light like the columns of a ruin. (*AJ*, 1)

The entry is, as Robert Con Davis describes it, "a striking model of visual ordering in nature." This organization is only possible if the observer is removed from the scene.[24] Her aloofness complements a sense of emotional distance in the passage's coolly descriptive tone. Conversely, a sense of the countryside's independence from human intervention is conveyed by anthropomorphism: the "countryside is populous" not with people but with gay, spreading, clustering, lengthening plants. Wildlife alone "peoples" the scene.

Adopting a certain geographic distance from the countryside literalizes the social and economic remove that separates observer from observed in picturesque convention.[25] By striking a picturesque stance, Dorothy Wordsworth positions herself as a middle-class observer of the natural environment and rural society, a perspective defined by its sociocultural investments. Recent attention to the politics of the picturesque—by John Barrell and Ann Bermingham, especially—makes clear that to assume the stance of the picturesque observer implied more than adopting a certain class position: it situated the observer within a more extensive historical matrix. To view the countryside in the 1790s was to consider the contentious setting of the period's social and economic unrest, produced by the converging pressures of the war, governmental repression of radical agitation at home, and the processes of parliamentary enclosure. The economic fluctuations of the war combined with poor harvests in 1794–95, and the escalation of agricultural industrialization, to produce unemployment, hunger, and widespread dislocation. These factors conspired to fill the landscapes that Dorothy Wordsworth describes with the figures of wandering beggars, soldiers, and domestic emigrants seeking more prosperous areas.

The first entry of the *Grasmere Journals* reports encounters with two female beggars, who lead what turns out to be a procession of vagrants through the succeeding entries: "At Rydale a woman of the village, stout & well-dressed, begged a halfpenny—she had never she said done it before—but these hard times!" (*GJ*, 1). A comment recorded in a May 1800 entry by the Wordsworths' neighbor John Fisher renders explicit the socioeconomic matrices of the scenes described in the *Journals*: "[H]e talked much about the alteration in the times, & observed that in a short time there would be only two ranks of people, the very rich & the very poor, for those who have small estates says he are forced to sell, & all the land goes into one hand" (*GJ*, 3). Fisher's comments address the relationship between parliamentary enclosure and poverty. W. E. Tate lends credence to this view of the circumstances of the rural economy: "[I]t seems clear that the dispossession of the small landed proprietor—before or after enclosure—was usual."[26] Tate links the process of enclosure with what Fisher refers to as a widening gap between the rich and poor, and J. M. Neeson concurs, arguing that enclosure "taught the small peasantry the new reality of class relations."[27] By rehearsing their histories, the vagrants who populate the domestic journals testify to these circumstances.

The rural scenes that Dorothy and William chronicle in the *Journals* and *Lyrical Ballads* provide particularly vivid evidence of the period's socioeconomic unrest. To "look on nature" in the 1790s was not to escape the sights of social turbulence, as has sometimes been assumed, since industrialization meant a collapsing of distinctions between country and city. Raymond Williams argues that "[b]y the late eighteenth century we can properly speak of an organized capitalist society, in which what happened to the market, anywhere, whether in industrial or agricultural production, worked its way through to town and country alike, as parts of a single crisis."[28] The incursions of enclosure, evident in the presence of surveyors and the physical processes of erecting fences, relegated the idea of nature as a retreat to the literary realm of pastoral. Bermingham argues that "the picturesque was suited to express the complexity of the historical moment": by valuing the ruins of a feudal system while suggesting that its time had passed, the picturesque was a cultural vehicle for facilitating changes from an agrarian society to a capitalist economy.[29] Middle-class tourists could appreciate the old order, from the secure perspective of modernity, thus satisfying a lingering conservative impulse toward a paternalistic agrarian society.

Dorothy Wordsworth's inquiry into the relationship of writer to rural scenes begins with her adoption of a picturesque stance, yet her practice of experimentation with conventional perspectives ultimately prevents her from assuming a static relationship to her surroundings. The journal reveals a continual interest in how her position in the landscape affects what she sees. A February 1798 entry describes a walk with Coleridge to Nether Stowey:

> A very clear afternoon. We lay sidelong upon the turf, and gazed on the landscape till it melted into more than natural loveliness. The sea very uniform, of a pale greyish blue, only one distant bay, bright and blue as a sky; had there been a vessel sailing up it, a perfect image of delight. Walked to the top of a high hill to see a fortification. Again sat down to feed upon the prospect; a magnificent scene, curiously spread out for even minute inspection, though so extensive that the mind is afraid to calculate its bounds. (*AJ*, 8)

The entry shows an interest in composing the countryside into a "landscape"; it is an "image of delight." Dorothy Wordsworth exercises her compositional abilities as a picturesque observer by defining the missing element in the tableau, "a vessel sailing up" the bay. Moreover, she and Coleridge follow picturesque directives by climbing to "the top of a high hill to see a fortification." The "prospect" seems arranged for their "delight" and her "minute inspection." Yet even in the process of exercising the picturesque observer's prerogatives in composing her environment, her relationship to it shows signs of being more dynamic than picturesque convention allows. Aspects of the sublime enter her description. This passage develops a concern with how her perspective is informed by spatial and temporal factors: by laying down and looking for an extended period of time, the scene is transformed—it "melts" into something "more than natural." By climbing to higher ground, her perspective shifts again, a change evident in her vocabulary, as she turns from the picturesque to the sublime.

Dorothy Wordsworth's introduction of the aesthetic category of the sublime is particularly important in defining her growing concern with her complicated relationship, as a writer, to her environment, since this convention involves a dynamic exchange between observer and landscape. In picturesque practice, the viewer consciously arranges the scene; in the sublime aesthetic, the observer's control is sharply diminished: when confronted with a "magnificent scene," she discovers that "[t]he mind is afraid" to "calculate its bounds." The sublime grants to the natural environment a power to affect the human observer. A shadow of Edmund Burke's sublime is detectable in Dorothy Wordsworth's description of the scene. Burke associates the experience of the sublime with fear, an extreme emotion incited by "terrible objects."[30] Her account also accords with Immanuel Kant's notion of the effect of great expanses on the mind: the sublime "is to be found in a formless object, so far as in it or by occasion of it *boundlessness* is represented, and yet its totality is also present to thought."[31] If we consider that the Wordsworths' natural surroundings were written over with evidence of the period's socioeconomic disturbances, then the experience of the sublime threatens to overwhelm the observer not only with nature's expansiveness, but also with the "boundlessness" of the poverty and despair that Dorothy Wordsworth confronts in chronicling her local environments.

I turn now to describe how her domestic journals develop what might be called the social sublime, prompted by the cumulative effect of the stories and evidence of destitution she records.[32] In the *Alfoxden Journal*, she is interested in how her physical location alters her view of her local surroundings; in the *Grasmere Journals*, she begins to consider how her socioeconomic position informs her literary representations of its scenes. If the picturesque obliquely raises the issue of how her presence in the landscape situates her in socioeconomic, as well as in aesthetic, terms, then the sublime makes clear that her relationship to the scenes she views is dynamic. The sublime involves her more explicitly with her rural surroundings, and she pursues the implications of that engagement in the *Grasmere Journals* and the *Narrative*.

The *Grasmere Journals* opens on 14 May 1800 with a well-known declaration of the speaker's detachment from her natural surroundings. Although Dorothy Wordsworth does not adopt the picturesque perspective in the entry—the *Grasmere Journals* is in general less interested in composing scenes than in chronicling domestic and local experience—her habitual reserve is intact. The entry is especially important because it contains a statement of authorial purpose: "I resolved to write a journal of the time till W & J return, & I set about keeping my resolve because I will not quarrel with myself, & because I shall give Wm Pleasure by it when he comes home again." Thus, the *Grasmere Journals* begins by raising the issue of how her personal circumstances—here her isolation—inform her point of view. She is concerned with her responsibility as an author; writing is associated with a duty to maintain an emotional equilibrium while she is alone. Beginning with a parting from her brothers, William and John, who leave for Gallow Hill to visit the Hutchinsons, Dorothy Wordsworth denies that her perspective is skewed by her emotional state, as if her objectivity as a writer would be compromised if she does not maintain a stern detachment from the landscape. Although the journal opens with tears, she claims that her authorial perspective is unaffected by sorrow:

> My heart was so full that I could hardly speak to W when I gave him a farewell kiss. I sate a long time upon a stone at the margin of the lake, & after a flood of tears my heart was easier. The lake looked to me I knew not why dull and melancholy, the weltering on the shores seemed a heavy sound. (*GJ*, 1)

The *Grasmere Journals* begins by trying to sustain an authorial distance from the natural objects of her attention, but her concession that the lake does in fact look "dull and melancholy" indicates doubts about the viability of a stance that replicates the picturesque's remove. The entry displays an embarrassment about, and resistance to, an acknowledgment of the influence of her emotions on her perceptions; she wants to maintain a sense of empirical objectivity, even at moments of personal distress. But her need to disclaim her emotions' effects on her view of her surroundings undercuts her claims.

This passage opens a work in which Dorothy Wordsworth begins to examine her encounters as a writer with her rural environment more directly, via the processes of sympathetic identification. She considers the implications of a practice central to the poetics that she, William, and Coleridge were simultaneously defining. In the entry above, she obscures an identification between the "melancholy" appearance of the lake and her own emotional state. In the Preface,

William elaborates a process of sympathetic identification necessary to "the wish of the Poet to bring his feelings near to those of the persons whose feelings he describes." "For short spaces of time," he must "let himself slip into an entire delusion, and even confound and identify his own feelings with theirs; modifying only the language which is thus suggested to him by a consideration that he describes for a particular purpose, that of giving pleasure" (*Prose*, 1:138). The poet must be prepared temporarily to lose himself in order to get "near" to the objects of his attention. Most immediately, this process raises the problem of difference, since as William suggests there is a distance that must be overcome between the poet and the objects of his attention—he strives to get "nearer" to them. In *Lyrical Ballads* and the *Alfoxden Journal* and *Grasmere Journals*, the distance between the "feelings" of the writer and the persons encountered is largely socioeconomic. Dorothy Wordsworth raises questions about the material relations between writer and rural environment that complicate any ideal sense of an exchange based solely on the writer's reflections and emotional responses.

Dorothy Wordsworth's increasing attention to her relationship to her rural environment becomes evident as her habitual detachment is either no longer possible or creates its own dilemmas.[33] An encounter with an old man whom Dorothy and William pass on their way to Rydal for mail shows how the detachment of the empirical observer fails her when she learns too much about the human figures she describes:

> As we came up the White Moss we met an old man, who I saw was a beggar by his two bags hanging over his shoulder, but from a half laziness, half indifference & a wanting to *try* him if he would speak I let him pass. He said nothing, & my heart smote me. I turned back & said You are begging? 'Ay' says he—I gave him a halfpenny. (*GJ*, 50)

Since she concedes that she had immediately recognized the man as a beggar, her crisis of conscience concerns denying the implications of that understanding. The man's demands are silent, but ignoring them does not ease their pressure. The exchange that William describes in the Preface is emotional and psychological; Dorothy acknowledges that many of their encounters with the rural poor involved a different kind of transaction: that of begging. She thus opens up for inquiry the socioeconomic content of these interactions. When she gives the man money, her sense of obligation to him as one of the rural poor expands into an understanding of the more extensive fabric of their relationship:

> William, judging from his appearance joined in I suppose you were a Sailor? 'Ay' he replied, 'I have been 57 years at sea, 12 of them on board a man-of-war under Sir Hugh Palmer.' Why have you not a pension? 'I have no pension, but I could have got into Greenwich hospital but all my officers are dead.' (*GJ*, 50)

The sailor's rehearsal of his history reveals an unexpected connection to those acting as his casual patrons: Dorothy and William learn that they are indebted to him for his service to England. Suddenly, an exchange based on the economy of charity is complicated by a political relationship shaped by national interest. The Wordsworths' discomfort with this new knowledge is evident in their persistence in establishing the precise nature of what the man is owed by the government and, by extension, by them as citizens.

Dorothy and William want to know why he is not receiving a pension, a question that further involves them in the man's circumstances. First, it suggests a suspicion about the beggar's claims, a skepticism Dorothy Wordsworth displays at other moments in the *Journals*—she prides herself on detecting deceitfulness in beggars, a quality that she never rewards. Here her doubt implicates her in the injustices the man has suffered, because it represents a momentary denial of his implicit claims. William's question reflects the central concern raised by the encounter: if the sailor has served the country, doesn't the state have a responsibility toward him? The man's reply confirms that he has lost what is rightly his. The discovery of one area of relationship discloses a more extensive involvement. The siblings' interest in his story would be enhanced by familial interest: their brother John had left Grasmere for his first voyage in September 1800 as captain of the *Earl of Abergavenny*. This encounter demonstrates the potential for the various encounters with vagrant figures in the journals to implicate the writer by revealing relations—and obligations—that might otherwise remain suppressed.

In listening to the individual histories she records in the *Grasmere Journals*, Dorothy Wordsworth begins to confront the broader historical context that produces wandering families, discharged soldiers, and stoic leech-gatherers. David Marshall's treatment of sympathetic identification suggests what she relinquishes: the middle-class comfort of a sense of detachment from rural poverty offered by picturesque perspective. The threat in these exchanges to the vagrant figures Dorothy and William encounter is more acute, since they become spectacles of suffering. Sympathy is often "associated with acts and scenes of violence which picture the subjects of their spectacles as victims." These persons must rehearse their histories, however painful or humiliating, to elicit the sympathy that moves a listener to offer financial relief. The beggar's role in these encounters requires accepting the status of victim. The spectator, on the other hand, risks the luxury of detachment by engaging these figures and hearing their stories. Marshall argues that one of the "disconcerting effects" of the "transport of sympathy" is "a loss or forgetting of self." By identifying with the sufferer, the spectator is in danger of entering too fully into the misery of another, of experiencing what Marshall calls the "'too much sameness' of sympathy."[34]

A politically benign but emotionally taxing instance occurs when Dorothy Wordsworth describes a local funeral in a September 1800 Grasmere entry. What she learns is crucial to the journals: by taking her rural environment as her subject she accepts a role in its events. Because Dorothy Wordsworth did not know the woman who had died, she could presumably remain a detached observer, but she discovers that her safe emotional distance is compromised by the act of writing about what she sees. She reports a coffin—"neatly lettered & painted black & covered with a decent cloth"—and the singing of a "funeral psalm":

> The corpse was then borne down the hill & they sang till they had got past the Town-end. I was affected to tears while we stood in the house, the coffin lying before me. There were no near kindred, no children. When we got out of the dark house the sun was shining & the prospect looked so divinely

beautiful as I never saw it. It seemed more sacred than I had ever seen it, & yet more allied to human life. The green fields, neighbours of the churchyard, were green as possible & with the brightness of the sunshine looked quite Gay. I thought she was going to a quiet spot & I could not help weeping very much. (*GJ*, 20)

Dorothy Wordsworth is sobered by what she witnesses, and the proof is her view of her natural surroundings, which afterward seem "more sacred" and "more allied to human life." She loses the rhetorical authority of apparent objectivity. There is also an emotional cost— "I could not help weeping very much." She has relinquished the claim to disengagement made in the first entry of the *Grasmere Journals*. She describes a loss of emotional control that results from getting "near" to these social scenes. She gains the requisite proximity to the "feelings" of the persons she encounters, but pays with involuntary sorrow.

Dorothy Wordsworth's investigations of her role as writer in her local community are carried out via these indirect means in the journals: her identifications—and, in other instances, disidentifications— with what and whom she sees. The journals do not offer explicit commentary on the social understandings that her entries generate, but rather register them in the workings of identification and, sometimes, in her resistance to it. Despite her susceptibility in the scene above to the communal grief of a funeral, in other instances, she is reluctant to pursue the implications of her identificatory exchanges with her rural environment and its inhabitants. This ambivalence manifests itself as a desire to suppress the recognitions of socioeconomic relationship that these encounters necessitate. A November 1801 entry recounts meeting a woman who "was travelling with her husband he had been wounded & was going to live with her at Whitehaven" (*GJ*, 42). Explaining that her husband had gone ahead of her, the woman relates her history, in the process observing that she had once shared her auditor's socioeconomic status:

'Aye' says she 'I was once an officers wife I, as you see me now. My first Husband married me at Appleby I had 18£ a year for teaching a school & because I had no fortune his father turned him out of doors. I have been in the West

Indies—I lost the use of this Finger just before he died he
came to me & said he must bid farewell to his dear children
& me—I had a Muslin gown on like yours—I seized hold of
his coat as he went from me & slipped the joint of my finger—
He was shot directly. (*GJ*, 42)

The woman stresses that, like Dorothy Wordsworth, she too had
once been financially and socially secure. She underscores her point
as she narrates her social fall: at the moment that she loses her husband, and hence her socioeconomic position, "I had a Muslin gown
on like yours." The woman notes a physical resemblance that suggests a more significant connection with her auditor: contingencies
had decided which woman would extend sympathy and which woman
would beg financial relief.

Dorothy Wordsworth is silent about the story's effect on her, but
a similar incident elicits troubled reflections on her role as writer in
her *Recollections of a Tour in Scotland*. This journal begins not long
after the *Grasmere Journals* ends, in January 1803; Dorothy, William, and Coleridge leave for Scotland on 15 August. In the *Grasmere
Journals*, Dorothy Wordsworth rarely compares her stable domestic
situation with the plight of the wanderers and beggars who pass Dove
Cottage, perhaps because the understandings they prompt about how
her sociocultural position as writer separated her from the persons
she describes are, literally and figuratively, too close to home. Yet on
her travels, she considers what it means to be a tourist rather than a
vagrant, and how her own mobility was enabled by her financial and
social position. An 11 September entry relates an encounter with a
woman waiting to cross Loch Lomond by ferry that provokes a disturbing comparison of their circumstances:

The ferryman happened to be just ready at the moment to go
over the lake with a poor man, his wife and child; the little
girl, about three years old, cried all the way, terrified by the
water. When we parted from this family, they going down
the lake, and we up it, I could not but think of the difference
in our condition to that poor woman, who, with her husband, had been driven from her home by want of work, and
was now going on a long journey to seek it elsewhere: every

step was painful toil, for she had either her child to bear or a
heavy burthen. *I* walked as she did, but pleasure was my object, and if toil came along with it, even *that* was pleasure,—
pleasure, at least, it would be in the remembrance.[35]

Dorothy Wordsworth's guilt about her privileged "condition" is produced by her recognition of similarity in difference: "*I* walked as she
did, but pleasure was my object." The passage reveals "the multiple
fissures between toil and pleasure, poverty and ease, physical com-
pulsion and mental freedom."[36] In the *Alfoxden Journal* and *Grasmere
Journals*, the questions of relationship produced by the identifications and disidentifications of these exchanges are registered as dis-
comforts, embarrassments, and occasionally as expressions of regret,
such as she feels after ignoring the "discharged soldier." But because
of the fragmentary form of the genre, the entries record these difficulties without drawing conclusions. In contrast, Dorothy Wordsworth's 1808 *Narrative Concerning George and Sarah Green* pursues the implications of these encounters and in the process collapses
more fully any remaining sense of her speaker's disinterestedness and
aesthetic remove from the rural scenes that fill her journals. The lessons of the domestic journals are finally brought home.

On the night of 19 March 1808, George and Sarah Green began
the trip home to Easedale from a day's outing to a farm sale in Lang-
dale. They had left one of their daughters (eleven years old) to take
care of five of their other children. In attempting their return, the
couple lost their way, perhaps because of the snow that began to fall.
Both George and Sarah fell from a rocky precipice; neither survived.
When their bodies were found four days later, a relief effort was
launched for the children, in an attempt to provide for them beyond
the usual parish allowance of two shillings per week for orphans
under ten years old. William drafted a brief account of the events,
which he mailed with a cover letter to acquaintances in London and
elsewhere; Thomas Monkhouse, Francis Wrangham, William Lisle

Bowles, and Sir Walter Scott were among those who responded. Mary Wordsworth organized a committee of local women who found homes for the children. William asked Dorothy to prepare a more extensive version of the incident, and by 4 May she had completed an account that also described the relief efforts for the children.

In the composition and circulation of the *Narrative*, Dorothy Wordsworth's sense of the writer's responsibility to the rural scenes she represents is experienced as a crisis. In the domestic journals, her audience is known, comprised of the family and friends to whom the journals circulated, instead of the anonymous readers she anticipates for the *Recollections of a Tour in Scotland*. In articulating her misgivings about publication to Samuel Rogers, Dorothy Wordsworth seems primarily concerned with presenting herself to the "public." In explaining why she won't publish the *Narrative*, her attention shifts to the natural and rural inhabitants who would be similarly introduced to an unknown readership and the kind of scrutiny she was determined to avoid for herself. The *Grasmere Journals* illuminates how her anxieties of authorship are matched by her reluctance to submit others to scrutiny. In the *Journals*, her habitual use of the category of sympathy, inherited from the tradition of sensibility, forges an identificatory relationship with the natural and human objects of her attention. Her sympathetic identification with the "melancholy" landscape in the first entry of the *Grasmere Journals* and her subsequent identifications with beggars and vagrants establish a tenacious bond between writer and rural environment that invests her with a sense of responsibility.

In Dorothy Wordsworth's account of the Greens' disaster, she discovers how the identificatory relations that sympathy encourages elucidate socioeconomic connections she had not yet fully addressed. She examines those relations in the process of telling the story, and the crisis this investigation produces manifests itself variously: formally, thematically, and as an anxiety about publication. In the *Alfoxden Journal* and the *Grasmere Journals*, her misgivings about the exchange between herself as writer and her local surroundings are often registered indirectly: in the *Narrative*, these complexities emerge more explicitly, in repeated digressions in her account and a lengthy footnote concerned with poverty and violence.

In the *Narrative*, Dorothy Wordsworth's habitually understated presence as observer of her rural environment is relinquished as she assumes the more prominent position of local historian. Her speaker is autobiographical, and she addresses her own role in the events related in the course of narration. Yet this figure bears unmistakable resemblance to her speaker in the journals. The *Narrative* reads as if her journal speaker had simply elaborated one of the stories she hears in the journals' litany of destitution. Moreover, the domestic journals and the *Narrative* are also closely connected by a shared context of rural poverty. Dorothy Wordsworth speculates that, had George and Sarah not died and left their children to be supported by the parish, the Greens might have become one of the wandering families of the journals. Their property was heavily mortgaged at their deaths. Dorothy Wordsworth details their circumstances before the accident:

> They must very soon have parted with their Land if they had lived; for their means were reduced by little and little till scarcely anything *but* the *Land* was left. The Cow was grown old; and they had not money to buy another; they had sold their horse; and were in the habit of carrying any trifles they could spare out of house or stable to barter for potatoes or meal. (N, 49)

This story within the *Narrative* could be told by one of the houseless, landless beggars who rehearse their histories in the *Grasmere Journals*.

Yet despite the prominent links between the domestic journals and the *Narrative*, in the latter Dorothy Wordsworth launches a more pointed assessment of her autobiographical speaker's role in observing, responding to, and describing her local surroundings. In considering the Greens, she must confront more directly her role as writer in the Grasmere community. Unlike the histories of the beggars who wander by Alfoxden House and Dove Cottage, the Greens' story of socioeconomic decline is rooted in her own neighborhood. In their history, she discovers a local story in which she plays a dual role, as neighbor and as chronicler.

In "Simon Lee," William Wordsworth arrests his poetic narrative of the debilitated man he encounters in order to consider how the reader might respond to the man's story. The poet is willing to interrupt himself so that he may instruct the reader in how to receive Simon Lee's history. William Wordsworth's poet is intent on prescribing the reader's response, a task that Wordsworth himself finds both urgent and impossible in his efforts to promote the volume in which the poem appeared, *Lyrical Ballads*. In refusing to publish the *Narrative*, Dorothy Wordsworth acts on an understanding of the writer's inability to direct reading audiences' reactions to the scenes that she presents to them. Unlike "Simon Lee," which interrupts the forward progress of the story for a moment of reflection and feeling, the *Narrative* completes its story. The account departs from the experimentation with the cultural traditions of the picturesque and the sublime that defines the domestic journals, and especially the *Alfoxden Journal*. Yet concerns about the role of the reader in consuming literary representations of the rural environment haunt the *Narrative*. Susan Levin observes the congruence between its subject and the materials of *Lyrical Ballads*.[37] William treated the tragedy himself in a ballad called "Elegiac Stanzas Composed in the Churchyard of Grasmere," written in April 1808 but unpublished until Thomas De Quincey printed it in an 1839 article in *Tait's Edinburgh Magazine*, entitled "Early Memorials of Grasmere." The Greens' history, like numerous scenes in the domestic journals, are of shared interest with William, and during the *Narrative*'s preparation the siblings were once again involved in a collaborative writing enterprise.

Dorothy Wordsworth's inquiry into responsibility for the event is at first limited to the immediate tragedy, the parents' deaths. Yet in the course of the *Narrative*, the family's broader disaster is revealed, along with its embeddedness in a local context of rural poverty. The *Narrative* is preoccupied with Dorothy Wordsworth's sense of social relationships and their obligations. Her discomfort with the implications of communal responsibility is evident in a half-expressed desire to blame Sarah Green. Initially, Dorothy Wordsworth suggests that the mother exercised poor judgment by leaving the children to attend the sale, a charge that implies a neglected maternal obligation to protect her children and, for their sake, herself. Dorothy Wordsworth adds that the woman had given birth to two children before her marriage, a disclosure that seems calculated to cast doubt on the woman's character. But the woman is also praised as an efficient household manager with well-behaved children. Dorothy Wordsworth seems to correct herself when she insists that "the awful event checks all disposition to harsh comments." Yet she closes the question of Sarah Green's culpability by concluding that "perhaps formerly it might be said, and with truth, the woman had better been at home" (N, 50). Despite her impulse to blame one of the victims, Dorothy Wordsworth does not conclude her investigation with Sarah Green's actions; instead, she elaborates the community's responsibility and her own. As she examines the socioeconomic relations that join the Grasmere households in England's unstable political and economic climate, she uncovers a more extensive fabric of interdependence. In the process, any remaining sense of detachment from the scenes that she describes is irreparably compromised.

Dorothy Wordsworth's sense of relationship to the family is established by the same practice of sympathetic identification that produces moments of embarrassment and discomfort in the journals. In a passage describing the place where the Greens had lost their way, she interposes a personal memory, imagining herself in their place. She makes the discovery of socioeconomic interdependence with the Greens by considering what it means to share the same natural environment. The act of recollection fosters a sense of relationship to them, as she recalls being lost in an area through which they had wandered.[38] She recounts losing her way in a mist above Easedale Tarn, and imagines following in their steps:

> Those foot-marks were now covered with fresh snow: the spot where they had been seen was at the top of Blea Crag above Easedale Tarn, that very spot where I myself had sate down six years ago, unable to see a yard before me, or to go a step further over the Crags. I had left W. at Stickell Tarn. A mist came on after I had parted with him, and I wandered long, not knowing wither. When at last the mist cleared away I found myself at the edge of the Precipice, and trembled at the Gulph below, which appeared immeasurable. Happily I had some hours of daylight before me, and after a laborious walk I arrived at home in the evening. (N, 45–46)

At the most basic level, this passage acknowledges that she shares with her neighbors a physical environment: a terrain that could be dangerous in bad weather; her mist could have been as fatal as their snow. In relating this memory, Dorothy Wordsworth feels an acute retrospective sense of her own danger, standing "at the edge of the Precipice." She remembers trembling in response to her narrow escape, but her anxiety is not relegated to the past.

Dorothy Wordsworth feels a connection to the Greens that inspires what she believed to be a premonition about the location of their bodies: the "neighborhood of this Precipice had been searched above and below, wherever foot could come; yet, recollecting my own dreadful situation, I could not help believing that George and Sarah Green were lying somewhere thereabouts" (N, 46). Her sympathetic identification does not produce clairvoyance—the bodies are found elsewhere. But another understanding produced by the process of recollection proves more accurate. Her involvement in the scenes she describes is confirmed when she learns that she and William had inadvertently contributed to the family's economic distress.

Dorothy Wordsworth concedes that the family's destitution was suspected before the accident, but emphasizes that its extent was revealed only when their house was inspected: "[W]hen the Neighbours went to look after the Children they found nothing in the house but two boilings of potatoes, a very little meal, a little bread, and three or four legs of lean dried mutton" (N, 49). In the wake of such revelations, Dorothy Wordsworth first attempts to absolve herself, explaining that "it was not known till now (at least by *us*) how much distressed they must have been: for they were never heard to murmur or complain" (N, 49). Yet investigating the family's circumstances leads her to consider more closely her role in them, and eventually she acknowledges disturbing links in the families' household economies. The Wordsworths had employed one of the daughters in Dove Cottage:

> We in our connection with them have had one opportunity of remarking (alas! we gained our knowledge since their death) how chearfully they submitted to a harsh necessity, and how faithful they were to their word. Our little Sally wanted two shifts: we sent to desire her Mother to procure them; the Father went the very next day to Ambleside to buy the cloth and promised to pay for it in three weeks. The shifts were sent to

Sally without a word of the difficulty of procuring them, or anything like a complaint. After her Parents' death we were very sorry (knowing now so much of their extreme poverty) that we had required this of them, and on asking whether the cloth was paid for (intending to discharge that debt) we were told by one of the Daughters that she had been to the shop purposely to make the inquiry, and found that, two or three days before the time promised, her Father had himself gone to pay the money. Probably if they had lived a week longer they must have carried some article of furniture out to barter for that week's provisions. (*N*, 80)

Dorothy Wordsworth's admission of her own contribution to the family's economic devastation quite literally brings home the somewhat vague responsibility she had felt toward the vagrant figures she describes in the journals. Here her economic and social links to poverty are more immediately established: she learns precisely how she had worsened the family's circumstances. After her parents' deaths, Sally continued to live with Dorothy, William, and Mary as part of the community effort for the children.

Yet Dorothy Wordsworth discovers that her sense of complicity in the *Narrative* and even her efforts to aid the children do not absolve her of responsibility. Once the social context of the disaster is understood, it is not easily suppressed. Her acute sense of involvement reemerges formally in two footnotes to the *Narrative*, the second of which begins with an enumeration of items the Greens did not possess—"things that were wanting even to the ordinary supply of a *poor* house" (*N*, 88). The list details the extent and precise nature of the family's deprivations. Dorothy Wordsworth pours over the Greens' circumstances in reporting these missing items, including salt and sugar, and recording the few things they did own and their worth when they were sold. Her distress is evident as the footnote expands into the rehearsal of another local tragedy, the drowning of Mary Watson's son. The link between the Greens' story and this woman's experience is extremely tenuous: a loved one's belief that she could find the lost persons.[39] Mary Watson had been sure that she could find a missing son when a search party could not, a conviction also held by one of the Greens' daughters about her parents. In a subsequent expansion of the footnote, Dorothy Wordsworth continues Mary Watson's tale to include yet another horrific event, her murder by another son. The lengthy note relates a chain of violent disasters and indicates an intense concern with catastrophe generated by the original event, the Greens' fatal fall.

Critics have interpreted the footnotes as a formal enactment of a desire to repress psychological material that the *Narrative* disturbs in its telling. Homans reads the second footnote as the return of a repressed autobiographical narrative, Dorothy Wordsworth's reaction to her own mother's "abandonment" of her at her death in 1778 when Dorothy Wordsworth was six.[40] Wolfson interprets the notes in light of "her peripheral obsession with figures of isolation and abandonment," arguing that the concern suppressed in this account is that of being separated from William.[41] The footnotes, with their almost gothic events, seem to me particularly resonant, and capable of multiple allusions. I locate in them yet another context, partially suppressed in the *Narrative* itself. What is the connection between Mary Watson's history and the story of the Greens? The relevance of her story to theirs seems so precarious that a question arises about the connection between them. The binding threads are locality and violence.

By associating the Greens' story with violence in a rural setting, Dorothy Wordsworth gestures toward a social context for it beyond the local community, one with which she and her readers were acutely familiar as a contemporary setting. The Greens' circumstances resound in a period in which rural social unrest had recently been the result of the kind of poverty that they experienced. The *Narrative* was consumed by a circle of readers in the wake of protests launched in response to economic hardship such as the food riots that had erupted in England in May–December 1795. The riots prompted a sharp parliamentary reaction after the carriage of George III was caught in a London crowd, and the king feared he had been shot. The "Two Acts" against "treasonable practices" and "seditious meetings," the legislative products of this event, were intended to shut down radical meetings, a measure aimed in part at the radical speaker John Thelwall, Coleridge's acquaintance who wanted to join him, Dorothy, and William in the neighborhood of Nether Stowey and Alfoxden. The Greens' pride would seem to dissociate them entirely from the direct action taken by the rioters just over a decade before. Some protesters, for instance, targeted wheat bound for export and for the cities and attacked mills; the Albion Flour Mill in London was burned twice, once apparently by arson. This kind of action sometimes proved effective; the threat of violence secured certain prices on food items in Newcastle.

In contrast, the Greens had taken pains to make sure the extent of their impoverishment was not known to their neighbors. The *Narrative* lingers over circumstances that had, in other families, provided the justification for action and for retribution. The Greens' story provides ample justification for social protest. Dorothy Wordsworth's account of it betrays a persistent concern with violence and loss that suggests a broader national anxiety about responsibility for the poor and a fear that no one was assuming it. This concern emerges also in the *Grasmere Journals* in Dorothy Wordsworth's account of her encounter with the man William describes as the discharged soldier. As the *Narrative*'s footnotes suggest, these broader socioeconomic issues continue to inform her treatment of rural scenes, including her decisions against publication. Her decision not to publish the account, even two years after the fatal accident, shows her still struggling with the implications of her role as author and neighbor in the Greens' devastating history.

Critics have been ambivalent about the Wordsworths' participation in the relief effort for the Green children.[42] Michael Friedman analyzes William's role and discovers "a Tory humanist conception of a community structured by social rank and degree and a belief that such a hierarchic community must be preserved."[43] He points to letters that William wrote recommending against raising more than the £300 that was donated to the children's support. William imagines that more money "would have excited much envy and unkindly feeling among the poor families of this neighborhood" (*Wordsworth Letters*, 2:239). He also wants to prevent the dissemination of an idea that others in distress could expect similar assistance. Finally, William makes an argument similar to one used by John Gibson Lockhart in the *Edinburgh Review* in reference to John Clare: Lockhart recommends to Clare's "patrons" that they do not financially enable the "peasant poet" to abandon agricultural labor, because he might be morally ruined by the change in social status. William suggests that the children might be "puffed up with vanity and pride" and learn to "associate unworthy feelings of complacency with the melancholy end of their parents" (*Wordsworth Letters*, 2:40).

Dorothy Wordsworth's desire to protect the children from the exposure of publication must be interpreted partly as a middle-class desire to manage the experience of an impoverished rural class who inspired fear. Yet she is also acutely conscious of her own role in this process, aware of the potential for exploitation in her account of the children's circumstances. Because her subject is children, she is particularly aware of her capacity to harm or to protect them. As if in an effort to shield them from exposure, Dorothy Wordsworth defines her audience narrowly as "a friend"—possibly Joanna Hutchinson, to whom the *Narrative* is dedicated. Levin shows how, "[i]n a technique reminiscent of William's in beginning 'Michael,' she invites the reader into the narrator's intimate circle by immediately addressing her as one who knows Grasmere, assuming her familiarity with the village and the people in it."[44] Dorothy Wordsworth precludes the threatening unfamiliarity of a broader audience.

In the December 1810 letter to Catherine Clarkson, she is anxious about her own power as writer: she would be responsible for subjecting the children to "curiosity." Yet it is also a lack of power that disturbs her: once she has submitted the *Narrative*, and the children, to the literary marketplace she cannot control how they will be read or the effects on them of this public legibility. Dorothy Wordsworth articulates how the object of the writer's and readers' mutual attention is subjected to the desires of both parties. Publishing the *Narrative* would constitute the children's second disempowerment at her hands, since they had already lost to her the representation of their circumstances. She accepts responsibility for her understanding that the relationship between writer and rural environment is built on power relations in which she has socioeconomic strength, ratified by literacy. By refusing to publish the *Narrative*, Dorothy Wordsworth acts upon her understanding of her socioeconomic status in the rural community whose stories she writes. Yet by declining to enter the literary marketplace, except on several rare instances with closely monitored circumstances, she also forfeits her chance to use this power, even on behalf of the children. She rejects the public forum in which she could exercise the rhetorical agency she understood so clearly, and about which she was so skeptical. Although she interrogates the power relations of the exchange between writer and rural environment that informs her prose works and her brother's early lyric experiments, she keeps her explications of its dynamics private and thereby relinquishes the social efficacy of her rhetorical power.

By declining to publish her prose works, Dorothy Wordsworth removes herself from the vagaries of the literary marketplace that William Wordsworth, Smith and Clare come to understand by submitting themselves to its influence. She theorizes the dangers of the public visibility that each discovers in the course of their careers. By assuming the role of "Author," her contemporaries avail themselves of the rhetorical power that comes with the high costs that Dorothy Wordsworth tallies. In Clare's work the poet's strong identification with his native Northamptonshire is a kind of advocacy for those scenes, that were threatened as he was by the movement for agricultural "improvement" that visited Northamptonshire beginning in 1809 with the Helpston Act of Enclosure. Yet William Wordsworth's, Smith's and Clare's successes and failures attest to the profound limitations that the writer has in lyricism's potential to persuade. They also act out another lesson of Dorothy Wordsworth's unpublished prose works: that popular success could grant rhetorical power but also could subordinate the writer to an audience's desires, a threat especially acute for Smith and Clare, since they needed the full power of the lyric's "eloquence" (to return to Mill's term) for their families' support.

FIVE

John Clare's Poetics and the Politics of Loss

> A way of seeing has been connected with a lost phase of living,
> and the association of happiness with childhood has been
> developed into a whole convention, in which not only innocence
> and security but peace and plenty have been imprinted, indelibly,
> first on a particular landscape, and then, in a powerful extension,
> on a particular period of the rural past, which is now connected
> with a lost identity, lost relations and lost certainties, in the
> memory of what is called, against a present consciousness,
> Nature.
> —Raymond Williams on Clare

In a prescient reading of a contemporary's poetry, John Keats identified the aspect of John Clare's poetics that would effectively exclude Clare from—and include Keats in—the Romantic canon. Keats's comments were reported to Clare by their mutual publisher, John Taylor, as part of the publisher's effort to persuade Clare to diversify his poetic style. Taylor felt that if Clare were to sustain the popular success of *Poems Descriptive of Rural Life and Scenery* (1820), he must provide readers with variety by modifying his habitual focus on natural detail. Taylor reports Keats's observations to Clare: "I think he wishes to say to you that your Images from Nature are too much introduced without being called for by a particular Sentiment." Taylor goes on to qualify Keats's critique, while at the same time subtly reinforcing it, by reassuring Clare that "his Remark is only applicable now & then when he feels as if the Description overlaid & stifled that which ought to be the prevailing Idea."[1] Although Taylor seems not to have held Clare to the changes that Keats advised, literary history for a long time certainly did.

Keats's reading of Clare precisely delineates the various hierarchies—between poet and nature, reflection and observation, subjectivity and description—that would define prevailing twentieth-century expectations of Romantic lyricism, expectations that Clare did not meet. Clare's focus in many of his poems on the latter terms—nature, observation, and description—contributed to his categorization as "minor poet." Moreover, a conventional premium on the former qualities—the poet, reflection, and subjectivity—influenced which "Clare" readers would see. Twentieth-century anthologies of the period's poetry have favored Clare's late, so-called asylum verse—written 1837–64, from his initial voluntary institutionalization until his death—for its visionary qualities and its concerns with identity and its dissolutions. A haunting figure in critical accounts of the period's lyric poetry, a "mad" Clare at one time seemed more "Romantic" than the attentive observer of his native Northamptonshire.

Today the question of Clare's Romantic status is far less pressing, because of a broadening of the field's traditional chronological and generic boundaries and a simultaneous burgeoning of Clare studies. Once cast as "the Wordsworthian shadow," Clare is now in a position to revise the critical expectations that excluded him from the canon, including assumptions about the period's lyric "norms."[2] The long period during which Clare lingered on the threshold of Romanticism can now in turn provide valuable information on the terms that kept him there. More specifically, Clare challenges a persistent view of Romantic lyricism as a poetics of privacy by demonstrating how two key features long deemed to foster the mode's insulation from social concerns may instead comprise a poem's social content: the poet's turn to nature and a concern with subjectivity, which encompasses questions of identity.

In Clare's hands, the bond between poet and nature serves not to remove the poet from social concerns but rather to further a variety of social critiques. In M. H. Abrams's field-defining terms, nature was only the catalyst for the lyric's real focus: the poet's recollections and recognitions. The poet-nature exchange was hierarchical, and nature was ultimately peripheral to the poem's central concerns. Abrams's paradigm prompted a variety of theoretical challenges: a deconstruction of the myths of poetic originality and autobiographical self-definition; an early feminist critique of the implicit hierarchy between a masculine poet and a feminized nature; and a new historical argument that casts the turn to nature as an "escape" from political commitment and the lyric itself as the ideal vehicle of the Romantic ideology. Despite the sharp disagreements recorded by these counterparadigms, the poet's turn to nature has been consistently equated with a desire to transcend or to suppress the constraints of materiality. None of these paradigms sufficiently glosses Clare's handling of nature. Feminist and new historicist critics have shown that the poet-nature exchange is laden with political meaning. Clare demonstrates, however, that the exchange accommodates not only what might be termed this negative historical content—of subordination or evasion—but also a more active involvement in contemporary issues.

In one sense, this claim is not news to Clare's readers and critics, who have long realized that his acute attention to his rural environment had political overtones in a period of intensified parliamentary enclosure, a process that transformed Helpston and its surroundings for purposes of "agricultural improvement." A recent interest in "green criticism" has effectively articulated the case for a strong environmentalist strain in Clare's poetry and prose.[3] Yet the case for Clare as a protoenvironmentalist has courted another risk: of relegating his social politics to a lesser status and thereby forfeiting an adequate sense of the range of Clare's critiques and the lyric's potential as their poetic vehicle. The lessons of Clare's lyric poems remain only half-learned if we attend solely to his advocacy of nature, even if environmentalism is understood as having a significant social component. An adequate assessment of the poet-nature exchange requires sustained attention to the first term in the equation: the poet himself. For many of Clare's lyrics make a case for not only his rural environment and its inhabitants but also for himself as a "peasant poet" trying to make a career in a literary marketplace in which he was largely powerless. Having closely watched the agonizing decline from popularity, independence, and health of Robert Bloomfield, "the farmer's boy," Clare was deeply concerned with the group of poets whose struggles were defined not only by their social subordination but also by their acute vulnerability in their careers. With the same poetic strategies that he uses to protest enclosure, Clare addresses the extreme dependence upon middle- and upper-class reading audiences, patrons, and publishers whom he shared with other "labourer poets."[4]

Clare discovers in the lyric a formal vehicle that fosters an attention to the workings of subjectivity, a focus that effectively foregrounds identity's tenuousness. He investigates what might be called the material aspects of identity: the ways in which a sense of self is shaped by social forces. He thus mines a rhetorical capacity within the lyric that prevailing views of the mode neglect. Clare's habitual response to a pervasive sense of dissolution was to describe in vivid detail that which is subject to change. He regularly employs lyric strategies to grant the vulnerable places, animals, and persons in his poems a heightened visibility. In several of the late poems, the lost object is Clare himself, a crisis with both economic and psychological causes, which he confronts with the same strategies he had used to address the effects of enclosure: by continuing to insist on his own identity in the face of its disintegration. In this way, his poems work against the threat of erasure that seems such an omnipotent force in his works.[5] For Clare, the act of reasserting the identity of both places and of sentient beings (animal and human) in rich poetic detail was to establish a sense of their integrity and their rights. The poet's identification as "peasant poet" with indigenous flora and fauna draws analogies between the circumstances of those most vulnerable to legislative, economic, and seasonal changes. In Clare's hands, the lyric becomes the vehicle of a subtle but devastating critique of their mutual losses.

Clare's version of the poet-nature exchange is illuminated by Coleridge's theorization of the English sonnet, a paradigm particularly relevant to Clare because of his frequent use of the form. In his "Introduction to the Sonnets" (1796), Coleridge praises as "the most exquisite" sonnets those "in which moral Sentiments, Affections, or Feelings, are deduced from, and associated with, the Scenery of Nature." He finds that sonnets that closely link feeling and the natural scene "create a sweet and indissoluble union between the intellectual and the material world."[6] Clare discovers that this "union" could foster a meaningful alliance between the two parties, that the lyric facilitates an impulse to find resemblances between self and surroundings. In his poems, the poet's sympathetic identification with the landscape often has disturbing implications for both poet and place, since the poet aligns himself with a natural world that he describes as subject to the incursions of the governmental and landed interests who were profoundly transforming the countryside and the rural economy.

Clare discovers that the lyric convention of the poet's sympathetic identification with the natural scene can convey a keen sense of the poet's presence, even when nature assumes the foreground. Thus, Clare's lyric poems are preoccupied with questions of identity, but not in the ways that we have come to expect, for as Keats perceives, Clare rejects a premium on expressivity extant from the poets' day to ours. Clare's close association with his rural environment was fostered not only formally—via his poet's sympathetic identification with his surroundings—but also by the promotional apparatuses of his publishers. In *Poems Descriptive*, Taylor introduces Clare to reading audiences as "a Northamptonshire peasant," and thus publicly identifies Clare with the scenes that he describes by the public persona of "peasant poet." This bond is ratified in the poems that follow this introduction and also in Clare's subsequent volumes (in *The Village Minstrel, and Other Poems*, published the following year, Clare becomes "*the* Northamptonshire peasant," italics mine). Thus when Clare's poems lament nature's sufferings at the hands of enclosure's agents, he also manages to register his own suffering as an inhabitant who loves its scenes. Moreover, Clare is linked to the landscape not only as one of the rural poor, whose lives often enter into his songs and ballads, but also as the poet who wrote about those scenes. In poems such as "The Lamentations of Round Oak Waters" and "The Lament of Swordy Well"—among those Johanne Clare calls his "vocation poems"—the subtext of Clare's career emerges as an explicit concern.

More often, however, Clare uses the lyric's identificatory bond between the poet and nature to draw analogies between their different kinds of suffering, comparisons that often register social critiques, but within the safe guise of metaphors and similes. Such circumspection—made possible by the lyric's capacity for indirection—was necessary for Clare, whose forums and what he could say in them were strictly delimited by his economic and social dependence.[7] His career required regular shows of gratitude to his readers, patrons, and even the sympathetic Taylor. His impoverished circumstances have been widely discussed by critics. It will suffice here to recall his reliance upon his patrons, particularly Lord Radstock and the middle-class Eliza Louisa Emmerson; upon a popular audience; and upon his publishers James Hessey and, especially, Taylor. Clare's public identity— as "the Northamptonshire peasant"—was carefully constructed in his volumes of poetry, a process overseen by these figures, who often disagreed about how he should be presented. Taylor cast Clare in the role of natural genius; subsequent efforts to shape his public figure are evident in the pressure from his patrons to exclude poems deemed improper—either politically or sexually—for a "labourer poet."

A more public effort to orchestrate Clare's persona came in John Gibson Lockhart's advice to the poet's patrons about keeping him in his place. After the publication of *Poems Descriptive*, Lockhart, who admits to having read only extracts of Clare's poems, urges that the poet's "generous and enlightened patrons ought to pause ere they advise him to become any thing else than a peasant." He holds up Burns's career as an admonition to Clare's patrons: "Let them pause and think of the fate of the far more highly-gifted Burns, and beware alike of the foolish zeal and the sinful neglect of *his* countrymen."[8] The anxiety with which Clare's persona was managed by critics, publishers, and patrons is explicable in the context of post-Napoleonic economic and social instability, for as Elizabeth Helsinger points out: "Especially in an already politicized rural scene, the peasant poet could not be a neutral figure."[9]

Clare's poetic strategies evolved within these social restrictions. Zachary Leader has warned against an easy equation of these monitory figures, emphasizing that Clare often requested and agreed with Taylor's judgments on his poetry, at times even asking his publisher to rewrite passages that were proving difficult. Leader's argument counters a critical temptation to discount Clare's sustained efforts to exercise some control over his career by acknowledging only his subjection to others. This reminder about a critical tendency to patronize the poet and to villainize the publisher also points, however, to another way in which Clare was subject to others: he asked for Taylor's help because he understood that the publisher, better educated and socially situated, was necessary to his hopes of writing his way out of continually strained economic circumstances. As Leader observes, Clare wanted "to meet public expectations" partly because "literary success offered the possibility of escape from arduous and ill-paid manual farm labour," and Taylor was crucial to this aim.[10] In the lyric, Clare found a poetic means of articulating his anxiety, despair, and his anger about his own plight as "the Northamptonshire peasant" in poems that make a passionate case for his beloved Helpston and a more covert case for the poet who wrote about the place.

Despite Clare's frank celebration of rural life in numerous works, many of his best known poems—including "Helpstone" (c. 1809–13), "The Lamentations of Round-Oak Waters" (1818), "The Lament of Swordy Well" (c. 1821–24), "Remembrances" (c. 1832), and "I Am" (c. 1844)—concern the perplexity of change and reflect a career-long interest in it. These poems, however, dramatize not a singleness of theme or tone but rather a multiplicity of loss. "Helpstone" is an elegy for childhood pleasures and their setting; "Remembrances" mourns the loss of familiar surroundings occasioned by Clare's move to Northborough; "I Am" eulogizes a faltering sense of identity that became an obsession during his late, unstable years. As even this brief list of poems suggests, both the number and kind of lost objects and the perpetrators of those losses proliferate across his career. The culprits Clare cites include time, parliamentary acts of enclosure, and the fickleness of the readers, publishers, and patrons on whom he depended.

My argument that many of Clare's lyrics effectively convey social critiques requires careful attention to the mechanisms of his lyricism, because his poems on enclosure have seemed to some critics to forfeit viable political arguments. Certainly, there is nothing inherently political about Clare's treatments of loss, even in poems that address the alterations wrought by enclosure. When the agent of change is identified as "Inclosure," or "wealth," then the poems take on overtly political overtones. Yet in a poem like "Helpstone," it is difficult to assign blame, because the causes of change are twofold: the poet's own maturation and the processes of enclosure. In naming two agents of loss as the source of the environment's transformation, Clare might seem to compromise his stance against enclosure, since ultimate responsibility for the changes he laments remains unassignable. In making his case for the predominance of a "sense of place" in Clare's poetry, John Barrell suggests that the poem's multiple agents of loss produce thematic confusions that compromise the poem's political salience.[11] Yet I would argue that in "Helpstone," the poem that opened his first volume, *Poems Descriptive*, an effective poetics and politics of loss is already operative, although its practice becomes subtler across the course of Clare's career.

"Helpstone," which was probably written between 1809 and 1813, is often compared to Oliver Goldsmith's *Deserted Village*, and it also suggests Thomas Gray as an important source of Clare's pervasive elegiac tone and his concern with obscurity.[12] Clare's initial success was based on his assumption of already familiar, cultural roles: his strong echoes of Gray's immensely popular *Elegy Written in a Country Church-yard* and his public appearance as a "peasant poet," in the wake of Stephen Duck, Ann Yearsley, Burns, and Bloomfield.[13] The poem begins with an address to the town of Helpston, which he describes in terms that recall the forgotten village of Gray's *Elegy:*

> Unletterd spot unheard in poets song
> Where bustling labour drives the hours along
> Where dawning genius never met the day
> Where usless ign'rance slumbers life away
> Unknown nor heeded where low genius trys
> Above the vulgar & the vain to rise.
> (lines 5–10)

The town and its inhabitants barely exist: the place is "unletterd," "unheard," and "unknown." Place and people have failed to register their presence. This "obscurity"—to use a term repeated several times in the poem—identifies village, animals, and humans with each other on the basis of a shared forgottenness.

The speaker's identification with the objects of his attention, neglected by others, is important for understanding how Clare often introduces his poet into the scene by identifying him with the natural entities already described. With a reticence familiar from Gray's speaker in the *Elegy,* the poet of "Helpstone" appears belatedly and then only as the second term in a comparison between birds who seek "food & 'better life' in vain" (line 25) and himself: "So little birds in winters frost & snow / Doom'd (like to me) wants keener frost to know" (lines 23–24). Clare's poet echoes Gray's speaker in the "Sonnet on the Death of Mr. Richard West," with an important difference: Gray's speaker defines himself as different from the birds who participate in dawn's renewal, while in Clare's poem the birds, like all of nature, seem to sympathize with the speaker in his desolation. The impact of the poet's delayed entrance in "Helpstone" is further diminished by its parenthetical nature. This opening establishes as a primary purpose in the poem the task of registering the unrecognized worth of this forgotten place by an equally unnoted figure: "Hail scenes obscure so near & dear to me / The church the brook the cottage & the tree" (lines 47–48). The poet's role is to acknowledge and to appreciate, while the "scenes" he observes retain center stage. He is important for noticing what has been overlooked, but as he draws attention to these lost objects, he himself remains obscure. We learn little about the poet other than his strong affection for the place and his immense sadness at seeing any piece of it disappear.

The poet's identification with the place establishes an intimate connection between them, one whose history is rehearsed in the course of the poem. But its trajectory becomes unclear when the cause of its dissolution is rendered uncertain. "Helpstone" opens with echoes of the *Elegy* and develops into a rehearsal of the "Ode on a Distant Prospect of Eton College," with the speaker mourning a vanished childhood free from foreboding about the future:

> Dear native spot which length of time endears
> The sweet retreat of twenty lingering years
> & oh those years of infancy the scene
> Those dear delights where once they all have been
> Those golden days long vanish'd from the plain
> Those sports those pastimes now belovd in vain.
> (lines 51–56)

We know that Clare was at most twenty years old when he wrote the poem, and this biographical framework heightens our sense of the intense literariness of the speaker's elegy for youth. When he makes a wish for the future near the end of the poem, however, his apparent distance from his childhood seems to close:

> Thou dear beloved spot may it be thine
> To add a comfort to my life['s] decline
> When this vain world & I have nearly done
> & times drain'd glass has little left to run
>
> . . . .
>
> May it be mine to meet my end in thee.
>
> (lines 165–76)

These lines reflect more accurately the autobiographical speaker's youthful perspective, looking toward a distant decline rather than back to a lost childhood. They may in fact recuperate a stance somewhat incongruous for a young poet. But between these two moments—looking back and looking forward—come lines that disrupt this tenuously held position. In the middle of the poem, the speaker blames the loss of these fondly remembered scenes not on the inexorable processes of maturation but rather on social forces that have altered the landscape.

In the middle of the poem the speaker makes his case against enclosure's transformation of the scenes that he remembers:

> Now all laid waste by desolations hand
> Whose cursed weapons levels half the land
> Oh who could see my dear green willows fall
> What feeling heart but dropt a tear for all
> Accursed wealth oer bounding human laws
> Of every evil thou remains the cause.
>
> (lines 123–28)

In these lines we witness the felling of trees and the devastation of "half the land," so that when the poet expresses a desire to return to these scenes, the obvious question arises: do the scenes remain or have they been altered beyond recognition, as is suggested in several lines? Midway through the poem the speaker bids farewell to the landscape he remembers: "Ye perishd spots adieu ye ruind scenes" (line 145). Did they perish because of natural processes of change that have altered the speaker as well as the landscape, or has the countryside undergone a premature decline at the hands of social forces? Barrell speculates that the poem may have been written at two different points, before the Helpston Enclosure Act of 1809 had affected the countryside and then several years later, when its effects were evident.[14] This possibility can account for the discrepancies I have been outlining in practical terms. But there is an irresolution about the agency of change in "Helpstone" that persists beyond this poem and that makes the conflict's clarity here valuable.

The apparent conflation of the causes of hopelessness in "Helpstone" may be read as the result of a protracted process of composition, but it may also be read as indicative of something larger in Clare's work: a practice of subtle comparison that discreetly conveys a point that could not be made more overtly. It is of course possible that there are multiple causes for the desolation of childhood scenes, that the natural decline of aging coexists with the destruction of the enclosure acts. Yet in "Helpstone" they are not simultaneous but analogous, since Clare does not finally sort out the differences between the effects of maturation and those of enclosure. This comparison of the agents of change produces two broad rhetorical effects in "Helpstone": an identification on the poet's part between himself and his natural surroundings and an association of the oppressive forces with each other. These analogies suggest that the countryside and its inhabitants, both animal and human, are mutually vulnerable to a range of powerful forces. By comparing enclosure to a force as impersonal and as inexorable as time, Clare projects an overwhelming helplessness in the face of parliamentary acts that were transforming his natural environment and its social existence. Moreover, Clare's comparisons of the sufferers of change significantly define his poet's perspective on his world: a position of a susceptibility that he shares with his environment. His response to his circumstances sometimes takes the tone of protest, but more often finds expression in lamentation—a word that appears often in Clare's works. It may seem as if Clare chooses lamentation over protest, but as Johanne Clare argues, "[h]is mourning was always quickened by anger."[15]

Clare's strategy of comparing an abstract entity such as time with a human, political force like enclosure runs the risk of muting his polemical point about enclosure. There is a rhetorical danger in equating an unstoppable natural force with a social one that could be challenged. But several important political points are established by Clare's deft comparisons: first, that the poet's extreme disenfranchisement made time and enclosure seem similarly inexorable forces to him; and second, that enclosure was altering rural life as permanently as years. Clare's comparison of the sufferers of these two different kinds of change makes another important point: his identification with his rural environment suggests that, as one of the rural poor, he has no more hope of halting the changes he witnesses than do the birds and trees. The speaker establishes an alliance of mutual subjection after comparing his lot with that of the birds: "But now alas those scenes exist no more / The pride of Life with thee (like mine) is oer" (lines 115–16). Clare elevates the birds to fellow sufferers, a gesture of sympathetic identification that, as Jonathan Bate makes clear, has political implications: "Clare extends *égalité* from mankind to the non-human world."[16]

William Empson's comment on Gray's *Elegy* is helpful in articulating Clare's poetics and politics of loss: he describes the *Elegy* as "an odd case of poetry with latent political ideas."[17] Clare's political ideas retain something of Gray's latency, yet they emerge explicitly often enough to alert us to their presence throughout his works. Helsinger brings Clare's dilemma into sharp focus in her discussion of the poem when she describes his "impossible desire to win an audience for his poetry and economic support for his poetic career from those whom his poem can barely avoid identifying as the authors of his distress."[18] Clare's patrons did not miss his more explicit statements about abuses of power, and in fact Radstock strongly objected to particular lines in "Helpstone" (including lines 125-28, quoted above) as expressing radical sentiments. The struggle over "Helpstone" indicates just how much was at stake for Clare, his patrons, and his publishers in the poet's treatments of enclosure.

In May 1820, Clare wrote to Taylor requesting that certain lines be excised in the next edition because of pressure he was receiving not only from Radstock, but also from Emmerson and Captain Markham E. Sherwill, who had written to Clare earlier in the year in response to the appearance of *Poems Descriptive* (also enclosing a contribution for Clare's parents).[19] Taylor was ambivalent about Radstock's pressure, both on political grounds and because Radstock was trespassing on editorial territory. But after initially resisting Radstock's interference, Taylor cut ten lines from the fourth edition.[20] The shift of meaning effected is significant. Prior to the revision, the

poet observes his surroundings and laments "all laid waste by desolations hand, / Whose cursed weapons levels half the land" (lines
123–24). The agent of this devastation is then identified: "Accursed
wealth" is the "cause" of "every evil," including the "loss of labour"
and of trees. The poet goes on to describe the effects on the rural
poor:

> Victims of want those wretches such as me
> Too truly lay their wretchedness to thee
> Thou art the bar that keeps from being fed
> & thine our loss of labour & of bread
> Thou art the cause that levels every tree
> & woods bow down to clear a way for thee
> (lines 129–34)

When these lines are omitted, the "desolation" he witnesses is rendered more existential than political. Moreover, the "weapons" de-
plored may be found in time's arsenal, rather than among the imple-
ments of "agricultural improvement." Yet even though Radstock won
this skirmish, his emendations do not disable Clare's broader poetic
argument against enclosure.

"Remembrances," one of several poems written in response to
Clare's 1832 move from Helpston to Northborough, a village roughly
three miles distant, anchors a case for the political salience of the
comparisons in "Helpstone" of the agents and victims of catastrophic
change. The experience of being removed from his childhood scenes
seems to have encouraged in Clare the sense of a threat to his identity, a disturbance that would become the explicit subject of some of
his late poems and prose fragments. The move was made possible by
one of his patrons, Lord Fitzwilliam, who rented the cottage to Clare,
an offer the poet accepted in hopes of gaining a measure of financial
security for his family. "Remembrances" laments ruptured connections
to his former environment at Helpston, a loss caused by Clare's circumscribed economic position, which made the move to Northborough

seem desirable. The poem memorializes a "ruin of the past" (line 10), and again the poet refers both to his own history and to that of his surroundings. The disparities of this comparison are not as glaring as in the earlier poem and for that reason they may go unnoticed, even though they have survived into the poet's middle period. However, their importance is underlined when we consider that "Remembrances" belongs to Clare's maturity and is marked not by a disentanglement of the analogies in "Helpstone" but rather by their more thorough integration.

The close identification between the poet and his environment already evident in an early poem like "Helpstone" gains added resonance in "Remembrances" by its relevance to a career in sharp decline. The relocation's promise of greater economic stability would have been hard to refuse for a poet whose first volume far outsold those that followed. Four editions of *Poems Descriptive* were called for within a year of its publication (over three thousand copies altogether), but *The Village Minstrel* (1821) sold far fewer copies, and his subsequent volumes further declined in sales. Many reasons have been given for the waning of interest in Clare, including a general decrease in poetry's popularity at about this time and a sense among his readers that after his success he was perhaps not the "peasant" he had been when first introduced to the public. More immediate problems surrounded the publication of Clare's volumes after *Poems Descriptive*, including delays that may have wearied his audience's enthusiasm for the "Northamptonshire peasant." Taylor's acquisition of the *London Magazine* in 1821 (with Hessey) seems to have slowed his editing and preparation of *The Village Minstrel*, and when it appeared in September, Eliza Emmerson, who had urged its publication before a London audience left the city for holidays, lamented to Clare, "The season is sadly against the sale."[21] The delays for his next volume extended beyond months to years; Taylor wrote to Clare in August 1823 suggesting a new volume to be called *The Shepherd's Calendar*. The collection did not appear until 1827, and then sold poorly. By the time of Clare's final volume, Taylor had given up publishing poetry and Clare initially sought to raise money by subscription for a collection to be called "The Midsummer's Cushion" which finally appeared, substantially reshaped by Emmerson's involvement with the project, as *The Rural Muse* (1835). Clare's struggles to publish his poems were exacerbated by the continuing precariousness of his finances and health. Father to a large family, Clare supplemented his poetic production with agricultural labor, a combination of employment that compromised both tasks by wearing him down physically and emotionally when he repeatedly failed to secure a steady, adequate income.

"Remembrances" begins with an extended explanation of an opening statement of loss: "Summer pleasures they are gone like to visions every one." The poet elaborates how maturity brought with it an understanding that "such raptures meet decay" (line 5). Clare begins, then, with a rehearsal of adult disillusionment reminiscent of Gray's poet in the *Elegy* and his own poet in "Helpstone." The poem also contains echoes of the "Eton Ode," although they seem fainter because the allusions are more muted, as if Clare has integrated Gray's sentiment into a language of his own. Midway through the poem he assigns a cause to the changes he enumerates: "O I never thought that joys would run away from boys / Or that boys would change their minds and forsake such summer joys" (lines 51–52). His explanation of what has changed is twofold here. Again time has forsaken the poet, even as the poet has abandoned his previous pleasures. Blame is assigned to time and to the speaker in these lines even as another, political cause is not precluded.

An unannounced turn to political commentary comes slightly less than halfway through the poem:

> . . . —O I never call to mind
> These pleasant names of places but I leave a sigh behind
> While I see the little mouldywharps hang sweeing to the wind
> On the only aged willow that in all the field remains
> And nature hides her face where theyre sweeing in their chains
> And in a silent murmuring complains.
>
> (lines 35–40)

The poet's sighs for a ruined past are joined by the murmuring complaints of nature at the sacrifice of wildlife in the shapes of willows and moles. The latter image recurs later in the poem, in a comparison between enclosure and Napoleon: "Inclosure like a Buonaparte let not a thing remain / It levelled every bush and tree and levelled every hill / And hung the moles for traitors—though the brook is running still / It runs a naked brook cold and chill" (lines 67–70). In these lines Clare makes a characteristic move, personifying a force like enclosure so that it seems less abstract. By giving enclosure human features he identifies a culprit. A similar moment occurs in "Helpstone" when we see "desolations hand" ruining "half the land." Both poems assign devastation to human actors, but "Remembrances" goes one step further by attributing to enclosure not just human features, but specifically those of Napoleon. The simile does more than remind the reader of enclosure's human agency: it characterizes enclosure as a political force with a disregard for those vulnerable to its dictates and a motivation of territorial gain. By assigning the roles of aggressor and victims to the processes of enclosure, Clare recasts as carnage parliamentary acts professedly designed for the improvement of the national economy. The passage's political references are multiple, and Clare's use of prosopopoeia complex: the countryside too is given human features as the moles become persons hung for acts of treason. Critics have suggested that Clare's imagery is drawn from the aftermath of the Swing Riots in 1830, for which some of the participants were hanged.[22] He thereby draws parallels between the power exerted by Napoleon and the British government, a highly polemical analogy between fallen imperialist ambitions and British justice.

Yet despite the pointedness of Clare's representation of enclosure in "Remembrances," his political stance is muted on several counts. Agents of loss proliferate, and our sense of each is thereby diminished, as in "Helpstone." Moreover, Clare's war imagery bleeds into other sections of the poem, and to different ends. Just before the striking personification of enclosure as Napoleon, comes another battle, this one without human tyranny:

But alack I never dreamed that the world had other toys
To petrify first feelings like the fable into stone
Till I found the pleasure past and a winter come at last
Then the fields were sudden bare and the sky got overcast
And boyhoods pleasing haunts like a blossom in the blast
Was shrivelled to a withered weed and trampled down and done

Till vanished was the morning spring and set that summer sun
And winter fought her battle strife and won.

(lines 53–60)

Here the fields are decimated not by enclosure's "levelling" but by a
winter of the soul. The fields are transformed not by governmental
acts but by the speaker's maturation; it is his perspective that changes.
Here maturity is the destructive force, coexisting and seemingly coin-
ciding with enclosure's transformations. This attribution of loss to
causes personal and more broadly political cannot be explained by
multiple points of composition, as was possible in "Helpstone." Other
explanations more integral to Clare's poetics—and his politics—must
be sought.

Two broad points may be made about Clare's habitual equation
of the agents of change in these poems. The first concerns the historical situation that Clare was addressing; the second, his manner of
addressing it. The extent of enclosure's effects—as well as its import
for different sections of the rural community—has been heavily de-
bated by historians, with one division occurring between those who
view it as catastrophic for the rural poor and those who contend that
enclosure was just the final, most visible step in a long process of
dispossessing laborers of rights of ownership and use. E. P. Thompson argues that for Clare and his contemporaries, enclosure was symbolic of the displacement and disempowerment of the rural poor in
early-nineteenth-century England, since "[l]and always carries associations—of status, security, rights—more profound than the value
of its crop." J. M. Neeson makes a related case, arguing that part of
the trauma of enclosure for the rural poor was that it made dramatically evident the widening economic gap between themselves and
landowners: "Perhaps this separation was a long time coming," yet
"[e]nclosure had a terrible but instructive visibility." It "taught the
small peasantry the new reality of class relations."[23] Thus protest
against enclosure could be both specific to the cause and critical of
broader social injustices. Railing against enclosure might also indict
the grabbing of power and wealth that the landed aristocracy effected at the beginnings of the Napoleonic Wars abroad and the con-
current counterrevolutionary repression of social unrest at home.

Enclosure made all too apparent the widening gap between landed power and dispossessed commoners, and Clare's response was to keep visible the multiple victims involved. By maintaining a dual focus on natural and human sufferers in many of his poems, he allows his readers to overlook neither. The image of enclosure hanging "the moles for traitors" (line 69) in "Remembrances" generates two scenes: that of the moles' destruction as their homes are destroyed and of the sacrifice of human livelihood by the same set of political changes. In the image of the moles "sweeing in their chains" (line 39) Clare reminds readers that the resistance to enclosure was, of course, human. It is tempting to read the moles merely as stand-ins for persons; the image of their hanging is a convenient way of smuggling into the poem a more incendiary point than a lamentation of changes to the natural world. Yet it is important to recognize that neither human nor natural world gains precedence in Clare's account of his changing surroundings. Even in poems in which no humans appear, Clare makes it clear that wherever the natural world is visible, the human realm is implicated, both as perpetrator and as victim.

From his earliest poems, Clare cites forgetfulness as one of the agents of detrimental change. Just as the sources of loss are multiple in his works, so forgetfulness has both benign and culpable manifestations. On the one hand, the loss of a vital countryside that Clare laments is part of the inevitable consequence of maturation, an adult forgetfulness that Wordsworth had articulated in the "Intimations Ode." But Clare also claims that his natural environment is neglected by persons in a position to perpetuate or to prevent deleterious changes. "Forgetfulness" about the consequences of enclosure on Northamptonshire by the landed gentry and governmental agents was culpable negligence—a willful disregard—according to Clare. Both contemporary accounts and recent historical treatments support his association of parliamentary enclosure with loss for land-poor or landless rural inhabitants, although this is a charge disputed then and now. A comment in Arthur Young's *General Report on Enclosures* (1808) supports Clare's association of enclosure with negligence. The report makes the case for carrying out enclosure on a larger scale by documenting "a general knowledge of the advantages which have attended Enclosures, and of the means by which those benefits have accrued to the Public."[24] Although Young's report is optimistic about the effects of enclosure and seeks to justify an expansion of the process, an appendix elaborating the "Effect on the Poor" is telling. The appendix chronicles the disadvantages and—far fewer—advantages reported by actual inhabitants of various parishes.

The most frequent complaint is the loss of grazing rights and the resulting loss of cows. The comments recorded lend anecdotal evidence to Clare's complaint in "To a Fallen Elm" (c. 1821) that when "[t]he common heath became the spoilers prey," then "labours only cow was drove away" (lines 59, 62). From the parish of Tutvy: "To my knowledge, before the enclosure, the poor inhabitants found no difficulty in procuring milk for their children; since, it is with the utmost difficulty that they can procure any milk at all." We learn: "Cows lessened from 110 to 40." We need only remember the import of these losses—a cow, calves, milk, butter, and cheese—to understand the significance of Clare's lament.[25] Thus, his concern with neglect draws on contemporary discourses about enclosure's effects. The list of "Effects on the Poor, of the Enclosures which took place during the first Forty Years of His present Majesty" reads like a series of losses: "Fewer hands employed" in Bradwell; "Less work for the people" in Castlethorp; "Live-stock of the poor gone" in Willington; "Deprived of their cows, and great sufferers by loss of their hogs" in Passenham, Northamptonshire. A marginal comment in the list attempts to distinguish the effects of human failure from the effects of enclosure itself, concluding hopefully "[t]hat the injury, which, in these cases, seems really to have been received, flowed from inattention to the property or customs of the poor, and by no means of necessity from enclosure."[26] But this partial defense actually concedes one of Clare's main points: that neglect of—or "inattention" to—the poor has resulted in overwhelming loss and permanent change to their ways of life. Historians have argued that in the wake of enclosure, the peasantry was finally transformed into a rural working class.

By ostensibly focusing solely on the issue of enclosure, Clare could remain—usually—within the bounds of subjects and sentiments acceptable for a "peasant poet" while at the same time insinuating a broader critique. Enclosure was a cause that could take a distinctly nonradical stance: a wounded aesthetic sense of landscapes disfigured. Clare sometimes makes explicit the human costs of enclosure, but a tradition of appreciating and praising nature made possible a less-politicized reading of many of his works, or at least a limitation of his platform to a protest of his beloved nature's destruction. Taylor seems to have understood the relative safety provided by the portrait of Clare as a "peasant poet" grieving over changes in his natural surroundings. Taylor emphasizes the aesthetic, rather than political, motivations of Clare's edgy lamentations for natural scenes in his introduction to *The Village Minstrel.* Taylor shrewdly anticipates readers' discomfort with "some apparently discontented stanzas about the middle" of the title poem and offers as an "excuse" the "state of dreary misery in which he then lived," before his first volume was published.[27] The extent of Taylor's anxiety about the emergence of Clare's anger in the collection is indicated by his continuation of this theme. Taylor follows up his explanation of Clare's "discontent" with a lengthy account of an anecdote related to him by Clare in a March 1821 letter, which casts the poet in the role of nature's defender rather than that of radical.

In the letter, Clare describes his anguish at plans to fell "my two favourite Elm trees at the back of the hut." Taylor quotes the poet's narration of the loss, in an account that echoes his statements against enclosure's exploitations: "[T]he savage who owns them thinks they have done their best & now he wants to make use of the benefits he can get from selling them." Taylor even includes Clare's description of the reprisals he would enact: "O was this country Egypt & was I but a caliph the owner shoud loose his ears for his arragant presumption & the first wretch that buried his axe in their roots shoud hang on their branches as a terror to the rest." It is initially surprising that Taylor includes this fantasy of physical retribution, but it soon becomes apparent that Taylor includes Clare's desire for revenge in order to defuse its impact, or rather to have Clare deflate it himself, for the poet goes on to voice second thoughts: "[Y]et this mourning over trees is all foolishness they feel no pains they are but wood cut up or not." Moreover, Clare concedes, "was People all to feel & think as I do the world coud not be carried on—a green woud not be ploughd a tree or bush woud not be cut for firing or furniture & every thing they found when boys would remain in that state till they dyd." Finally, Clare reduces himself to an eccentric lover of trees when he confesses with apparent embarrassment, "[T]his is my indisposition

& you will laugh at it."[28] Clare's volumes, however, repeatedly state a desire for the immutability that he describes as laughable; and, moreover, his anger in the letter sometimes surfaces in the poems that follow. In introducing the anecdote, Taylor cautiously suggests that "[t]he regret of a poet for the loss of some object in nature, to which many of the dearest recollections of his earliest and happiest days had attached themselves, is always vehement; but who can wonder at or condemn it?" The publisher divined that Clare's love of his native countryside was at least a plausible excuse for a polemic against enclosure, a safeguard against charges of radicalism necessary in light of his patrons'—and especially Radstock's—censoring of his poems. "Remembrances," nevertheless, remained unpublished until 1908.

What Taylor and Clare's patrons understood was that the poet was in fact participating in a viable tradition of enclosure protest that extended in Northamptonshire beyond the date of Helpston's final Award in 1820. Countering a long-held assumption that rural inhabitants with little or no land offered almost no resistance to enclosure, Neeson documents a persistent—if, in the end, largely ineffectual—practice of "argument and obstruction" that took a variety of forms, legal and illegal: "local and parliamentary counter-petitions, the refusals to sign bills, the bills lost or delayed, the letters written to enclosers, the hostile fence-breaking before and after enclosure, the riots, the thefts of boundary marks and field books, the expressions of concern and apprehension found in diaries and poems, the malicious rumours, and the advertisements and letters sent to the *Northampton Mercury.*"[29] Situating Clare's poems against enclosure within the context of a pervasive and sustained protest on the part of his Northamptonshire neighbors registers just how much was at stake for Clare, his patrons, and his publishers in printing poems that would have been too easily recognized as part of this opposition.

Enclosure was, however, not the only, or perhaps even the riskiest, cause for Clare to espouse; by making his own case as a laborer poet, the poet risked alienating those who made his career possible. I have suggested that Clare uses his poet's sympathetic identification with his natural surroundings to establish a moving alliance that lends an almost human identity to his native Northamptonshire. In making the case for his native environs, Clare also renders more sympathetic the poet who becomes so closely associated with those scenes. The interdependence of human and natural worlds in Clare's writings is so thorough that we detect the human world in natural objects, and vice versa. Whenever he talks about the landscape and its wildlife, he refers to himself; at the same time, whenever he explicitly laments his own situation, he also publicizes his threatened rural environment. In defining what he calls (quoting Clare) a new "green language," Raymond Williams describes "the investment of nature with a quality of creation that is now, in its new form, internal; so that the more closely the object is described, the more directly, in a newly working language and rhythm, a feeling of the observer's life is seen and known."[30]

In "The Lamentations of Round-Oak Waters" (1818) and "The Lament of Swordy Well" (c. 1821–24), the landscape pleads its own case, but proves most persuasive about the sufferings of the "peasant poet." One of Clare's characteristic poetic strategies for treating enclosure's losses is a complicated prosopopoeia, a trope that literalizes his efforts to give places a humanlike identity. At its most straightforward, Clare's practice of prosopopoeia clarifies the human agency in seemingly abstract processes. In "Helpstone" we see "desolations hand / Whose cursed weapons levels half the land" (lines 123–24); in "Remembrances," Clare gives enclosure Napoleon's features, comparing "Inclosure" to "a Buonaparte" (line 67). But Clare also gains a subtler point with prosopopoeia: the absolute inseparability of natural and human lives affected by enclosure.[31] Clare's use of prosopopoeia is closely related to the eighteenth-century inscription. Like an inscription, many of Clare's poems allow places to speak for themselves. The effect is to amplify what Geoffrey Hartman calls a "sense of hidden life" in nature. But in Clare's poetry—unlike in an inscription—this life is no longer "so hidden, retired, or anonymous that it is perceived only with difficulty."[32] Clare's places—or the poet who speaks for them—rehearse their stories in great detail, having secured a passerby to listen and hopefully to respond. This use of prosopopoeia lends credence to the tales of devastation and, equally important, seems to absolve the poet of responsibility for any political overtones that might emerge in his poems.

In "The Lamentations of Round-Oak Waters" and "The Lament of Swordy Well," prosopopoeia becomes dramatic monologue, as the places Clare names deliver their own stories and protest their own destruction.[33] In these poems, both nature and the poet make their own cases more frankly—although still via the careful use of lyric form. These poems make explicit the alliance between rural laborers and the environment. Swordy Well proves savvy about the political advantage of adopting human speech: "'Though Im no man yet any wrong / Some sort of right may seek / And I am glad if een a song / Gives me the room to speak'" (lines 41–44). Having claimed its right to be heard, Swordy Well goes on to make one of Clare's blunter comments about enclosure, an explanation of how "'vile enclosure'" (line 183), named as culprit near the end of the poem, has reduced the place to the status of "'parish slave'" (line 184).

But my keenest interest in these poems is how they foreground the specific nature of the poet's plight: he suffers not just as one of the rural poor, but as the poet who writes about the place. "The Lamentations of Round-Oak Waters" adds to the list of complainants the poet himself, and not just as rural inhabitant, but as poet. This rhetorical turn occurs formally: two voices are heard as the poet, who sits beside the stream, begins "[r]ecounting many a woe" (line 4), when the stream interjects, adding its own complaints to his. As in "Helpstone" and "Remembrances," a close identification between human and natural worlds produces multiple meanings. Speaker and landscape nearly merge in the poem, and the convergence of their lamentations enhances the claims of each. Most immediately, the stream's complaint is humanized, but the poet also benefits from their mutual identification, for in these poems sympathy is also extended from the landscape to the poet. The poem's title heightens the identification of speaker and stream to the point of confusion, by making it unclear whose lamentations the poem records. Are the complaints those of the speaker for the stream, or those of the stream for itself? The first line of the poem suggests the former, as the speaker recalls his visit to the stream, "Opress'd wi' grief a double share." At the poem's opening, his surroundings sympathize with him: "My naked seat without a shade / Did cold and blealy shine / Which fate was more agreable made / As sympathising mine" (lines 5–8). The comparison seems an unsurprising use of pathetic fallacy, but suddenly nature's sympathy is verbalized when the "genius of the brook" (line 45) begins talking, taking pity on the poet and lamenting his plight.

In a departure from conventional expectations of the Romantic lyric, the speaker rather than the landscape is obscured as the poem develops. Although the effect is certainly a foregrounding of the countryside's devastation, something else has been introduced into the poem: the poet has been identified with natural scenes so closely that when he goes on to elaborate their destruction, it is impossible not to be aware of his own desolation. What he gains by emphasizing nature is an association of himself with highly visible physical alterations in the landscape:

> 'Dire nakedness oer all prevails
> Yon fallows bare and brown
> Is all beset wi' post & rails
> And turned upside down.'
>   (lines 97–100)

The poet takes advantage of the graphic nature of enclosure's effects on the environment by drawing an analogy between the sudden appearance of "post & rails" and detrimental effects on his own life that were less tangible. By making speaker and landscape "equals," Clare intertwines their narratives of decline, and the poet's own story gains a kind of physical drama by aligning it with the environmental changes described: everything is "turned upside down."

Again, Clare's analogies show strains: it is unclear exactly how the poet's sorrows are related to the stream's. At one point the genius loci claims that the poet mourns because the stream has been altered, but the poet does not in fact relate the landscape's changes to his own in his initial lament. Yet Clare's polemical edge is sharpened when a common oppressor of poet and stream is named. Near the beginning of the poem, the speaker explains that it is "money'd men" who "make a sport and prove their might / O' me a fellow worm" (lines 21–24), while the stream ends its complaint with a charge against "cruel foes with plenty blest," who, "ankering after more," determine "[t]o lay the greens & pastures waste / Which profitted before" (lines 189–92). Although the outlines of this critique may be found in "Helpstone," here Clare explicitly attributes a common etiology for the human and natural sufferings that his poems on enclosure describe—financial gain. Both poet and stream name their powerful antagonists, a move that brings the poet's own trials into sharper focus.

In "Helpstone," the poet introduces the figure of "low genius," who "trys / Above the vulgar & the vain to rise" (lines 9–10); in "Lamentations," the nature of the poet's dilemma is clearer. But it is the stream that explains their shared history, and thus Clare continues his self-protective practice of making his own case indirectly, by comparing his case to the stream's plight. The stream begins with the poet's childhood, describing the poet in terms that complement its subsequent lament for the countryside. We learn that the genius loci chose the poet to hear its lamentations, and thus it is the stream who forges their alliance: "For to none else could I lament / And mourn to none but thee" (lines 131–32). The stream chooses the poet because he is "[t]he worlds make gamely sport and scorn" (line 39); like his surroundings, he is at the mercy of powerful forces.

The stream's account of the poet's history reveals that the poet's sorrows, which go virtually unelaborated, must have more to do with his particular position than with a more general condition he shares with his contemporaries, who are excluded from the intimate bond between poet and stream. The speaker is singled out not only because of the extent of his misery, but also for his difference from his neighbors. As a boy he shunned "[t]he sports which they so dearley lov'd" (line 77), fleeing "[f]rom all their Gambols rude / In some lone thicket to consceal / Thyself in Sollitude" (lines 82–84). The genius loci is careful to distinguish between those who ordered the fields to be altered and those who carried out these wishes: "But sweating slaves I do not blame / Those slaves by wealth decreed / No I should hurt their harmless name / To brand 'em wi' the deed" (lines 165–68). But the stream also elevates the poet above these "poor moilers" (174), because he alone can adequately sympathize with the place: "So while the thoughtles passes by / Of sence & feelings void / Thine be the Fancy painting Eye / On by'gone scenes employ'd" (lines 153–56). The stream casts the poet as both "Son of Poverty" (line 38) and man of feeling. His "sence and feelings" (line 154) identify him as a

172   FIVE

poet and indicate that the poem's most important subtext is his vocation. Although as "peasant poet," his vocation and class are insepa-
rable, the poem's focus is not the poet's rural existence but rather his
struggle to support himself with poetry.³⁴ This poem too remained
unpublished until 1935. The fate of the "low genius" of "Helpstone"
becomes of increasing concern in late poems that focus on identity
and its dissolutions.

Critics have often made a general distinction between Clare's early
poetics—his meticulously detailed descriptions of natural scenes—
and the later, visionary lyricism of the asylum years, from 1837 until
his death in 1864. The late poems have been more popular among
anthologists and critics than his richly descriptive poems on nature
because of the former's seemingly visionary quality and philosophical questions about identity. This hierarchy has begun to be obscured
in recent criticism, but only lately have critics questioned one of the
products of this familiar dichotomy, what Nicholas Birns calls "a
premature classification of Clare's career into an orderly progress (or
regress)."³⁵ Clare mines the identificatory relationship between poet
and natural environment for its multiplicity of meaning throughout
his career. Thus, the lyric practice of comparison that I have been
describing constitutes additional evidence against this conventional
model of progress. What I have termed a poetics and politics of loss
encompasses poems lamenting enclosure, poems on the impoverished
lives of the rural poor, and poems that focus on the poet who feels
estranged from his neighbors because of his vocation. This is not to
say that Clare's perspective on the vulnerability and obscurity that he
shares with the landscape does not change in the course of a career
that briefly made him a popular figure, while ultimately restricting
him to a life of continuous and insufficiently remunerative poetic and
agricultural labor. In "Helpstone," the speaker shares with the landscape a seemingly benign obscurity, while later he is not just overlooked, but neglected. This rough trajectory in his works makes sense
in the context of Clare's declining career.

From the moment of his initial success, Clare was continually reminded of the likely outcome of his popularity, not only by the insistence of his own pressing economic circumstances but also by cultural models like Burns and Bloomfield, for as Williams says of the "labourer poets," "the extravagant praise was so regularly followed by neglect."[36] Bloomfield wrote to Clare in July 1820 after having read *Poems Descriptive*, addressing Clare as "Brother Bard, and fellow labourer."[37] When Clare sent Bloomfield a copy of his second volume, *The Village Minstrel*, he received a letter from Bloomfield comparing their careers that must have been both gratifying and ominous: "I write with such labour and difficulty that I cannot venture to praise, or discriminate, like a critic, but must only say that you have given us great pleasure." In 1822, within two years of his emergence as a successful "peasant poet," Clare was given this distressing portrait of his future self by the author of the extremely popular volume, *The Farmer's Boy*, who died in poverty the following year. Bloomfield's identification with Clare proved prescient: "[S]ick and ill as I continually feel, I can join you heartily in your exclamation—'What is Life?'"[38] After Bloomfield's death in 1823, Clare wrote to a mutual acquaintance, Thomas Inskip, reporting his own bad health and then turning to Bloomfield's misfortunes:

> I heard of Bloomfields death & it shockd my feelings poor
> fellow you say right when you exclaim 'who would be a poet'
> ... I am grievd to hear of his family misfortunes were are the
> icy hearted pretenders that came forward once as his friends—
> but it is no use talking this is always the case—neglect is the
> only touchstone by which true genius is proved.[39]

Clare's persistent concern with the deleterious effects of "neglect" emerges here. Although he makes an effort to recuperate "neglect" as the mark of "genius," his own poems work hard to prevent forgetfulness. What Helsinger says about "Helpstone" is true of Clare's poems in general: there is an expectation "that the power to rescue both village and poet from obscurity rests with the reader."[40]

The broad contours of Clare's career render readily comprehensible a marked shift in his poems' tone and concern—from cautious hope to deep discouragement, gratitude to resentment. An impression of stylistic differences between the richly descriptive early poems and the more philosophical later poems has been ratified by a wide-spread familiarity with Clare's career—his biography has in general been better known than the works themselves. Yet many of the late, reflective works share with even the earliest poems a pervasive sense of loss and dissolution. The key difference is Clare's object of atten-tion: in the early poems, loss is generally manifested in the speaker's lamentations of changes in the landscape; in the late poems on iden-tity, he himself becomes the lost figure. An understanding of how Clare's lyric practices establish identifications and alliances between the poet and his environment in his early and middle years provides a way of understanding the later poems. In them the balance has simply shifted from an intense focus on natural objects to a more attentive scrutiny of subjectivity, yet the natural world remains a felt presence even in poems that focus intensely on the poet himself. By the time of Clare's late philosophical poems on personal losses, his autobiographical speaker was so firmly associated with his rural environment that his losses were inevitably tied to its shifting fortunes.

Many of these late pieces strongly resemble his early descriptive poems in their concerns with the vagaries of identity and obscurity, forgetfulness and forgottenness. If Clare's enclosure poems attribute a culpable neglect to the government and landed classes, his poems and prose fragments on identity lament the poet's neglect by "friends." In "An Invite to Eternity" (1847), the speaker's account of how he became lost to the world is a story of being forgotten. The poem is one of many late verses to Mary, presumably Mary Joyce, a child-hood friend and early love. One of Clare's persistent delusions after he became mentally unstable was that he had two wives, Patty (Martha) Turner, whom he had actually married in 1820, and Mary Joyce, who had died in 1838. In this poem, Mary is the imagined companion in a state of profound obscurity: "Say maiden wilt thou go with me / Through this sad non-identity / Where parents live and are forgot / And sisters live and know us not" (lines 13–16). The effect of feeling forgotten by persons close to him is not only a sense of obscurity, but something more debilitating, a "sad non-identity." Being lost to the world induces a loss of self. The poem "I Am"—written the previous year—makes a similar statement of loss, and once again the cause is neglect: "I am—yet what I am, none cares or knows; / My friends forsake me like a memory lost" (lines 1–2). Being forgotten is being "forsaken."

The prose fragment "Self identity" (1841) serves as an admonition not to lose the final vestige of self, the assurance that at least he exists:

> A very good common place counsel is *Self Identity* to bid our own hearts not to forget our own selves and always to keep self in the first place lest all the world who always keeps us behind it should forget us altogether—forget not thyself and the world will not forget thee—forget thyself and the world will willingly forget thee till thou art nothing but a living-dead man dwelling among shadows and falshood.[41]

Here, to forget is to betray; there is nothing benign about it. In the sonnet "I Am," the speaker seems just able to retain self-remembrance: "I feel I am;—I only know I am, / And plod upon the earth, as dull and void: / Earth's prison chilled my body with its dram / Of dullness, and my soaring thoughts destroyed" (lines 1–4). Now he only "feels" he is. There was a time when the poet "was a being created in the race / Of men disdaining bounds of place and time" (lines 7–8), he remembers, "But now I only know I am,—that's all" (line 14).

In these poems and prose pieces, Clare's long-standing concern with enclosure's obliteration of natural entities closely parallels his anxieties about his own disappearance on the literary scene. In one of his last poems, a sonnet "To John Clare" (1860) he reaffirms their alliance by envisioning himself as a child in his native environs: "Well honest John how fare you now at home / The spring is come & birds are building nests / The old cock robin to the stye is come / With olive feathers & its ruddy breast" (lines 1–4). Poet and place are restored, together, to a Northamptonshire Eden, where "[t]he pigs sleep in the sty the bookman comes" (line 9). The poem's tone, reflected in the opening self-address, is casual and tranquil, but the sonnet conveys a more troubling meaning, since poet and place are restored, but only in his own preenclosure and prepublishing era; the books that "John Clare" reads are children's literature. Moreover, there is a distinction reflected in the poem's mode of address between the seemingly autobiographical speaker and "John Clare," so that poet and place remain not just irrecoverable but actually alien enough to be recalled as familiar but distant "ruins of the past."

As the dates of these works indicate, Clare's concern with "self-identity" escalates after his institutionalization, first at High Beech Asylum, near Epping Forest, Essex, in 1837. In July 1841, he decided to leave the asylum and walk home to Northborough, but his psychological state made his tenure there brief, and by late December he had been returned to the Northamptonshire General Lunatic Asylum, where he remained until his death in 1864. Although I have been arguing that Clare's writings on identity in the 1840s cannot be severed from his poems on enclosure, I would add a caveat: just as Clare's muted literary critiques of enclosure must be read in the context of his difficult career, these musings on identity must be considered with his institutionalization in mind. Credence should be given to one undeniable difference from the early poems—the debility of mental illness. These poems have always startled critics with their lucid investigations of the mechanisms of identity; their insights have even encouraged skepticism about whether in fact Clare was mentally ill. I am uncomfortable with this suggestion, which risks diminishing another kind of material suffering that Clare endured, a prolonged physiological deterioration, the causes of which remain obscure despite a critical temptation to cast Clare in the role of mad poet.[42]

These late writings on identity in the 1840s must be contextualized within his psychological decline, but they cannot be relegated entirely to the obsessions of a mind troubled by its own dissolution, because they pursue themes of identity's material manifestations and losses that were present even in his earliest poems. The late visionary works belong to a period in which Clare's incapacitation sometimes seems to threaten becoming an external force like the seasons or enclosure in its ability to overwhelm him, at least momentarily. It is all the more remarkable, then, that within this new existence, defined by alternating periods of lucidity and delusion, Clare persists in a long-standing investigation of the vicissitudes of identity and the consequences of such deleterious changes, concerns that he increasingly made his explicit subject rather than the indirect object of inquiry, as was necessary to a poet struggling to support himself by publishing. The late lyrics continue, in the wake of a faltering sense of self, the close association of poet and place which together had comprised "the Northamptonshire peasant."

Clare's career reiterates, in different terms, lessons that Charlotte Smith learned about the lyric's possibilities for social engagement and its liabilities for the poet. Like Smith, Clare finds in the lyric the means of popular success, though his was far more short-lived. Moreover, he discovers the mode's rhetorical capacity for responding both to enclosure and to the plight of the "labourer poets" whose careers were so closely tied to its scenes. Despite his poet's frequently under- stated presence, Clare's lyric poems present to reading audiences an appealing poetic persona who laments losses personally felt but so- cially imposed. Readers responded to the highly personal appeal of Smith's and Clare's lyric speakers, yet this kind of popularity fore- grounded the poet in the poems, with deleterious consequences for both. Their prominence in the works had the unwelcome effect of drawing attention to the poets themselves, thus submitting them to critical commentary along gender and class lines. Smith was censured as a woman writer when her works took on political themes too explicitly, and Clare was censured as a "labourer poet" whose topics and tenor should be monitored. Thus the success of their lyric strat- egies may be gauged not only by their popularity but also by the unwelcome interventions of patrons, publishers, and critics who wanted a say in defining their public personae.

The circumstances in which Clare pursued his chance for a po- etic career diverged widely from Smith's. Both poets, however, were in precarious positions in the literary marketplace, because as a woman and a "laborer poet," respectively, they had limited access to the cul- tural role of poet, and because they wrote with an urgent need for their published volumes to generate a substantial portion of their families' income. Their careers unfolded in the context of a profound change in Europe, "from an oral-scribal to a print society."[43] Each had patrons even as each actively participated in a new kind of liter- ary production based on print technology and the economy of the marketplace. Both poets also ventured into the often difficult waters of subscription, a means of publication by which a list of subscribers—some of whom would likely be patrons—would help a writer or a publisher to defray the costs of publication while also reassuring the publisher that a certain number of copies would be sold. Clare possessed considerably less power than Smith in the exchanges involved in each of these modes of literary production. She addressed patrons as a member of the landed gentry who had suffered misfortune not of her own making, while Clare's patrons required displays of gratitude proper for a "peasant poet."[44] Smith's genteel origins also gave her a distinct, albeit limited advantage (as a woman), in negotiating her works' publication, while Clare remained at a profound disadvantage throughout his career in his dealings with patrons, publishers, critics, and readers. His dependence upon reading audiences is reflected in the very terms of his fleeting success, for Clare appeared on the literary scene when the fashion for "uneducated poets" was already waning, and the viability of his career depended upon the continued demand for the literary productions of a "peasant poet."

The autobiographical aspect of Clare's poems was fostered by Taylor's casting of Clare as "the Northamptonshire peasant" and by his lyricism's focus on the poet's subjectivity. *Poems Descriptive* introduced the poems as the sincere expressions of Clare's love of his native surroundings, and critics often responded to the life that seemed to be visible through the poems, as if the lyric mode provided a looking glass into his interesting existence.[45] Taylor fostered this perception by effectively subordinating the works to the life in the introduction's opening gesture: "The following Poems will probably attract some notice by their intrinsic merit; but they are also entitled to attention from the circumstances under which they were written." Taylor emphasizes a feature conventionally associated with Romantic lyricism: a sense of authentic expression. The poems are "the genuine productions of a young Peasant, a day-labourer in husbandry, who has had no advantages of education beyond others of his class." Taylor thematizes the lyric mode's autobiographical content in a portrait of Clare composing poems in the fields: "He could not trust his memory, and therefore he wrote them down with a pencil on the spot, his hat serving him for a table; and if it happened that he had no opportunity soon after of transcribing these imperfect memorials, he could seldom decypher them, or recover his first thoughts."[46] Taylor thus envisions for readers the poems that follow in the poet's own hands.

Taylor provides cues for responding to Clare that were taken by critics from a variety of critical and political perspectives. This strategy surely fostered the poet's initial success, but its deleterious consequences became apparent in the response to Clare's appearance on the critical scene in *Poems Descriptive*. Like Smith, Clare received sympathetic responses from readers in the form of poems and letters that were either sent to him or published in newspapers. Eliza Emmerson's patronage was motivated by her own sympathetic reading of Clare's poems, which she articulated in verse in a poem published in the *Morning Post* in the same month in which *Poems Descriptive* appeared: "Lines written by a Lady, and Presented with a volume of 'Clare's Poems' to a Noble Friend." In publicly representing her experience of Clare's poetry and her pity for his plight, Emmerson adopted the familiar gestures of sensibility. In modeling the appropriate response to the pathos of Clare's volume, Emmerson encouraged a similar sympathy in other readers, including Radstock, the "Noble Friend" to whom her poem was addressed. She successfully implored him, "Oh! take this little volume to thy care— / And be the friend of Genius—and of 'Clare!'"[47]

Clare, like Smith, found not only readers but also critics who were willing to champion him by instructing their readers in the proper response to poems and the life they seemed to chronicle. In its review of *Poems Descriptive,* the *Eclectic Review* provides almost a conduct manual, derived from the conventions of sensibility, for reading Clare's poems. The critic predicts that the poems will generate "a genuine and powerful interest" that

cannot fail to be excited by the perusal of these exquisitely vivid descriptions of rural scenery, in every lover of nature, who will feel a sort of affinity to the Author; and the recollection that the sensibility, the keenness of observation, and the imaginative enthusiasm which they display, have discovered themselves in an individual of the very humblest station in society, in a day-labourer, whose independence of spirit alone has sustained him above actual pauperism, will be attended by sensations similar to those with which he would recognise some member of his own family in a state of degradation.[48]

The critic—the poet Josiah Conder—describes the poet in terms familiar from Smith's reviews. He suggests that because Clare's own "sensibility" is expressed in the poems, his readers will respond since they will "discover themselves" in him. Just as William Cowper felt that he heard his own voice echoed back to him in reading Smith's poems, Clare's readers will find in him their own best qualities.[49] As a result of this recognition, the reader "will feel a sort of affinity to the author" that will be experienced as kinship: he will experience "sensations similar" to those of encountering "some member of his own family." Yet there will be pathos in this readerly experience, because of the loved one's appearance "in a state of degradation."

John Scott's positive, unsigned review of *Poems Descriptive* in Taylor's *London Magazine* likewise reads the poet in the poems and approves of the volume because he approves of Clare. Just as the critic for the *Eclectic Review* recommends, Scott finds the poet in the poems, for "[t]he sentiment is every where true, and often deep." Scott feels confident in sketching his own portrait of the poet:

An intense feeling for the scenery of the country, a heart susceptible to the quietest and least glaring beauties of nature, a fine discrimination and close observation of the distinguishing features of particular rural seasons and situations, and, a melancholy sense of the poet's own heavy,—and as he has had too much reason to consider it,—hopeless lot;—such are the qualities of character most prominent in these poems, and which shed over them a sweet and touching charm, in spite of some inaccuracies and incoherencies in their language and arrangement.

Because the poet's "qualities" infuse his poems, reading the poems provides unmediated access to his personality.

This kind of poet-reader relationship dictates rules for readerly response, which Scott models himself and then prescribes. He concludes his review by pointedly instructing his readers that "[i]f any person can read the compositions it contains, and afterwards reflect without emotion on the fate of the author, should he still be doomed to pursue the weary way in which his life hath hitherto proceeded, either such person is very differently constituted from what we would wish to be, or our estimate of the poetical merit of the book is more grossly wrong than we are willing to believe it will be found." Scott joins Clare's cause by making the poet's case to his readers. Yet his sympathetic response to Clare bears traces of a monitory stance that other critics would assume with less-benign intentions. Scott praises the poet's "faith" in "Providence" despite "the calamity of his fortune." Because he writes for Taylor's periodical, Scott might be expected to agree with Taylor's reading of Clare. Yet the *Antijacobin* sounds a similar note of approval from a very different political perspective. The critic compliments Clare on his response to his impoverishment in terms that recall Scott's, but that issue from an explicit desire to keep the "peasant poet" in his "station." The poet is praised because "no envious spirit, no carping discontent, is to be traced in Clare's Poems." The critic discovers the poet in the verse and concludes approvingly that "[r]esignation to his lot appears to be a prominent feature in his character, combined with that love of his native village, which frequently bears such potent sway in the mind of the unlettered rustic."[50]

Thus Clare's lyrics won sympathy for the poet while inviting admonitory comments on which poems were published and how Clare should behave. Several poems in *Poems Descriptive* that drew Radstock's ire for their frank treatment of female sexuality—including "Dolly's Mistake" and "My Mary"—were also criticized by the *Eclectic Review* and the *New Monthly Magazine*. These critical responses certainly encouraged Taylor to give in to Radstock's demands that these poems be excised from *Poems Descriptive;* the two poems disappeared in the third edition (whereas "Helpstone" lost its offending lines only in the fourth and final edition). The critic for the *Eclectic Review* also feels entitled to advise Clare's "friends" against providing support that would take him out of the fields and allow him to devote his full attention to poetry: "Let him still be suffered to live, and to labour too, in the presence of Nature, but to live free, and to labour for an object that shall sustain and compensate his exertions."

Clare's career replayed the lessons William and Dorothy Wordsworth acquired in the course of William's publishing career and
Dorothy's ambivalent history of almost entirely unpublished writing:
that the lyric's focus on an autobiographical speaker was the source
of both its eloquence and its risks to the poet. By foregrounding the
poet, the mode submitted that figure to wide-ranging commentary
on the life as well as the poems. Dorothy may have been prescient in
deciding never to assume for herself that position, from which William increasingly withdrew by means of a developing rhetoric of disinterestedness. Clare and Smith, however, were in no position to affect a detachment that, in William's hands, would become a consolatory myth of the lyric poet aloof from the reading "Public," that he
ostensibly dismissed in 1815.

Even though Clare lost far more in his exchanges with reading
audiences than William Wordsworth did, and despite Clare's own
deep ambivalence about popular success, his efforts to salvage his
career in his last two collections betray an unexpected faith that he
might still win a responsive "Public." *The Shepherd's Calendar* and
The Rural Muse mark a return, after Taylor's elaborate biographical
and critical introductions to *Poems Descriptive* and *The Village Minstrel,* to a direct solicitation of readers, which he had also attempted
at the very beginning of his career.[51] In the preface to *The Shepherd's
Calendar,* he redefines his relationship to his readers by distancing
the poems from the "peasant poet": "I leave the following Poems to
speak for themselves." He expresses a desire to let the poems stand
or fall on their own: "I feel that confidence in my readers' former
kindness, to rest satisfied, that if the work is worthy the reward it is
seeking, it will meet it; if not, it must share the fate of other broken
ambitions, and fade away."

Clare's acts of self-presentation in his last two prefaces continue
to reflect a confidence in lyric poetry's rhetorical capacity for engaging readers, which he held in common with his publishers, patrons,
and critics. Clare acted on an understanding that he shared with
Radstock and Emmerson: that a sympathetic poet might reach readers, both on issues of national concern, such as enclosure, and on his
own behalf. Clare's purpose in self-portraiture differed sharply from
his patrons' efforts to mute in his public figure the anger that sur-

faced in some of his poems. Likewise, Clare's intentions diverged from Taylor's desire to present the poet cautiously to middle- and upper-class readers. These agents attempted to define Clare's poet to different ends, but they were alike in understanding just how much was at stake in a lyric poet's prominence on the literary scene.

Notes

Preface

1. Walter Benjamin, "Theses on the Philosophy of History" (1940), in *Illuminations*, ed. Hannah Arendt, trans. Harry Zohn (New York: Schocken, 1968), 254.

2. I use the term "mode" rather than "genre" because, as Tilottama Rajan explains, criticism has "centered Romantic discourse in the mode (though not the genre) of lyric, with significant consequences for our view of the period." Thus, lyricism defines poems such as *The Prelude* too long to be considered lyrics according to a familiar criterion of brevity. Lyricism also emerges in the period's drama and even its prose, not only in the form of the actual poems that Ann Radcliffe and Charlotte Smith put into the mouths of their protagonists, but also as bursts of lyrical prose in novels. See Rajan, "Romanticism and the Death of Lyric Consciousness," in *Lyric Poetry: Beyond New Criticism*, ed. Chaviva Hošek and Patricia Parker (Ithaca: Cornell University Press, 1985), 195.

3. In his 1988 essay, "The I Altered," Stuart Curran influentially outlined the contours of a highly productive field for feminist investigation by enumerating some of the many publishing women poets who have since been incorporated into the Romantic canon. See *Romanticism and Feminism*, ed. Anne K. Mellor (Bloomington: Indiana University Press, 1988), 185–207.

4. Anne Janowitz trains new light on the lyric poems of the period's communitarian political movements. See "Class and Literature: The Case of Romantic Chartism," in *Rethinking Class: Literary Studies and Class Formations*,

ed. Wai Chee Dimock and Michael T. Gilmore (New York: Columbia University Press, 1994), 239–66.

5. Jerome J. McGann, *The Romantic Ideology* (Chicago: University of Chicago Press, 1983), 82. McGann's manifesto deems Wordsworth "exemplary" of the Romantic ideology, and the early major works of Romantic new historicism follow his lead, including Marjorie Levinson's *Wordsworth's Great Period Poems* (Cambridge: Cambridge University Press, 1986); David Simpson's *Wordsworth's Historical Imagination* (New York: Methuen, 1987); and Alan Liu's *Wordsworth: The Sense of History* (Stanford, Calif.: Stanford University Press, 1989). Clifford Siskin makes a point relevant to my argument: "Discussions of Wordsworth's originality, achievement, and 'anti-climax'—his lyrical flowering—for example, have effectively functioned as arguments for the origin (*Lyrical Ballads*), character (greater Romantic lyric), and duration (short) of Romanticism." See *The Historicity of Romantic Discourse* (New York: Oxford University Press, 1988), 19.

6. Perhaps the most memorable statement of this view is McGann's emphatic representation of canonical Romantic poetry as characterized by the hope "that poetry by its nature can transcend the conflicts and transiences of this time and that place" (*Romantic Ideology*, 69). This quotable claim is more often recalled, however, than McGann's subtle caveat that an accompanying drive in Romantic poetry reveals the impossibility of this ideal. I quarrel with his early statement of these concerns in *The Romantic Ideology* to the extent that his influential project insists that "high" Romantic poetry is defined by a single desire and its failures. McGann complicates his own account of the ideological implications of a Wordsworthian poetics of displacement in *The Beauty of Inflections* (Oxford: Clarendon Press, 1988).

Chapter 1. The History of an Aura

1. Thomas Babington Macaulay, for instance, characterizes Milton in similar terms in 1825: "It is the part of the lyric poet to abandon himself, without reserve, to his own emotions." See "Milton," which first appeared in the August 1825 issue of the *Edinburgh Review*. Rpt. *Critical and Historical Essays* (Boston: Houghton Mifflin, 1900), 1:95. Abrams discusses the importance of Immanuel Kant's *Critique of Judgment* in defining poetry by its disinterestedness in *The Mirror and the Lamp* (London: Oxford University Press, 1953).

2. McGann, *Romantic Ideology*, 1.

3. Musing on how to define the form, Northrop Frye at first proposes "that a lyric is anything you can reasonably get uncut into an anthology," but eventually focuses on its relationship to music, since "the very word lyric implies a musical instrument." See "Approaching the Lyric," in *Lyric Poetry*, ed. Hošek and Parker, 31, 34. In his *Glossary of Literary Terms*, Abrams categorizes the lyric as

"any fairly short poem, consisting of the utterance by a single speaker, who expresses a state of mind or a process of perception, thought, and feeling." See *A Glossary of Literary Terms*, 6th ed. (Forth Worth, Tex.: Harcourt Brace, 1993), 108.

4. W. R. Johnson, *The Idea of Lyric: Lyric Modes in Ancient and Modern Poetry* (Berkeley: University of California Press, 1982), 6, 21.

5. Critics in literary fields other than Romanticism have assumed the lyric's sociohistorical aspects. Illuminating treatments include Richard Halpern, "The Lyric in the Field of Information: Autopoesis and History in Donne's *Songs and Sonnets*," in *Critical Essays on John Donne*, ed. Arthur F. Marotti (New York: G. K. Hall, 1994), 49-76; Howard D. Weinbrot, "William Collins and the Mid-Century Ode: Poetry, Patriotism, and the Influence of Context," in *Context, Influence, and Mid-Eighteenth-Century Poetry*, by Howard D. Weinbrot and Martin Price (Los Angeles: William Andrews Clark Memorial Library, University of California, 1990), 1-39. See also Diana E. Henderson's *Passion Made Public: Elizabethan Lyric, Gender and Performance* (Urbana: University of Illinois Press, 1995) and Christopher Martin's *Policy in Love: Lyric and Public in Ovid, Petrarch and Shakespeare* (Pittsburgh, Pa.: Duquesne University Press, 1994).

6. Siskin, who helps define the new historical equation of Romantic lyricism with apostasy in *The Historicity of Romantic Discourse*, productively reopens this issue in a subsequent essay. He echoes Jonathan Culler's 1985 claim that New Criticism's decontextual approach, which is indebted to Frye's emphasis on "voice," "remains the only theory of the lyric to gain wide currency and influence." See Siskin, "The Lyric Mix: Romanticism, Genre, and the Fate of Literature," *Wordsworth Circle* 25 (1994): 7–10; and Culler, "Changes in the Study of the Lyric," in *Lyric Poetry*, ed. Hošek and Parker, 38.

7. M. H. Abrams, *Natural Supernaturalism* (New York: Norton, 1971), 334–35. Abrams returns to the parallels between Wordsworth's, Auden's, and his own political disappointments in "Revolutionary Romanticism, 1790–1990," in *Wordsworth in Context*, ed. Pauline Fletcher and John Murphy (Lewisburg, Pa.: Bucknell University Press, 1992), 19–34.

8. E. P. Thompson, "Disenchantment or Default? A Lay Sermon," in *Power and Consciousness*, ed. Conor Cruise O'Brien and William Dean Vanech (London: University of London Press, 1969), 178.

9. Ibid., 152.

10. John Stuart Mill, *Autobiography* (London: Oxford University Press, 1963), 112–26.

11. Sharon Cameron, *Lyric Time: Dickinson and the Limits of Genre* (Baltimore: Johns Hopkins University Press, 1979).

12. Theodor W. Adorno, "On Lyric Poetry and Society" (1957), in *Notes to Literature*, edited by Rolf Tiedemann, translated by Shierry Weber Nicholsen (New York: Columbia University Press, 1991), 1:39-40, 45-46. Untranslated quotations

are from "Rede über Lyrik und Gesellschaft," in *Gesammelte Schriften* (Frankfurt-am-Main: Suhrkamp, 1974), 2:52.

13. Benjamin, "The Work of Art in the Age of Mechanical Reproduction" (1936), in *Illuminations*, 217–51.

14. Because I am concerned with the construction of a canonical lyricism which is implicitly (and sometimes explicitly) coded masculine, I frequently refer to the poet as "he" when discussing the definitions I am challenging.

15. Siskin argues that "[t]he denial of essential generic traits is the key to the viability of any contemporary genre theory." See *Historicity of Romantic Discourse*, 22.

16. Mill, "What Is Poetry?" 4–5.

17. Ibid., 8–13.

18. In his account of the lyric, Jonathan Culler explains that "[p]oetry lies at the center of the literary experience because it is the form that most clearly asserts the specificity of literature, its difference from ordinary discourse by an empirical individual about the world." Drawing on Roman Jakobson, Culler describes how the lyric transforms material existence, an account that reiterates, in poststructuralist terms, Mill's example of the lion: "The poem is a structure of signifiers which absorbs and reconstitutes the signified." See *Structuralist Poetics* (Ithaca: Cornell University Press, 1975), 162-63.

19. Matthew Arnold, "Preface to *The Poems of Wordsworth*" (1879), in *The Complete Prose Works of Matthew Arnold*, ed. R. H. Super (Ann Arbor: University of Michigan Press, 1973), 9:36–55.

20. T. S. Eliot, "The Three Voices of Poetry," in *On Poetry and Poets* (New York: Farrar, Straus and Cudahy, 1957), 96. The "third voice" is "the voice of the poet when he attempts to create a dramatic character speaking in verse." The essay was originally given as an Annual Lecture of the National Book League in 1953, and published for the National Book League by Cambridge University Press. Hence, Eliot's essay was in circulation before Frye's 1957 *Anatomy of Criticism*.

21. Frye, *Anatomy of Criticism* (Princeton: Princeton University Press, 1957), 249, 271.

22. Frye, "Approaching the Lyric," 35.

23. Although I argue that Abrams naturalizes Mill's category of disinterestedness by associating it with specific features, it is important to acknowledge Abrams's circumspection about Mill's rhetoric. He observes that "whatever Mill's empirical pretensions, his initial assumption about the essential nature of poetry remains continuously though silently effective in selecting, interpreting, and ordering the facts to be explained." (The principle concerned is poetry's expression of feeling.) *Mirror and Lamp*, 23.

24. Abrams, "Structure and Style in the Greater Romantic Lyric" (1965), *Romanticism and Consciousness*, ed. Harold Bloom (New York: W. W. Norton, 1970), 202.

25. Abrams, *Mirror and Lamp*, 84.

26. The term is Liu's, in *Wordsworth*, 223.

27. Abrams, "Structure and Style," 201.

28. Ibid., 224.

29. Siskin, "Lyric Mix," 8, 9.

30. In "The Internalization of Quest-Romance" (1969), in Bloom, ed., *Romanticism and Consciousness*, Bloom agrees that "Wordsworth's Copernican revolution in poetry is marked by the evanescence of any subject but subjectivity, the loss of what a poem is 'about.'" See *Romanticism and Consciousness*, 8. The volume also contains Abrams's "Structure and Style" and "English Romanticism: The Spirit of the Age."

31. Eliot, "Three Voices," 110.

32. Abrams, "Structure and Style," 202.

33. Abrams, "English Romanticism: The Spirit of the Age" (1963), in Bloom, ed. *Romanticism and Consciousness*, 101, 107, 118.

34. Rajan observes that "New Historicism simply accepts the image of Wordsworth it inherits, situating lyric as a socially symbolic act of avoidance." See "The Erasure of Narrative in Post-Structuralist Representations of Wordsworth," in *Romantic Revolutions*, ed. Kenneth R. Johnston, Gilbert Chaitin, Karen Hanson, and Herbert Marks (Bloomington: Indiana University Press, 1990), 366.

35. Levinson, *Wordsworth's Great Period Poems*, 80.

36. Ibid., 82.

37. McGann, *Romantic Ideology*, 88.

38. Ibid., 89.

39. Rajan, "Erasure of Narrative," 366.

40. As I discuss in chapter 4, Homans subsequently revises her assessment of Dorothy Wordsworth's prose, which she reconceives as employing a rhetoric of the literal, by which the writer speaks from the object's position. See *Women Writers and Poetic Identity: Dorothy Wordsworth, Emily Brontë, and Emily Dickinson* (Princeton: Princeton University Press, 1980), 4.

41. Meena Alexander, *Women in Romanticism: Mary Wollstonecraft, Dorothy Wordsworth and Mary Shelley* (Houndmills, U.K.: Macmillan Education, 1989).

42. Homans, *Women Writers*, 8.

43. Mellor, *Romanticism and Gender* (New York: Routledge, 1993).

44. Susan J. Wolfson, "Individual in Community: Dorothy Wordsworth in Conversation with William," in Mellor, ed., *Romanticism and Feminism*, 146.

45. Mill, "What is Poetry?" 6.

46. Liu, *Wordsworth*, 51.

47. Levinson, *Wordsworth's Great Period Poems*, 18.

48. Helen Vendler challenges new historical and historical materialist readings of Romantic lyricism by interrogating a standard of mimesis. See *"Tintern*

Abbey: Two Assaults," in *Wordsworth in Context*, ed. Fletcher and Murphy, 173–90.

49. Claudia Brodsky Lacour, "Contextual Criticism, or 'History' v. 'Literature,'" *Narrative* 1 (1993): 97.

50. Peter J. Manning, "Placing Poor Susan: Wordsworth and the New Historicism," in *Reading Romantics: Texts and Contexts* (New York: Oxford University Press, 1990), 300.

51. Simpson, *Wordsworth's Historical Imagination*, 5. Only recently have critics begun to recognize that the period's lyricism might offer the possibility for a different sense of self: in her study of Chartist poetry, Janowitz makes the case for "the double intention within the Romantic poetic," which she identifies as "its individualism and its communitarian ends." See "Class and Literature," 257. Andrea K. Henderson demonstrates that numerous, and often conflicting, conceptual models of subjectivity were operative in the period; see *Romantic Identities: Varieties of Subjectivity, 1774–1830* (Cambridge: Cambridge University Press, 1996). For a cogent argument that "the Romantic self cannot be regarded as an asocial entity," an argument that pays careful attention to the lyric's auditors, see Michael Macovski, *Dialogue and Literature: Apostrophe, Auditors, and the Collapse of Romantic Discourse* (New York: Oxford University Press, 1994), 12.

52. Levinson, *Wordsworth's Great Period Poems*, 58. Liu, *Wordsworth*, 24, 56.

53. Benjamin, "On Some Motifs in Baudelaire," in *Illuminations*, 159–60.

54. Ibid., 157.

55. Benjamin, "A Berlin Chronicle," in *Reflections*, ed. Peter Demetz, trans. Edmund Jephcott (New York: Schocken, 1978), 14.

56. Liu, *Wordsworth*, 50–51.

57. Frances Ferguson too reminds us of the potential "conflict between the well-made story and moral action." Her reassessment of "Romantic memory" investigates the relationship between the individual and "the claims of the collective." See "Romantic Memory," *Studies in Romanticism* 35 (1996): 518, 510.

58. Benjamin, "Theses," 257, 255, 263.

59. Simpson's critique of Raymond Williams's emphasis on voice (both the historian's and the individual voices of an era) is helpful here; his cautions might also be directed at Benjamin's historical materialism and at the possibilities for the lyric's historical engagement for which I have been arguing. Simpson examines Williams's "history of voices" and finds wanting a theoretical framework that would afford a better view of what Williams calls "the true generalities of class formation." Simpson argues for a theoretical and sufficiently panoramic historical perspective to supplement "the range of specificities indicated by family, community, occupation, gender, education, and sheer idiosyncrasy." See "Raymond Williams: Feeling for Structures, Voicing 'History'," *Social Text* 10 (1992): 24–25.

60. Samuel Taylor Coleridge, *The Collected Works of Samuel Taylor Coleridge*, vol. 14, pt. 1, ed. Carl Woodring (Princeton: Princeton University Press, 1990), 446. William Hazlitt, *The Complete Works of William Hazlitt*, ed. P. P. Howe (London: J. M. Dent, 1930), 5:48.

61. Wordsworth, *Prose*, 1:138.

62. Coleridge, *Collected Works*, vol. 7, pt. 2, ed. James Engell and W. Jackson Bate (Princeton: Princeton University Press, 1983), 23.

63. Abrams borrows the term "coalescence" from Coleridge in *Biographia Literaria*. See "Structure and Style," 219.

64. David Marshall, *The Surprising Effects of Sympathy* (Chicago: University of Chicago Press, 1988), 179, 146, 103.

65. Frye, "Towards Defining an Age of Sensibility" (1963), in *Poets of Sensibility and the Sublime*, ed. Harold Bloom (New York: Chelsea House, 1986), 15-16. McGann makes a cogent case that in order to understand many of the period's women writers, we must fathom a tradition of sensibility, the key to which was for a long time lost due to the predominance of canonical models of Romanticism. See *The Poetics of Sensibility: A Revolution in Literary Style* (Oxford: Clarendon Press, 1996).

66. Marilyn Butler, *Romantics, Rebels and Reactionaries* (Oxford: Oxford University Press, 1981), 31.

67. Janet Todd, *Sensibility: An Introduction* (London: Methuen, 1986), 2.

68. Todd explains that "[i]n all forms of sentimental literature, there is an assumption that life and literature are directly linked, not through any notion of a mimetic depiction of reality but through the belief that the literary experience can intimately affect the living one." See ibid., 4.

69. Jon P. Klancher, *The Making of English Reading Audiences, 1790-1832* (Madison: University of Wisconsin Press, 1987).

70. Johnson, *Idea of Lyric*, 6.

71. W. B. Yeats, *Autobiographies* (London: Macmillan, 1961), 97.

72. A recent defense of the reader's role in lyric poetry urges this kind of attention, but stops short of granting the reader an active role. Timothy Bahti, following Vendler, argues that "the role of the silent reader that lyric aims for is for him or her to be the recipient, the goal and end, of the lyric." See *Ends of the Lyric* (Baltimore: Johns Hopkins University Press, 1996), 7.

73. Elizabeth A. Fay has launched a persuasive challenge to this conventional antithesis in her treatment of Dorothy and William Wordsworth's literary collaboration. I discuss in chapter 4 her argument regarding Dorothy Wordsworth. *Becoming Wordsworthian: A Performative Aesthetics* (Amherst: University of Massachusetts Press, 1995).

74. Joanna Baillie, *A Series of Plays, 1798* (Oxford: Woodstock, 1990), 23.

75. Michael McKeon, "Writer as Hero: Novelistic Prefigurations and the

Emergence of Literary Biography," in *Contesting the Subject: Essays in the Post-modern Theory and Practice of Biography and Biographical Criticism*, ed. William H. Epstein (West Lafayette, Ind.: Purdue University Press, 1991), 17.

76. Samuel Johnson, *Rambler*, no. 60 (13 October 1750), in *The Works of Samuel Johnson*, ed. W. J. Bate and Albrecht B. Strauss (New Haven: Yale University Press, 1969), 3: 321, 319.

77. Johnson, *Idler*, no. 102 (29 March 1760), in *The Works*, 2:312.

78. Unsigned review of *Elegiac Sonnets*, 5th ed., *European Magazine* 16 (1789): 264.

79. Paul Magnuson, "The Politics of 'Frost at Midnight,'" *Wordsworth Circle* 22 (1991): 3.

80. Jerome Christensen makes the case for a shift in critical vocabulary from "vocation" to "career" in "Byron's Career: The Speculative Stage," *ELH* 52 (1985): 59–84. As Christensen acknowledges, Richard Helgerson's treatment of the career of the Renaissance poet was instrumental to a critique of poetic vocation in Romantic studies. See Helgerson's *Self-Crowned Laureates: Spenser, Jonson, Milton and the Literary System* (Berkeley: University of California Press, 1983).

81. Boehm makes a cogent case that ignoring the careful decisions that poets and publishers made about a volume's appearance has compromised a sense of how actively reading audiences were sought: "There is a tendency to overlook this impulse in modern critical views, and to emphasize instead the Romantic author's repudiation of the marketplace." See "The 1798 *Lyrical Ballads* and the Poetics of Late Eighteenth-Century Book Production," *ELH* 63 (1996): 4, 57, 478.

Chapter 2. "Dost thou not know my voice?"

1. Anna Letitia Barbauld, introduction to *The Old Manor House*, by Charlotte Smith, in *The British Novelists* (London: F. C. and J. Rivington, 1810), 36:iii.

2. Unsigned "Sonnet to Mrs. Smith," *European Magazine* 10 (1786): 125.

3. Richard Phillips, *British Public Characters of 1800–1801* (London: Richard Phillips, 1801), 3:65.

4. Frye, *Anatomy of Criticism*, 271.

5. Abrams, "Structure and Style," 201–29.

6. Bishop C. Hunt Jr. describes a copy of the fifth edition (1789) owned by Wordsworth at Cambridge, which contains Wordsworth's marginalia. Hunt provides an extensive account of Smith's influence on Wordsworth in "Wordsworth and Charlotte Smith," *Wordsworth Circle* 1 (1970): 85–103.

7. William Wordsworth, *The Poetical Works of William Wordsworth*, ed. William Knight (London: Macmillan, 1896), 7:351. Kari Lokke explains that Wordsworth's citation of this poem is particularly significant, because the poem represents Smith's self-conscious statement of her poetic enterprise. See "Char-

lotte Smith and Literary History: 'Dark Forgetfulness' and the 'Intercession of Saint Monica,'" *Women's Studies* 27 (1998): 259-80.

8. Stuart Curran, *Poetic Form and British Romanticism* (New York: Oxford University Press, 1986), 32.

9. Coleridge, "Introduction to the Sonnets" (1796), in *The Complete Poetical and Dramatic Works of Samuel Taylor Coleridge*, ed. James Dykes Campbell (London: Macmillan, 1938), 543.

10. In her preface to *The Banished Man* (1794), Smith reports, "In the strictures on a late publication of mine, some Review (I do not now recollect which) objected to the too frequent allusion I made in it to my own circumstances." See *The Banished Man* (London: T. Cadell, Jr. and W. Davies, 1794), 1:viii. Other defenses against charges of egotism are found in the prefaces to *Marchmont* (1796) and to volume 2 of *Elegiac Sonnets* (1797).

11. William Jones to J. Shore, Esq. (16 August 1787), in *Memoirs of the Life, Writings and Correspondence of Sir William Jones*, by John Shore, Lord Teignmouth (London: John Hatchard, 1804), 2:139.

12. Unsigned notice of *Elegiac Sonnets, Gentleman's Magazine* 56 (1786): 334.

13. From the first edition, *Elegiac Sonnets* contains poems other than sonnets, but the sonnets continually outnumber them. These poems, like the sonnets, multiplied with expanding editions. "Metastasio" is Pietro Trapassi (1698–1782).

14. The lines Smith puts in her own mouth are Egeon's. Smith slightly misquotes him: "Oh! Time has Changed me since you saw me last, / And heavy Hours with Time's deforming Hand, / Have written strange Defeatures in my Face." Shakespeare's lines are quoted correctly in my epigraph.

15. Unsigned review of *The Emigrants, British Critic* 1 (1793): 403.

16. One of a group of Smith's letters housed by the Princeton University Library contains instructions for an engraver about altering the frontispiece portrait and one of the collection's engravings. I quote the letter at length in "Charlotte Smith's Letters and the Practice of Self-Presentation," *Princeton University Library Chronicle* 53 (1991): 50–77.

17. Michael Fried, *Absorption and Theatricality: Painting and Beholder in the Age of Diderot* (Chicago: University of Chicago Press, 1980), 108.

18. Unsigned notice of *Elegiac Sonnets, Gentleman's Magazine* 56 (1786): 333.

19. Marshall, *Surprising Effects of Sympathy*, 5, 107.

20. Coleridge, "Introductions to the Sonnets," 543.

21. William Cowper to Charlotte Smith (26 October 1793), in *The Correspondence of William Cowper*, ed. Thomas Wright (London: Hodder and Stoughton, 1904), 4:462.

22. Marshall, *Surprising Effects of Sympathy*, 128.

23. Cowper to William Hayley (29 January 1793), in *Correspondence of William Cowper*, 4:363.

24. Vendler and Bahti consider the role of the lyric's reader carefully, but

each views that role as more passive and subordinate than I do. Vendler describes a lyric poem as *"a role offered to a reader."* Her notion of the reader's identification with the poetic speaker is absolute: "[T]he reader is to be the voice speaking the poem" (*"Tintern Abbey:* Two Assaults," 184). Vendler's decisive account of the reader's capacity for sympathetic identification with the lyric speaker explains something important about that relationship: its potential for intensity. I view the relationship as more of a precarious exchange, however, and I would instead emphasize the potential for marked ambivalence by both parties. For Bahti's account of this relationship, see chapter 1, n. 70.

25. For Abrams's account of the significance of sincerity to Romantic poetry, see *Mirror and Lamp,* 317–19. For "the lyric as poetic norm," see ibid., 84–88. A number of critics have complicated Romantic accounts of sincerity. See Lionel Trilling, *Sincerity and Authenticity* (Cambridge: Harvard University Press, 1971) and Judith Pascoe, *Romantic Theatricality* (Ithaca: Cornell University Press, 1997).

26. Judith Phillips Stanton, "Charlotte Smith's 'Literary Business': Income, Patronage, and Indigence," in *The Age of Johnson,* ed. Paul J. Korshin (New York: AMS Press, 1987), 375–401.

27. This account of Smith's life appears in a section entitled "Memoirs of Eminent Persons," *Monthly Magazine* 22 (1807): 246.

28. Culler, *Structuralist Poetics,* 166. Culler follows Frye's claim that in the lyric "we turn away from our ordinary continuous experience in space or time, or rather from a verbal mimesis of it." According to Frye, this detachment requires a rejection of "the kind of language we use in coping with ordinary experience." Frye, "Approaching the Lyric," 31, 34.

29. Cameron, *Lyric Time,* 203.

30. Stafford Harry Northcote, Viscount St. Cyres, "The Sorrows of Mrs. Charlotte Smith," *Cornhill Magazine,* n.s., 15 (1903): 686–96.

31. Leigh Hunt, *The Book of the Sonnet,* ed. Leigh Hunt and S. Adams Lee (Boston: Roberts Brothers, 1867), 1:85.

32. Adela Pinch, *Strange Fits of Passion: Epistemologies of Emotion, from Hume to Austen* (Stanford, Calif.: Stanford University Press, 1996).

33. Todd, *Sensibility,* 4.

34. Sir Walter Scott, *The Miscellaneous Prose Works of Sir Walter Scott* (Edinburgh: Robert Cadell, 1849), 2:64.

35. John Clare, *The Natural History Prose Writings of John Clare,* ed. Margaret Grainger (Oxford: Clarendon Press, 1983), 34.

36. Curran, "The I Altered," 200.

37. Unsigned review of *The Emigrants, European Magazine* 24 (1793): 42.

38. Donald Greer, *The Incidence of the Emigration during the French Revolution* (Cambridge: Harvard University Press, 1951), 112.

39. Florence May Anna Hilbish, "Charlotte Smith, Poet and Novelist 1749-1806" (Ph.D. diss., University of Pennsylvania, 1941), 151.

40. The *Gentleman's Magazine* noticed and praised *Elegiac Sonnets* early in its publication history (in 1786). The periodical also published poems and letters from readers addressed to her. For its initial notice of the sonnets, see *Gentleman's Magazine* 56 (1786): 333–34.

41. Margery Weiner, *The French Exiles, 1789–1815* (London: John Murray, 1960), 103.

42. For instance, in Levinson's reading of "Tintern Abbey" in *Wordsworth's Great Period Poems,* memory obliterates an awareness of social history. Liu's definition of memory in Wordsworth's poetry as "the supervision of time by selfhood" similarly stresses the subjugation of a social environment to subjectivity. See *Wordsworth,* 204.

43. Benjamin, "On Some Motifs in Baudelaire," 159. Pinch makes a relevant argument in her reading of Jane Austen's *Persuasion:* she defines lyricism in the novel as "a particular way of rendering consciousness' apprehension of the social." She too turns to Benjamin for aid in constructing a model of the lyric as social. See "Lost in a Book: Jane Austen's *Persuasion," Studies in Romanticism* 32 (1993): 99.

44. The *European Magazine* was less pleased, complaining that "no particular character, or even species of misfortune, is suffered to dwell long enough upon the mind to produce any very great and concentrated degree of anxiety and interest." The result is that "[w]e pity *all* too much to suffer acutely *any* one." Yet the critic concedes Smith's success in making readers aware of the ongoing violence across the Channel, worrying that "[t]here is but too much reason to fear, that this creature of her imagination has been many times realized in the course of the last two years, and that similar scenes are transacting at the very hour in which we are amusing ourselves with the contemplation of these fictitious sorrows!" Unsigned review of *The Emigrants, European Magazine* 24 (1793): 45.

45. Unsigned review of *The Emigrants, Analytical Review* 22 (1793): 91.

46. Review signed "E.," *Monthly Review* 12 (1793): 375.

47. As Mary Poovey has argued, women writers faced the necessity of remaining "proper ladies," and were chastened when they were judged to have lapsed from rigorous social codes. See *The Proper Lady and the Woman Writer* (Chicago: University of Chicago Press, 1984).

48. Stanton, "Charlotte Smith's 'Literary Business,'" 393.

49. Ibid., 376–77.

50. Unsigned review of vol. 2 of *Elegiac Sonnets, Analytical Review* 26 (1797): 158–59.

51. Curran, introduction to *Poems of Charlotte Smith,* xxi.

52. Stanton makes a cogent case that "after her first three conventional novels, Smith had begun [in *The Old Manor House*] to test the limits of what a woman might write." Derek Roper points out that, with the exception of the *Critical Review,* the major periodicals viewed this novel positively. He argues that Smith's

decline in popularity began with her next novel, *The Banished Man*, since this and subsequent novels were "of less interest." See Stanton's introduction to *The Old Manor House*, ed. Anne Henry Ehrenpreis (Oxford: Oxford University Press, 1989), ix; and Roper, *Reviewing Before the "Edinburgh," 1788–1802* (London: Methuen, 1978), 130.

53. Unsigned review of *The Banished Man*, *British Critic* 4 (1794): 623. Unsigned review of *The Banished Man*, *Analytical Review* 20 (1794): 254.

54. Unsigned review of *The Banished Man*, *European Magazine* 26 (1794): 276. A reviewer for the *Critical Review* makes a related charge about *Letters of a Solitary Wanderer*. The critic suggests that "the story of the Hermit speaks to every one's bosom; and the affectionate sensibility of Frank Maynard is equally interesting and pathetic." Yet the critic goes on to suggest: "To similar tales of domestic life and domestic feelings perhaps Mrs. Smith might, with propriety, confine her exertions." Unsigned review of *Letters of a Solitary Wanderer*, *Critical Review* 32 (1801): 39.

55. Unsigned review of *Beachy Head, with other Poems*, *British Critic* 30 (1807): 170, 174.

Chapter 3. William Wordsworth and the Uses of Lyricism

1. Abrams makes this case influentially in *Natural Supernaturalism*, basing his argument on the understanding of Wordsworth as "the great and exemplary poet of the age." Abrams's portrait of this representative figure was drawn largely from the Prospectus to *The Excursion*. James K. Chandler's critique of the Romantic idea of a representative poet examines the implications of Wordsworth's exemplary status for Romantic studies. See Abrams, *Natural Supernaturalism*, 14. See Chandler, "Representative Men, Spirits of the Age, and Other Romantic Types," in *Romantic Revolutions*, 104–32.

2. Coleridge to Robert Southey (14 August 1803), *The Collected Letters of Samuel Taylor Coleridge*, ed. Earl Leslie Griggs (Oxford: Clarendon Press, 1956), 2:977.

3. Abrams, "Spirit of the Age," 107.

4. Liu, *Wordsworth*, 35.

5. Levinson, *Wordsworth's Great Period Poems*, 37.

6. Wordsworth, citing Coleridge's admonition, makes this aim public in the 1815 Essay, Supplementary to the Preface. See *The Prose Works*, 3:80.

7. Abrams, *Natural Supernaturalism*, 14.

8. My chapter title alludes to Abrams's closing meditation in *The Mirror and the Lamp* on "the use of Romantic poetry," which he defines as a humanism

fostered by the poet's display of disinterested emotion. As my title suggests, I'm interested in a sense of Romantic lyricism's multiple and often contradictory uses.

9. Klancher argues that Wordsworth's prose works (including letters), have influenced subsequent definitions of the poet's relationship to readers, most significantly a definition of literature as "a discourse without social audiences." Klancher feels that Wordsworth's influence extends to his present-day academic readers, who have adopted the role of Wordsworth's deferred ideal audience. He cites Abrams as important for fostering this critical identification. See *The Making of English Reading Audiences*, 4–5, 17.

10. Peter T. Murphy, *Poetry as an Occupation and an Art in Britain, 1760–1830* (Cambridge: Cambridge University Press, 1993), 195.

11. Abrams, *Mirror and Lamp*, 25.

12. Stephen Parrish makes the case that the "reader's response" was Wordsworth's "central concern through all his critical writing, altering little throughout his career." What changes is the "artful means," as Parrish puts it, by which he courts readers, here by declaring his indifference toward them. See *The Art of the "Lyrical Ballads"* (Cambridge: Harvard University Press, 1973), 8.

13. Francis Jeffrey, review of *The Excursion*, by William Wordsworth, *Edinburgh Review* 24 (1814): 1–31. The review was published 6 December 1814.

14. Kenneth R. Johnston, *Wordsworth and "The Recluse"* (New Haven: Yale University Press, 1984), 335. Wordsworth's revisionary strategies succeeded in muddying the waters around a central issue: whether or not his attitude toward reading audiences changes from the 1800 *Lyrical Ballads* to the 1815 *Poems*. Abrams views Wordsworth's notion of audience in the 1815 Essay as simply an expansion upon the ideas of the 1800 Preface and thus sees development rather than revision (*Mirror and Lamp*, 108–10). This critical narrative of continuity follows Wordsworth's account of a process of development in the 1815 Essay. Klancher disputes this version, arguing that "Wordsworth's effort to remake the existing audience of 1800 ends, in 1815, by inventing an audience in imagination he was unable to form in the world" (*Making of English Reading Audiences*, 143).

15. Marlon B. Ross describes self-possession as "an ideology that owes nothing to any source outside the desiring self." See *The Contours of Masculine Desire: Romanticism and the Rise of Women's Poetry* (New York: Oxford University Press, 1989), 10.

16. Wordsworth, *The Excursion*, lines 60-63. Quotations from the Prospectus are taken from *Prose Works*, vol. 3.

17. Murphy charts a pronounced change from the solicitude of the Preface to *Lyrical Ballads* to the antagonism of the 1815 Essay (*Poetry as Occupation and Art*, 182–84).

18. Arguing that there is a basic difference in the way that Wordsworth and

Coleridge handled their radical pasts, Nicholas Roe contrasts Coleridge's renunciations and denials of a former radical self with Wordsworth's revisionary biography. Roe speculates that the difference can be traced to their divergent futures after their radical years: "For Wordsworth as the writer of *The Prelude* revolutionary disappointment was compensated in his power and calling as a poet; for Coleridge it issued as breakdown and creative paralysis." See *Wordsworth and Coleridge: The Radical Years* (Oxford: Clarendon Press, 1988), 3.

19. Richard J. Onorato, *The Character of the Poet: Wordsworth in "The Prelude"* (Princeton: Princeton University Press, 1971), 16.

20. Coleridge, *Collected Works*, vol. 5, pt. 1, ed. R. A. Foakes, 118.

21. Simpson classes together Coleridge, Mill and Arnold as representing an ideal, apolitical Wordsworth. He points out that Arnold's selection of particular poems as representative "privileges the spiritual over the intellectual, the natural over the social, and the resolved statement over the transcription of crisis or struggle." See *Wordsworth's Historical Imagination*, 9.

22. Coleridge to George Coleridge (c. 10 March 1798), in *Collected Letters*, 1:397.

23. Dorothy Wordsworth to Jane Pollard (16 February [1793]), in *Wordsworth Letters*, 1:89.

24. William Wordsworth to James Webbe Tobin (6 March [1798]), in *Wordsworth Letters*, 1:210–11.

25. William Wordsworth declares in 1830, "The preface which I wrote long ago to my own Poems I was put upon by the urgent entreaties of a friend, and heartily regret I ever had any thing to do with it; though I do not reckon the principles then advanced erroneous." Letter to John Abraham Heraud (23 November [1830]), in *Wordsworth Letters*, 5:352.

26. John E. Jordan, *Why the* Lyrical Ballads? (Berkeley: University of California Press, 1976), 172. Charles Ryskamp goes further, finding the title "not especially appropriate to the volume." Nevertheless, Ryskamp discovers the originality of *Lyrical Ballads* to be largely their "psychological subtlety," a quality that has been considered constitutive of Wordsworth's lyricism, and he identifies as the most original poems several lyrical poems, including "Tintern Abbey." See "Wordsworth's *Lyrical Ballads* in Their Time," in *From Sensibility to Romanticism*, ed. Frederick W. Hilles and Harold Bloom (New York: Oxford University Press, 1965), 359, 365.

27. John Stoddart, review of *Lyrical Ballads* (1800), by Wordsworth and Coleridge, *British Critic* 17 (1801): 131.

28. Parrish brings into focus the two points that critics often cite as comparisons: "[A] 'lyrical' ballad was lyrical in two respects—its passion . . . arose, as in any lyric, from the mind of the speaker or the dramatic narrator of a ballad tale, and it was heightened by the employment of 'lyrical' or rapid metre so as to convey this passion to readers unaccustomed to responding to the common language

of men in common life." See "'Leaping and Lingering': Coleridge's Lyrical Ballads," in *Coleridge's Imagination*, ed. Richard Gravil, Lucy Newlyn, and Nicholas Roe (Cambridge: Cambridge University Press, 1985), 106.

29. Curran, *Poetic Form*, 182.

30. The social realism of the novel, not the ballad, is the kind of narrative with which lyricism is usually contrasted. But this distinction has encouraged broader assumptions of essential differences between lyric and narrative modes.

31. Cameron, *Lyric Time*, 206. Don H. Bialostosky counters a tradition of viewing the poem as bringing together narrative and lyric forms, proposing instead that the poem experiments exclusively with a narrative poetics in juxtaposing and bringing together two different "tales" of Simon Lee. See *Making Tales: The Poetics of Wordsworth's Narrative Experiments* (Chicago: University of Chicago Press, 1984), 74–81.

32. Siskin calls lyricism "the primary site for the Author's deep transcendence of form." See "Lyric Mix," 8. Liu describes Wordsworthian lyricism as an "*émigré* flight from narrative" (*Wordsworth*, 51).

33. Abrams, "Structure and Style," 211–12, 225.

34. Clare, "Sketches in the Life of John Clare," in *John Clare by Himself*, ed. Eric Robinson and David Powell (Ashington and Manchester: Mid Northumberland Arts Group and Carcanet, 1996), 18.

35. In a November 1801 entry of the *Grasmere Journals*, Dorothy Wordsworth associates "Simon Lee" with this context. The passage describes the increasing economic vulnerability of Thomas and Peggy Ashburner, their neighbors at Town End. Dorothy relates how the family was forced to sell some of their land because of debts; William treats this history in the poem "Repentance." Dorothy reports a conversation with Peggy: "[T]hen she told me with what pains & industry they had made up their taxes interest &c &c—how they all got up at 5 o'clock in the morning to spin & Thomas carded, & that they had paid off a hundred pound of the interest." Having sent the Ashburners some goose and received honey and 'a thousand thanks' in return," Dorothy quotes her brother—"'alas the gratitude of men has &c.'" Although the Ashburners are clearly not at the same level of economic desperation as either Simon Lee or Parker Clare, her allusion to "Simon Lee" in this context signals a working awareness of the nature of the economic pressures on rural families in the area at this time (*GJ*, 41).

36. E. P. Thompson, *The Making of the English Working Class* (New York: Vintage, 1966), 221.

37. Simpson, *Wordsworth's Historical Imagination*, 153.

38. Geoffrey H. Hartman, *Wordsworth's Poetry, 1787–1814* (New Haven: Yale University Press, 1964; reprint, Cambridge: Harvard University Press, 1987), 150.

39. Heather Glen observes about Wordsworth's ballads, including "Simon Lee," that they "demand a new kind of activity of their readers: not the passive

acceptance of a finished literary product, but a creative engagement with that which is suggestively unresolved." Glen is, however, ultimately skeptical about the extent of Wordsworth's challenge to readers' expectations in *Lyrical Ballads*. She cites a contemporary context of similar verse in magazines and the educated, liberal audience that Wordsworth could assume already existed for such periodicals as the *Monthly Magazine*. See *Vision and Disenchantment: Blake's "Songs" and Wordsworth's "Lyrical Ballads"* (Cambridge: Cambridge University Press, 1983), 54.

40. Ibid., 239.

41. Critics have often focused on the reader's role in the poem, but their assessments of how it is defined vary greatly. Carl Woodring, for instance, suggests that "[i]n 'Simon Lee' he asks the reader to examine his own psychological reasons for expecting a protagonist and an episode less humble than those the poem gives him." See *Wordsworth* (Boston: Houghton Mifflin, 1965), 23.

42. Mary Jacobus, *Tradition and Experiment in Wordsworth's "Lyrical Ballads" (1798)* (Oxford: Clarendon Press, 1976), 207. Bialostosky concurs, arguing that the poet "puts himself on the line not just as a poet but as a man and appeals for the kindness and thoughtfulness of others after recognizing his own thoughtless unkindness" in inadvertently demonstrating Simon Lee's debility (*Making Tales*, 81).

43. Michael H. Friedman discovers an opportunity for the poet to disavow a debility he fears in himself by projecting devastation onto another person whom he then aids, in the process gaining a sense of his own relative strength. *The Making of Tory Humanist: William Wordsworth and the Idea of Community* (New York: Columbia University Press, 1979), 30. Thomas Hutchinson's interpretation of the poem lays an early foundation for critiques such as Friedman's, which emphasize the exploitative nature of the exchange: "The object of *Simon Lee* seems to be to vindicate the instinctive character of the emotion of gratitude as against Godwin, who represented it as an unjust and degrading sentiment, having its origin in the unequal distribution of wealth, influence, etc." See his edition of *Lyrical Ballads* (1798; reprint, London: Duckworth, 1898), 234.

44. Abrams, "On Political Readings of *Lyrical Ballads*," in *Romantic Revolutions*, 328. Levinson, *Wordsworth's Great Period Poems*, 37.

45. Onorato's discussion of the relationship between mind and landscape in the poems is especially relevant to McGann's and Levinson's readings. Discussing a passage in Book II of *The Prelude*, he argues that "[t]he person is represented as sitting in the landscape, but the landscape then seems to be in his own mind; he is and is not himself, is and is not there." *The Character of the Poet: Wordsworth in "The Prelude,"* 59.

46. Liu, *Wordsworth*, 32.

47. John Barrell, *Poetry, Language and Politics* (Manchester: Manchester University Press, 1988), 148. Bialostosky makes a strong case for revaluing the ballads' narrative experiments in *Making Tales*.

48. Johnston, "The Politics of 'Tintern Abbey,'" *Wordsworth Circle* 14 (1983): 9.

49. Liu makes an argument for the recovery of a social sense in the *Memorial Tour* sonnets, but he locates the openness to history in the interstices between the sonnets, rather than in the poems themselves.

50. Chandler, *Wordsworth's Second Nature* (Chicago: University of Chicago Press, 1984), 9. Fred V. Randel associates the term with Wordsworth's abandonment of Annette Vallon and Caroline. See "The Betrayals of 'Tintern Abbey,'" *Studies in Romanticism* 32 (1993): 379–97.

51. Levinson emphasizes that the five-year anniversary commemorates the death of Marat, the event that signaled to some English radicals that the revolution had gone wrong, "the true cause destroyed by the false, the republic betrayed by the tyrant" (*Wordsworth's Great Period Poems,* 22). According to this interpretation, Wordsworth in 1798 would be recalling a moment whose import confirmed his subsequent retreat from radical politics. She also interprets the 1793 visit as a return to nature after the political trauma of revolutionary France and views this poet as the self that he wants to commemorate in 1798, as part of his consolatory narrative. Although Levinson concedes that this return "could not have been so renewing nor so unambivalent as he later chose to suggest, given the state of his personal night and of national affairs," nevertheless she views his ability to revise this moment as plausible (18). My argument is that Levinson understates the scale of the complications involved in a recollection of himself in 1793.

52. Johnston, "Politics of 'Tintern Abbey,'" 12.

53. Robert Langbaum's description of the poem as a "dramatic lyric" emphasizes the exchange between speaker and silent auditor. But Langbaum views this theatrical quality as antithetical to lyricism: "When we consider how dramatic the Romantic lyric is, in the arrangement of its events, the role of its observer and the dialogue-like style of its address, we can only wonder whether it can properly be called a lyric at all." Yet Langbaum points to a contradiction that exists only if Romantic lyricism is deemed inherently asocial, and therefore antithetical to the kind of social dynamic that a dialogue, however one-sided, implies. See *The Poetry of Experience* (New York: Norton, 1957), 53–54. Parrish and Sheats have both made cases for the importance of the dramatic and the rhetorical in *Lyrical Ballads.* Sheats describes the ballads not as "romantic effusions" but as "complex, sophisticated, and deliberately pragmatic presentational structures." See *The Making of Wordsworth's Poetry, 1785-1798* (Cambridge: Harvard University Press, 1973), 204. Parrish finds continuity between the more expressly dramatic forms of the ballads and Wordsworth's subsequent autobiographical lyrics, including the "Intimations Ode." He makes an important argument for the dramatic nature of many of the poems in *Lyrical Ballads*, but he exempts those, like "Tintern Abbey," which are "spoken solely by the poet in his own character."

Yet the argument he makes—that many of the poems are dramatic in following the "fluxes and refluxes of the mind" while imitating the "real language of men"—also applies to "Tintern Abbey" (*Art of the "Lyrical Ballads,"* 83).

54. Homans, *Women Writers*, 21. In *Poetry, Language and Politics*, Barrell makes a related argument about Dorothy Wordsworth's role, saying that in this period women and children, like primitives, were thought to speak something closer to a "language of the sense." As such, she gives him access to a vital language he has lost.

55. Mellor, *Romanticism and Gender*, 19.

56. Siskin locates in the Preface a new definition of the audience that is also operative in "Tintern Abbey," with Dorothy standing in for the readers William was trying to reach. Siskin views Wordsworth's rejection of personification, along with "poetic diction," as an effort to establish a new community of readers, a company of "flesh and blood," as William puts it. Dorothy represents the ideal audience for William, one that will sympathetically identify with him, allowing his feelings to become her own. "Appeals" such as William's apostrophe to Dorothy in the poem, "dramatically voiced in a variation of what Wordsworth called the 'language of conversation,' are supposed to elicit the sympathetic identification that forges communal norms *and* the possibilities of deviation from them." See *Historicity of Romantic Discourse*, 81. While it seems clear that the addresses to Dorothy in this poem and to Coleridge in *The Prelude* are prescriptive, I am more skeptical about William's success and even his confidence of success in directing her future thoughts.

57. Ibid., 82.

58. McGann notes that she is "of course, the reader's surrogate" (*Romantic Ideology*, 88), but that, as Levinson suggests, she is "a decidedly feeble gesture toward externality" (*Wordsworth's Great Period Poems*, 38).

59. Klancher, *Making of English Reading Audiences*, 14.

60. Once again, my interest is not in countering a new historical reading, but rather in suggesting that its account of the poet's subjectivity and the genre in which it is elaborated is too narrow, that it accounts for only one, conservative impulse in the poem. In Levinson's account, a social context—here the evidence of the Industrial Revolution written on England's landscape—is "transformed" into an ideal place relevant only to the personal history of the poet. Levinson describes the "transformational grammar" by which this re-vision of the abbey is accomplished (*Wordsworth's Great Period Poems*, 83). This concept is related to Liu's definition of lyricism as a "transform" of history's narrative (*Wordsworth*, 51). In McGann's words, "what might have been a picture *in* the mind (of a ruined abbey)" is replaced "with a picture *of* the mind" (*Romantic Ideology*, 87).

61. Chandler, *Wordsworth's Second Nature*, 9. Bloom points out that the term "betrayal" has "sexual implications," a point that lends support to my argument that thoughts of Annette Vallon and their separation, however unavoidable

and amicable, haunt this section of the poem. See *The Visionary Company*, rev. ed. (Ithaca: Cornell University Press, 1971), 138. Onorato argues that Wordsworth's use of the term in reference to nature reflects an association of nature with his mother, who "betrayed" him by dying (*Character of the Poet: Wordsworth in "The Prelude,"* 34–35). David Bromwich observes that Wordsworth seems like "someone who thinks his life is in need of an apology." Bromwich focuses on a sense of "dread" associated with revolutionary France in the poem in "The French Revolution and 'Tintern Abbey,'" *Raritan* 10 (1991): 4.

62. John Thelwall, *Poems Chiefly Written in Retirement* (London: Richard Phillips, 1801).

63. Coleridge to Thelwall [21 August 1797], *Collected Letters*, 1:343.

64. Émile Legouis prints two letters from Annette (which were apparently sent together) to William and Dorothy, dated 20 March 1793. They indicate that the Wordsworths had mentioned this scheme in previous letters. See *William Wordsworth and Annette Vallon*, revised by Pierre Legouis (1922; reprint, Hamden, Conn.: Archon, 1967).

65. Mary Moorman, *William Wordsworth: The Early Years, 1770–1803* (Oxford: Clarendon Press, 1957), 1:221–22.

66. Chandler, *Wordsworth's Second Nature*, 11.

67. Levinson argues that in his passionate embrace of nature in "Tintern Abbey" he was fleeing his political engagements in France: "more like a man / Flying from something that he dreads, than one / Who sought the thing he loved." Onorato makes more explicit the Freudian model implicit in Levinson's reading: he argues that Wordsworth in 1793 experienced a regressive desire to return to the period before his mother's death (*Wordsworth's Great Period Poems*, 36).

68. Thomas Carlyle, *Reminiscences*, ed. Charles Eliot Norton (London: J. M. Dent, 1972), 360–61.

69. Roe, *Wordsworth and Coleridge*, 40.

70. Mark L. Reed, *Wordsworth: The Chronology of the Early Years* (Cambridge: Harvard University Press, 1967), 147.

71. Wordsworth, *The Prelude, 1799, 1805, 1850*, ed. Jonathan Wordsworth, M. H. Abrams, and Stephen Gill (New York: Norton, 1979).

72. Sigmund Freud, "Mourning and Melancholia," in *The Standard Edition of the Complete Psychological Works of Sigmund Freud*, ed. James Strachey and Anna Freud (London: Hogarth, 1957–62), 14:243–58.

73. Thompson, "Disenchantment or Default," 155.

74. As I argue in chapter 1, Benjamin's materialist account of memory is at sharp odds with Levinson's and Liu's description of the faculty central to Romantic lyricism. According to Liu, "Wordsworth's secular god is Memory," which works to "conserve identity" (*Wordsworth*, 56). What Liu refers to as Wordsworth's "rhetoric of *private* memory" (485) accords with Levinson's account of "Tintern Abbey" in that both credit memory with enormous powers of revision and repression,

while downplaying its more disruptive possibilities. Levinson's memory is Proust's *memoire voluntaire*, a "functional agency" for the transformation of social scenes into private landscapes. According to her, Wordsworth's "Mnemosyne," is "a deeply conservative muse" (*Wordsworth's Great Period Poems*, 51, 23). Bloom's "myth of memory" is relevant to these new historical accounts of recollection: he reads "Tintern Abbey" as developing the myth of memory's restorative power (*Visionary Company*, 140). The argument that the Wordsworthian act of remembrance is asocial enhances a view that his lyricism excludes the reader. But Parrish provides a counterargument in his claim that Wordsworth actually uses memory rhetorically in his poems, as a way to draw the reader into his thoughts: he describes how memory serves "to impose on experience the control of art." The rhetorical gain was "to distance both poet and reader from reality in such a way as to transfigure painful or shocking events and heighten their meaning" (*Art of the "Lyrical Ballads,"* 4).

75. Thomas Bowman became headmaster in June 1786 and resigned in January 1829. His son, who was a governor of Hawkshead Grammar School, recalls the books that his father had given to Wordsworth. The comments are found in his 1885 recollections of what his father had told him about Wordsworth: "'He wrote again—and I have his letter yet—saying that my father also introduced him to Langhorne's poems and Beattie's 'Minstrel' & Percy's 'Reliques,' and that it was in books or periodic works my father lent him that he first became acquainted with the poetry of Crabbe & Charlotte Smith & the two Wartons.'" See T. W. Thompson, *Wordsworth's Hawkshead*, ed. Robert Woof (London: Oxford University Press, 1970), 344.

76. Albert Goodwin, *The Friends of Liberty: The English Democratic Movement in the Age of the French Revolution* (Cambridge: Harvard University Press, 1979), 249–50.

77. Hilbish designates 1791 to 1793 Smith's French period, "because of her manifest interest in French affairs and the French." See *Charlotte Smith*, 151.

78. Unsigned notice in the Supplement to the *Gentleman's Magazine* 76 (1806): 1247.

79. Writing to Alaric Watts, Wordsworth commends a recent publication, apparently an anthology of sonnets, but admits, "I cannot but regret however that it does not contain a single specimen from my old Friend Charlotte Smith, who was the first *Modern* distinguished in that Composition." Letter to [?] Alaric Watts (10 January 1836), in *Wordsworth Letters*, 6:149–50. He recommends Smith's inclusion to another anthologist, Alexander Dyce, should his *Specimens of English Sonnets* (1833) go into a second edition. He suggests "a few more from Charlotte Smith, particularly 'I love thee, mournful, sober-suited night.'" Letter to Alexander Dyce (10 May [1830]), in *Wordsworth Letters*, 5:260. In another letter he recommends her inclusion in an edition of Dyce's "Specimens of British

Poetesses." Letter to Alexander Dyce (4 December 1833), in *Wordsworth Letters*, 5:663–64.

80. Unsigned notice of *Letters of a Solitary Wanderer* (vols. 1-2), *Antijacobin Review* 10 (1801): 318.

Chapter 4. Dorothy Wordsworth and the Liabilities of Literary Production

1. Homans sparked a reassessment of Dorothy Wordsworth's role in the field in *Women Writers and Poetic Identity*.

2. Dorothy Wordsworth to Lady Beaumont (20 April [1806]), in *Wordsworth Letters*, 2:24–25. The poems are "Address to a Child" and probably "The Cottager to Her Infant."

3. Dorothy Wordsworth to Catherine Clarkson (9 December 1810), in *Wordsworth Letters*, 2:454.

4. Fay, *Becoming Wordsworthian*, 119. She argues that what we have thought of as "the Wordsworthian" in literary history is in fact a joint production in which the siblings' contributions were equally significant: "[T]he Wordsworthian world view was a product of both of their imaginations working together, not her subservience to him or, the opposite, his exploitation of her abilities but a team collaboration to which William affixed the name 'Wordsworth' and claimed for his own" (15).

5. Arnold in fact specifies the years 1798–1808 as "the single decade" in which "almost all his really first-rate work was produced." He makes this pronouncement in his effort to canonize the Wordsworth of the shorter lyrics in his preface to his 1879 collection of Wordsworth (*Complete Prose Works of Matthew Arnold*, ed. Super, 9:42).

6. In her edition of the *Alfoxden Journal* and *Grasmere Journals*, Moorman traces various instances of Coleridge's borrowings for *Christabel*, written in April 1798, from the January and March entries of the *Alfoxden Journal*. Dorothy Wordsworth seems to have borrowed from *The Rime of the Ancient Mariner* in her repeated observations of "the horned moon" in her entries for 21 and 23 March. (Coleridge had written to Joseph Cottle that the poem was completed in February.)

7. William Wordsworth to Lady Beaumont (21 May 1807), in *Wordsworth Letters*, 2:145.

8. Jeffrey, review of *Poems, in Two Volumes* (1807), by William Wordsworth, *Edinburgh Review* 11 (1807): 216.

9. William Wordsworth wrote to Francis Wrangham requesting his help with the *Critical Review*, explaining that "the immediate sale of books is more under

the influence of reviews than is generally supposed, and the sale of this work is of some consequence to me." Wordsworth to Wrangham (12 July and 4 November 1807), in *Wordsworth Letters*, 2:155, 174.

10. Dorothy Wordsworth to William Wordsworth (31 March [1808]), in *Wordsworth Letters*, 2:207.

11. Dorothy Wordsworth to Richard Wordsworth (10 June 1802), in *Wordsworth Letters*, 1:358–61.

12. Dorothy Wordsworth to Jane Pollard (11 May 1808), in *Wordsworth Letters*, 2:236.

13. Dorothy Wordsworth to Lady Beaumont (11 June 1805), in *Wordsworth Letters*, 1:598.

14. Dorothy Wordsworth to Samuel Rogers (3 January 1823), in *Wordsworth Letters*, 4:181.

15. Homans, *Women Writers*, 57.

16. Homans, *Bearing the Word: Language and Female Experience in Nineteenth-Century Women's Writing* (Chicago: University of Chicago Press, 1986), 40–41, 56.

17. Alexander, *Women in Romanticism*, 6, 16, 12.

18. Moorman describes the note in her edition of the *Journals* (128).

19. George B. Parks argues that "emotional writing about nature in travel literature was first established as a fashion in England between 1736 and 1767." See "The Turn to the Romantic in the Travel Literature of the Eighteenth Century," *Modern Language Quarterly* 25 (1964): 30. Charles L. Batten Jr. contends that it was a "clearly defined convention of eighteenth-century travel literature" that the "writer must not talk about himself." Travel journalists often simply eliminated the "I" or substituted "you" or "we." These maneuvers were meant to deflect charges of "egotism," an anxiety that also prompted many to adopt a "humble style" and to deny any ambition for literary fame. See *Pleasurable Instruction: Form and Convention in Eighteenth-Century Travel Literature* (Berkeley: University of California Press, 1978), 40, 44.

20. Alec Bond proposes repositioning Dorothy Wordsworth's journals within the traditions of "the journal and travel book." See "Reconsidering Dorothy Wordsworth," *Charles Lamb Bulletin*, n.s., 47–48 (1984): 194–207.

21. Dorothy Wordsworth to Lady Beaumont (26 August [1805]), in *Wordsworth Letters*, 1:621.

22. In a July 1800 entry, Dorothy Wordsworth reports reading Richard Payne Knight's popular poem, *The Landscape* (1794) (*AJ*, 31). Between them, Knight, Gilpin, and Uvedale Price are credited with popularizing the aesthetic categories of the picturesque, the sublime, and the beautiful.

23. Robert Con Davis, "The Structure of the Picturesque: Dorothy Wordsworth's Journals," *Wordsworth Circle* 9 (1978): 47.

24. Ibid., 45. See also John R. Nabholtz, "Dorothy Wordsworth and Picturesque," *Studies in Romanticism* 3 (1963): 118–28.

25. The picturesque stance was fashionable for middle-class tourists in the mid to late eighteenth century, as travel was just becoming accessible to them. Dorothy Wordsworth became one of these tourists in the journals she kept on trips, including the *Recollections of a Tour Made in Scotland* (1803), the prose work she came closest to publishing.

26. W. E. Tate, *The English Village Community and the Enclosure Movements* (London: Victor Gollancz, 1967), 90.

27. J. M. Neeson, "The Opponents of Enclosure in Eighteenth-Century Northamptonshire," *Past & Present* 105 (1984): 138.

28. Raymond Williams, *The Country and the City* (New York: Oxford University Press, 1973), 98.

29. Ann Bermingham, *Landscape and Ideology: The English Rustic Tradition, 1740–1860* (Berkeley: University of California Press, 1986), 70, 83.

30. Edmund Burke, *A Philosophical Inquiry into the Origin of Our Ideas of the Sublime and Beautiful* (1759), ed. James T. Boulton (Notre Dame, Ind.: University of Notre Dame Press, 1958).

31. Immanuel Kant, *Critique of Judgement*, trans. J. H. Bernard, 2d ed. (New York: Hafner/Macmillan, 1951).

32. Fay provides a rich discussion of what she terms Dorothy Wordsworth's "feminine sublime" (*Becoming Wordsworthian*, 214–26).

33. Fay argues that the fragmentary journal form allows Dorothy Wordsworth to avoid "turning these estranged people into objects" (ibid., 208).

34. Marshall, *Surprising Effects of Sympathy*, 197, 6, 103.

35. Dorothy Wordworth, *The Journals of Dorothy Wordsworth*, ed. Ernest De Selincourt (Oxford: Oxford University Press, 1941), 1:369.

36. Elizabeth A. Bohls, *Women Travel Writers and the Language of Aesthetics, 1716-1818* (Cambridge: Cambridge University Press, 1995), 193.

37. Susan M. Levin recounts an episode particularly appropriate for *Lyrical Ballads*: "Seven-year-old John is taken by an old family friend who is 'feeble and paralytic' and who had previously spent his time outdoors with 'no Companion but his Dog and Staff.'" *Dorothy Wordsworth and Romanticism* (New Brunswick, N.J.: Rutgers University Press, 1987), 43. Michael H. Friedman observes that "[t]here is no discrepancy between the story of the Greens and the social world Wordsworth created in his own poetry" (*Making of a Tory Humanist*, 180).

38. Levin makes a similar point about this passage, saying that it registers her identification with the Greens. But Levin derives a different meaning from the comparison, focusing less on survivor's guilt than on affirmation: "The narrative becomes in part a reassertion of her own life." See *Dorothy Wordsworth and Romanticism*, 50.

39. Levin suggests as another connection a lesson that she argues that the *Narrative* promotes: that communal bonds are more important than familial bonds (ibid., 45).

40. Homans, *Women Writers*, 57–62.

41. Wolfson extends this argument to the passage considered earlier in describing "the peculiar manner in which she writes herself across the Greens' path—namely, her report of 'that very spot' where they disappeared." See "Individual in Community," 60.

42. Levin discusses Dorothy Wordsworth's role and concludes that "her assertions" about what should be done with the children "may be perceived as at once reactionary, utopian, naïve, and efficiently workable" (*Dorothy Wordsworth and Romanticism*, 44).

43. Friedman, *Making of a Tory Humanist*, 181.

44. Levin, *Dorothy Wordsworth and Romanticism*, 47.

Chapter 5. John Clare's Poetics and Politics of Loss

1. Clare, *Letters*, 99 n.

2. Bloom assigns Clare this "minor" role in *The Visionary Company*, 444–56.

3. In a prominent defense of Clare that won the poet considerable visibility, Jonathan Bate claims Clare as a protoenvironmentalist. Bate's argument, however, is strongly inflected by an antagonism toward Romantic new historicism, precisely for its definition of the turn to nature as an evasion of social responsibility. By reasserting the priority of Clare's environmentalism over his social politics, Bate misses an opportunity to do justice to the multiplicity of political impulses manifested in Clare's lyric poetry. See "The Rights of Nature," *John Clare Society Journal* 14 (1995): 7–15. For Bate's broader argument about environmentalism and Romantic new historicism, see *Romantic Ecology* (London: Routledge, 1991).

4. I borrow the term from the introduction to *John Clare: Selected Poetry and Prose,* ed. Merryn Williams and Raymond Williams (London: Methuen, 1986), 1–22.

5. Critics have warned about the dangers of such visibility, both for Clare and the environment he describes. For arguments that complicate an easy equation between identity and empowerment, see Adam Phillips, "The Exposure of John Clare," in *John Clare in Context*, ed. Hugh Haughton, Adam Phillips, and Geoffrey Summerfield (Cambridge: Cambridge University Press, 1994), 178–88; and Nicholas Birns, "'The riddle nature could not prove': Hidden Landscapes in Clare's Poetry," in *John Clare in Context*, ed. Houghton, Phillips, and Summerfield, 188–220.

6. Coleridge, "Introduction to the Sonnets," 543.

7. By claiming the continuity of a poetics and politics of loss in Clare's oeuvre,

I do not suggest that either were static in the course of a career that offered great promises and disappointments. Elizabeth Helsinger and John Lucas have traced detailed trajectories of the relationship between his poetics and politics. See Helsinger, "Clare and the Place of the Peasant Poet," *Critical Inquiry* 13 (1987): 509–31, and Lucas, "Clare's Politics," in *John Clare in Context*, ed. Haughton, Phillips, and Summerfield, 148–77.

8. John Gibson Lockhart, "Extracts from Mr. Wastle's Diary," *Blackwood's Edinburgh Magazine* 7 (1820): 322. Reprinted by Mark Storey in *Clare: The Critical Heritage* (London: Routledge & Kegan Paul, 1973), 103.

9. Helsinger, "Clare," 511.

10. Zachary Leader, *Revision and Romantic Authorship* (Oxford: Clarendon Press, 1996), 208.

11. Defining the precise nature and efficacy of Clare's political stance in his poems, and particularly those that address enclosure, has proven critically contentious. Barrell contextualizes Clare's poems in a range of eighteenth-century cultural and poetic traditions and concludes that his politics is often compromised by, for instance, conventions of nostalgia. See *The Idea of Landscape and the Sense of Place, 1730-1840* (Cambridge: Cambridge University Press, 1972). Johanne Clare responds to Barrell by making a strong case for the sociopolitical content of Clare's enclosure poems. Lucas, in turn, argues that she underestimates the radicalness of the poet's politics by suggesting that his resistance to enclosure is moral rather than political. Barrell revisits these questions in *Poetry, Language and Politics*, 100–136. Johanne Clare, *John Clare and the Bounds of Circumstance* (Kingston, Ont.: McGill-Queen's University Press, 1987).

12. As with many of Clare's poems, there is some uncertainty about dating. Robinson and Powell give 1809–13 as probable dates of composition, but Barrell speculates that "he must have been adding to it at least until 1815 or so" (*Idea of Landscape and the Sense of Place*, 110).

13. In the introduction to *Poems Descriptive*, Taylor casts Clare in the role of one of Gray's forgotten villagers with a reference to the *Elegy*'s "annals of the poor." See Taylor's introduction to *Poems Descriptive of Rural Life and Scenery*, 4th ed. (London: Taylor and Hessey, 1821), iii.

14. Barrell describes the process of Helpston's enclosure, the bulk of which occurred between 1813 and 1816. The final Award for Helpston was published in 1820. See *Idea of Landscape and the Sense of Place*, 106, 226–27.

15. Johanne Clare, *John Clare*, 48.

16. Bate, "Rights of Nature," 11.

17. William Empson, *Some Versions of Pastoral* (Norfolk, Conn.: James Laughlin, 1960), 4.

18. Helsinger, "Clare," 513.

19. Sherwill was a writer himself; his *Ascent to the Summit of Mont Blanc* appeared in 1826 and his *Poems* were published in 1832.

20. Taylor's reluctance ensured, however, that the changes appeared not in the third edition, as Clare's patrons had desired, but in the final, fourth edition. For a fuller account of the controversy, see Clare, *Letters of John Clare*, 68–69 n.

21. Emmerson's epistolary comments are quoted by John and Anne Tibble in *John Clare: His Life and Poetry* (Melbourne and London: William Heinemann, 1956), 81.

22. See E. P. Thompson, *Customs in Common* (New York: New Press, 1993), 184. In "Clare's Politics," Lucas elaborates other contexts for the poem's politics, including agitation leading up to the 1832 Reform Bill.

23. Thompson, *Makings of the English Working Class*, 230. Neeson, *Commoners: Common Right, Enclosure and Social Change in England, 1700-1820* (Cambridge: Cambridge University Press), 290-91.

24. This explanation of the report is found in a note at the front of the volume. Young is credited with the *General Report*'s authorship, although he did not compile all the reports contained in the volume. See *General Report on Enclosures, Drawn up by Order of the Board of Agriculture* (1808), rpt., ed. Sir John Sinclair (New York: A. M. Kelley, 1971), vi.

25. See Neeson on the contemporary worth of a cow, in *Commoners*, 311.

26. Young, *General Report*, 150–55.

27. Taylor, introduction to *The Village Minstrel and Other Poems* (London: Taylor and Hessey, 1821), 1:xix–xx.

28. Clare, *Letters*, 161. I quote from Clare's letter (dated 7 March 1821); Taylor's quotation in the Introduction reflects editing changes that for the most part regularize punctuation and spelling. One change is more significant: Taylor omits "& think" in Clare's concession, "was People all to feel & think as I do the world coud not be carried on. . . ." By emphasizing emotion over intellection, Taylor mutes a sense of a political argument in Clare's response to the elms' loss.

29. Neeson includes several of Clare's poems against enclosure in her account of a variety of oppositional practices (*Commoners*, 262, 286).

30. Williams, *Country and City*, 133.

31. In her discussion of the "enclosure elegies," Johanne Clare argues that "[i]n the identification of the labourer and the land through the suffering they shared at the hands of a common enemy Clare found the theme which organized all his responses to enclosure, and in *prosopopeia* [*sic*] he found the figure to convey this theme" (*John Clare*, 43).

32. Hartman, *Beyond Formalism* (New Haven: Yale University Press, 1970), 210.

33. This is Barrell's term for these poems.

34. Bridget Keegan makes an important related argument about *The Village Minstrel* in "Broadsides, Ballads and Books: The Landscape of Cultural Literacy in *The Village Minstrel*," *John Clare Society Journal* 15 (1996): 11–18.

35. Birns, "The riddle," 208.

36. Williams, *Country and City*, 135.

37. Clare, *Letters*, 94 n.

38. Frederick Martin prints Bloomfield's letter in *The Life of John Clare* (London: Macmillan, 1865), 140.

39. Clare to Thomas Inskip (10 August 1824), in Clare, *Letters*, 300–301.

40. Helsinger, "Clare," 513.

41. "Self identity," in *John Clare by Himself*, 271.

42. Roy Porter has recently surveyed what we know about Clare's mental state in the period leading up to and including his institutionalization. He concludes that diagnosis is impossible based on existing evidence and warns against a critical tendency, in the absence of medical surety, to project diagnostic interpretations onto Clare. See "'All madness for writing': John Clare and the Asylum," in *John Clare in Context*, 259–78.

43. Alvin Kernan, *Printing Technology, Letters and Samuel Johnson* (Princeton: Princeton University Press, 1987), 4.

44. Both Radstock and Emmerson directed Clare to express his "gratitude" toward his patrons. See Storey, *Clare: The Critical Heritage*, 61–62.

45. Not all of Clare's critics took Taylor's cue by viewing knowledge of the poet's life as important to reading his works. Some critics countered the publisher's plea for the poet by arguing that knowledge of the life should have no bearing on judging the poems. For instance, the *Monthly Review* says of the poems that "it would be useless to plead in their favour the disadvantages and difficulties with which their author has been obliged to struggle; because, though it is very honourable to him that he has surmounted them, they can neither add to nor detract from their poetic excellence." Unsigned review of *Poems Descriptive*, *Monthly Review* 41 (March 1820). Reprinted in Storey, *Clare: The Critical Heritage*, 74.

46. Taylor, introduction to *Poems Descriptive*, xv.

47. Emmerson's poem and several other poetic and epistolary responses from readers are reprinted in Storey, *Clare: The Critical Heritage*, 57–59; 81–83.

48. Unsigned review of *Poems Descriptive*, *Eclectic Review*, n.s., 13 (1820). Reprinted in Storey, *Clare: The Critical Heritage*, 88–89. Storey suggests Conder's possible authorship.

49. Cowper to Charlotte Smith (26 October 1793), Cowper, *Correspondence*, 462.

50. Although Scott borrows from Taylor's introduction, he supports his interpretation of Clare with the poems, citing "Helpstone" as evidence for his assessment of Clare's "character." Unsigned review of *Poems Descriptive*, *London Magazine* 1 (1820). Reprinted in Storey, *Clare: The Critical Heritage*, 79. Unsigned review of *Poems Descriptive*, *Antijacobin Review* 58 (1820). Reprinted in Story, *Clare: The Critical Heritage*, 105.

51. Before Taylor had been introduced to Clare's poems by Taylor's first cousin,

the bookseller Edward Drury, Clare had J. B. Henson of Market Deeping print an advertisement soliciting subscribers to a volume of poems, of which one, "The Setting Sun," was offered as a "specimen." Clare did not succeed in his immediate purpose of reaching his readers directly in this manner, but he did attract Drury's notice, which led to Taylor's interest in the poet (*Clare: The Critical Heritage*, 30).

Bibliography

Abrams, M. H. "English Romanticism: The Spirit of the Age" (1963). Reprinted in *Romanticism and Consciousness,* edited by Harold Bloom, 91–119. New York: Norton, 1970.

———. *A Glossary of Literary Terms.* 6th ed. Forth Worth, Tex: Harcourt Brace, 1993.

———. *The Mirror and the Lamp.* London: Oxford University Press, 1953.

———. *Natural Supernaturalism.* New York: Norton, 1971.

———. "On Political Readings of *Lyrical Ballads.*" In *Romantic Revolutions,* edited by Kenneth R. Johnston, Gilbert Chaitin, Karen Hanson, and Herbert Marks, 320–49. Bloomington: Indiana University Press, 1990.

———. "Revolutionary Romanticism, 1790–1990." In *Wordsworth in Context,* edited by Pauline Fletcher and John Murphy, 19–34. Lewisburg, Pa.: Bucknell University Press, 1992.

———. "Structure and Style in the Greater Romantic Lyric." Reprinted in *Romanticism and Consciousness,* edited by Harold Bloom, 201–29. New York: Norton, 1970.

Adorno, Theodor W. "Rede über Lyrik und Gesellschaft" (1957), in *Gesammelte Schriften, 2:49–68.* Frankfurt-am-Main: Suhrkamp, 1974. Translated under the title "On Lyric and Society" in *Notes to Literature,* by Shierry Weber Nicholsen, ed. Rolf Tiedemann (New York: Columbia University Press, 1991), 37–54.

Alexander, Meena. *Women in Romanticism: Mary Wollstonecraft, Dorothy Wordsworth and Mary Shelley.* Houndmills, U.K.: Macmillan Education, 1989.

Arnold, Matthew. Preface to *The Poems of Wordsworth* (1879). Reprinted in *The Complete Prose Works of Matthew Arnold,* edited by R. H. Super, 9:36–55. Ann Arbor: University of Michigan Press, 1973.

Bahti, Timothy. *Ends of the Lyric: Direction and Consequence in Western Poetry.* Baltimore: Johns Hopkins University Press, 1996.

Baillie, Joanna. *A Series of Plays, 1798.* Oxford: Woodstock, 1990.

Barbauld, Anna Letitia. Introduction to *The Old Manor House.* In vol. 36 of *The British Novelists.* i–viii. London: F. C. and J. Rivington, 1810.

Barrell, John. *The Idea of Landscape and the Sense of Place, 1730–1840.* Cambridge: Cambridge University Press, 1972.

———. *Poetry, Language and Politics.* Manchester: Manchester University Press, 1988.

Bate, Jonathan. *Romantic Ecology.* London: Routledge, 1991.

———. "The Rights of Nature." *The John Clare Society Journal* 14 (1995): 7–15.

Batten, Charles L., Jr. *Pleasurable Instruction: Form and Convention in Eighteenth-Century Travel Literature.* Berkeley: University of California Press, 1978.

Benjamin, Walter. *Illuminations.* Edited by Hannah Arendt. Translated by Harry Zohn. New York: Schocken, 1968.

———. *Reflections.* Ed. Peter Demetz. Trans. Edmund Jephcott. New York: Schocken, 1978.

Bermingham, Ann. *Landscape and Ideology: The English Rustic Tradition, 1740–1860.* Berkeley: University of California Press, 1986.

Bialostosky, Don H. *Making Tales: The Poetics of Wordsworth's Narrative Experiments.* Chicago: University of Chicago Press, 1984.

Birns, Nicholas. "'The riddle nature could not prove': Hidden Landscapes in Clare's Poetry." In *John Clare in Context,* edited by Hugh Haughton, Adam Phillips, and Geoffrey Summerfield, 188–220. Cambridge: Cambridge University Press, 1994.

Bloom, Harold. "The Internalization of Quest-Romance" (1969). Reprinted in *Romanticism and Consciousness,* edited by Harold Bloom, 3–24. New York: Norton, 1970.

———. *The Visionary Company*. Rev. ed. Ithaca: Cornell University Press, 1971.

Boehm, Alan D. "The 1798 *Lyrical Ballads* and the Poetics of Late-Eighteenth-Century Book Production." *ELH* 63 (1996): 453–87.

Bohls, Elizabeth A. *Women Travel Writers and the Language of Aesthetics, 1716–1818*. Cambridge: Cambridge University Press, 1995.

Bond, Alec. "Reconsidering Dorothy Wordsworth." *The Charles Lamb Bulletin*, n.s., 47–48 (1984): 194–207.

Bowstead, Diana. "Charlotte Smith's *Desmond*: The Epistolary Novel as Ideological Argument." In *Fetter'd or Free? British Woman Novelists, 1670–1815*, edited by Mary Anne Schofield and Cecilia Macheski, 237–63. Athens: Ohio University Press, 1986.

Bromwich, David. "The French Revolution and 'Tintern Abbey.'" *Raritan* 10 (1991): 1–23.

Burke, Edmund. *A Philosophical Enquiry into the Origin of Our Ideas of the Sublime and Beautiful* (1759). Edited by James T. Boulton. Notre Dame, Ind.: University of Notre Dame Press, 1968.

Butler, Marilyn. *Romantics, Rebels and Reactionaries*. Oxford: Oxford University Press, 1981.

Cameron, Sharon. *Lyric Time: Dickinson and the Limits of Genre*. Baltimore: Johns Hopkins University Press, 1979.

Carlyle, Thomas. *Reminiscences*. Edited by Charles Eliot Norton. London: J. M. Dent, 1972.

Chandler, James K. "Representative Men, Spirits of the Age, and Other Romantic Types." In *Romantic Revolutions*, edited by Kenneth R. Johnston, Gilbert Chaitin, Karen Hanson, and Herbert Marks, 104–32. Bloomington: Indiana University Press, 1990.

———. *Wordsworth's Second Nature*. Chicago: University of Chicago Press, 1984.

Christensen, Jerome. "Byron's Career: The Speculative Stage." *ELH* 52 (1985): 59–84.

Clare, Johanne. *John Clare and the Bounds of Circumstance*. Kingston, Ont.: McGill-Queen's University Press, 1987.

Clare, John. *John Clare by Himself*. Edited by Eric Robinson and David Powell. Ashington and Manchester, U.K.: Mid Northumberland Arts Group and Carcanet, 1996.

———. *The Natural History Prose Writings of John Clare* . Edited by Margaret Grainger. Oxford: Clarendon Press, 1983.

Coleridge, Samuel Taylor. *Collected Letters*. Edited by Earl Leslie Griggs. Vols. 1 and 2. Oxford: Clarendon Press, 1956.

——. *The Collected Works of Samuel Taylor Coleridge*. Vol. 5. Edited by R. A. Foakes. Princeton: Princeton University Press, 1987.

——. *The Collected Works of Samuel Taylor Coleridge*. Vol. 7. Edited by James Engell and W. Jackson Bate. Princeton: Princeton University Press, 1983.

——. *The Collected Works of Samuel Taylor Coleridge*. Vol. 14. Edited by Carl Woodring. Princeton: Princeton University Press, 1990.

——. "Introduction to the Sonnets" (1796). Reprinted in *The Complete Poetical and Dramatic Works of Samuel Taylor Coleridge*, edited by James Dykes Campbell. London: Macmillan, 1938.

Cowper, William. *The Correspondence of William Cowper*. Edited by Thomas Wright. London: Hodder and Stoughton, 1904.

Culler, Jonathan. "Changes in the Study of the Lyric." In *Lyric Poetry: Beyond New Criticism,* edited by Chaviva Hošek and Patricia Parker, 38–54. Ithaca: Cornell University Press, 1985.

——. *Structuralist Poetics*. Ithaca: Cornell University Press, 1975.

Curran, Stuart. "The I Altered." In *Romanticism and Feminism,* edited by Anne K. Mellor, 185–207. Bloomington: Indiana University Press, 1988.

——. Introduction to *The Poems of Charlotte Smith*. Edited by Stuart Curran. New York: Oxford University Press, 1993.

——. *Poetic Form and British Romanticism*. New York: Oxford University Press, 1986.

Davis, Robert Con. "The Structure of the Picturesque: Dorothy Wordsworth's Journals." *The Wordsworth Circle* 9 (1978): 45–49.

Eliot, T. S. "The Three Voices of Poetry." In *On Poetry and Poets,* 96–112. New York: Farrar, Straus and Cudahy, 1952.

Empson, William. *Some Versions of Pastoral*. London: Chatto and Windus, 1935.

Fay, Elizabeth A. *Becoming Wordsworthian: A Performative Aesthetics*. Amherst: University of Massachusetts Press, 1995.

Ferguson, Frances. "Romantic Memory." *Studies in Romanticism* 35 (1996): 509–33.

Freud, Sigmund. "Mourning and Melancholia." In *The Standard Edition of the Complete Psychological Works of Sigmund Freud,* edited by James Strachey and Anna Freud, 14:243–58. London: Hogarth, 1962.

Fried, Michael. *Absorption and Theatricality: Painting and Beholder in the Age of Diderot*. Chicago: University of Chicago Press, 1980.

Friedman, Michael H. *The Making of a Tory Humanist: William Wordsworth and the Idea of Community.* New York: Columbia University Press, 1979.

Frye, Northrop. *Anatomy of Criticism.* Princeton: Princeton University Press, 1957.

——. "Approaching the Lyric." In *Lyric Poetry: Beyond New Criticism,* edited by Chaviva Hošek and Patricia Parker, 31–37. Ithaca: Cornell University Press, 1985.

——. "Towards Defining an Age of Sensibility" (1963). Reprinted in *Poets of Sensibility and the Sublime,* edited by Harold Bloom, 11–18. New York: Chelsea House 1986.

Glen, Heather. *Vision and Disenchantment: Blake's "Songs" and Wordsworth's "Lyrical Ballads."* Cambridge: Cambridge University Press, 1983.

Goodwin, Albert. *The Friends of Liberty: The English Democratic Movement in the Age of the French Revolution.* Cambridge: Harvard University Press, 1979.

Greer, Donald. *The Incidence of the Emigration During the French Revolution.* Cambridge: Harvard University Press, 1951.

Hartman, Geoffrey H. *Beyond Formalism.* New Haven: Yale University Press, 1970.

——. *Wordsworth's Poetry: 1787–1814 .* 1964. Reprint, Cambridge: Harvard University Press, 1987.

Hazlitt, William. *The Complete Works of William Hazlitt.* Edited by P. P. Howe. London: J. M. Dent, 1930.

Helsinger, Elizabeth. "Clare and the Place of the Peasant Poet." *Critical Inquiry* 13 (1987): 509–31.

Hilbish, Florence May Anna. "Charlotte Smith, Poet and Novelist, 1749–1806." Ph.D. diss., University of Pennsylvania, 1941.

Homans, Margaret. *Bearing the Word: Language and Female Experience in Nineteenth-Century Women's Writing.* Chicago: University of Chicago Press, 1986.

——. *Women Writers and Poetic Identity: Dorothy Wordsworth, Emily Brontë, and Emily Dickinson.* Princeton: Princeton University Press, 1980.

Hunt, Bishop C., Jr. "Wordsworth and Charlotte Smith." *The Wordsworth Circle* 1 (1970): 85–103.

Hunt, Leigh. *The Book of the Sonnet.* Edited by Leigh Hunt and S. Adams Lee. Boston: Roberts Brothers, 1867.

Hutchinson, Thomas, ed. *Lyrical Ballads* (1798), by William Words-
    worth and Samuel Taylor Coleridge. London: Duckworth, 1898.
Jacobus, Mary. *Tradition and Experiment in Wordsworth's "Lyrical
    Ballads (1798)."* Oxford: Clarendon Press, 1976.
Janowitz, Anne. "Class and Literature: The Case of Romantic
    Chartism." In *Rethinking Class: Literary Studies and Social
    Formations,* edited by Wai Chee Dimock and Michael T. Gilmore,
    239–66. New York: Columbia University Press, 1994.
Jeffrey, Francis. Review of *Poems in Two Volumes* (1807), by William
    Wordsworth. *Edinburgh Review* 11 (1807): 214–31.
———. Review of *The Excursion,* by William Wordsworth. *Edinburgh
    Review* 24 (1814): 1–30.
Johnson, Samuel. *The Collected Works of Samuel Johnson.* Vol. 2.
    Edited by W. J. Bate, John M. Bullitt, and C. F. Powell. New
    Haven: Yale University Press, 1963.
———. *The Collected Works of Samuel Johnson.* Vol. 3. Edited by W.
    J. Bate and Albrecht B. Strauss. New Haven: Yale University Press,
    1969.
Johnson, W. R. *The Idea of Lyric: Lyric Modes in Ancient and Modern
    Poetry.* Berkeley: University of California Press, 1982.
Johnston, Kenneth R. "The Politics of 'Tintern Abbey.'" *The
    Wordsworth Circle* 14 (1983): 6–14.
———. *Wordsworth and "The Recluse."* New Haven: Yale University
    Press, 1984.
Jordon, John E. *Why the "Lyrical Ballads"?* Berkeley: University of
    California Press, 1976.
Kant, Immanuel. *Critique of Judgement.* Translated by J. H. Bernard.
    2d ed. New York: Hafner/Macmillan, 1951.
Keegan, Bridget. "Broadsides, Ballads and Books: The Landscape of
    Cultural Literacy in *The Village Minstrel.*" *The John Clare Society
    Journal* 15 (1996): 11–18.
Kernan, Alvin. *Printing Technology, Letters and Samuel Johnson.*
    Princeton: Princeton University Press, 1987.
Klancher, Jon P. *The Making of English Reading Audiences, 1790–
    1832.* Madison: University of Wisconsin Press, 1987.
Lacour, Claudia Brodsky. "Contextual Criticism, or 'History' v. 'Litera-
    ture.'" *Narrative* 1 (1993): 93–104.
Langbaum, Robert. *The Poetry of Experience.* New York: Norton, 1957.
Leader, Zachary. *Revision and Romantic Authorship.* Oxford:
    Clarendon Press, 1996.

Legouis, Émile. *William Wordsworth and Annette Vallon.* 1922. Reprint, revised by Pierre Legouis, Hamden, Conn.: Archon, 1967.

Levin, Susan M. *Dorothy Wordsworth and Romanticism.* New Brunswick, NJ: Rutgers University Press, 1987.

Levinson, Marjorie. *Wordsworth's Great Period Poems.* Cambridge: Cambridge University Press, 1986.

Liu, Alan. *Wordsworth: The Sense of History.* Stanford, Calif.: Stanford University Press, 1989.

Lokke, Kari. "Charlotte Smith and Literary History: 'Dark Forgetfulness' and the 'Intercession of Saint Monica.'" *Women's Studies* 27 (1998): 259–80.

Macaulay, Thomas Babington. "Milton" (1825). Reprinted in *Critical and Historical Essays.* Boston: Houghton Mifflin, 1900.

Magnuson, Paul. "The Politics of 'Frost at Midnight.'" *The Wordsworth Circle* 22 (1991): 3–11.

Manning, Peter J. *Reading Romantics: Texts and Contexts.* New York: Oxford University Press, 1990.

Marshall, David. *The Surprising Effects of Sympathy: Marivaux, Diderot, Rousseau, and Mary Shelley.* Chicago: University of Chicago Press, 1988.

Martin, Frederick. *The Life of John Clare.* London: Macmillan, 1865.

McGann, Jerome J. *The Romantic Ideology.* Chicago: University of Chicago Press, 1983.

McKeon, Michael. "Writer as Hero: Novelistic Prefigurations and the Emergence of Literary Biography." In *Contesting the Subject: Essays in the Postmodern Theory and Practice of Biography and Bibliographical Criticism,* edited by William H. Empson, 17–41. West Lafayette, Ind.: Purdue University Press, 1991.

Mellor, Anne K. *Romanticism and Gender.* New York: Routledge, 1993.

Mill, John Stuart. *Autobiography.* London: Oxford University Press, 1963.

———. "What is Poetry?" (1833). Reprinted in *Essays on Poetry,* edited by F. Parvin Sharpless, 3–22. Columbia: University of South Carolina Press, 1976.

Moorman, Mary. *William Wordsworth.* 2 vols. Oxford: Clarendon Press, 1957.

Murphy, Peter T. *Poetry as an Occupation and an Art in Britain, 1760–1830.* Cambridge: Cambridge University Press, 1993.

Neeson, J. M. *Commoners: Common Right, Enclosure and Social Change in England, 1700–1820.* Cambridge: Cambridge University Press, 1993.

———. "To Opponents of Enclosure in Eighteen-Century Northamptonshire." *Past & Present* 105 (1984).

Northcote, Stafford Harry, Viscount St. Cyres. "The Sorrows of Mrs. Charlotte Smith." *Cornhill Magazine,* n.s., 15 (1903): 683–96.

Onorato, Richard J. *The Character of the Poet: Wordsworth in "The Prelude."* Princeton: Princeton University Press, 1971.

Parks, George B. "The Turn to the Romantic in the Travel Literature of the Eighteenth Century." *Modern Language Quarterly* 25 (1964): 22–33.

Parrish, Stephen Maxfield. *The Art of the "Lyrical Ballads."* Cambridge: Harvard University Press, 1973.

———. "'Leaping and Lingering': Coleridge's Lyrical Ballads." In *Coleridge's Imagination,* edited by Richard Gravil, Lucy Newlyn, and Nicholas Roe, 102–16. Cambridge: Cambridge University Press, 1985.

Phillips, Richard. *British Public Characters of 1800–1801.* Vol. 3. London: Richard Phillips, 1801.

Pinch, Adela. "Lost in a Book: Jane Austen's *Persuasion.*" *Studies in Romanticism* 32 (1993): 97–117.

———. *Strange Fits of Passion: Epistemologies of Emotion, from Hume to Austen.* Stanford, Calif.: Stanford University Press, 1996.

Poovey, Mary. *The Proper Lady and the Woman Writer.* Chicago: University of Chicago Press, 1984.

Rajan, Tilottama. "The Erasure of Narrative in Post-Structuralist Representations of Wordsworth." In *Romantic Revolutions,* edited by Kenneth R. Johnston, Gilbert Chaitin, Kareñ Hanson, and Herbert Marks, 350–70. Bloomington: Indiana University Press, 1990.

———. "Romanticism and the Death of Lyric Consciousness." In *Lyric Poetry: Beyond New Criticism,* edited by Chaviva Hosek and Patricia Parker, 194–207. Ithaca: Cornell University Press, 1985.

Randel, Fred V. "The Betrayals of 'Tintern Abbey.'" *Studies in Romanticism* 32 (1993): 379–97.

Reed, Mark L. *Wordsworth: The Chronology of the Early Years, 1770–1799.* Cambridge: Harvard University Press, 1967.

Roe, Nicholas. *Wordsworth and Coleridge: The Radical Years.* Oxford: Clarendon Press, 1988.

Roper, Derek. *Reviewing Before the Edinburgh, 1788–1802.* London: Methuen, 1978.

Ross, Marlon B. *The Contours of Masculine Desire: Romanticism and the Rise of Women's Poetry.* New York: Oxford University Press, 1989.

Ryskamp, Charles. "Wordsworth's *Lyrical Ballads* in Their Time." In *From Sensibility to Romanticism,* edited by Frederick W. Hilles and Harold Bloom, 357–72. New York: Oxford University Press, 1965.

Scott, Sir Walter. *The Miscellaneous Prose Works of Sir Walter Scott.* Edinburgh: Robert Cadell, 1849.

Sheats, Paul D. *The Making of Wordsworth's Poetry, 1785–1798.* Cambridge: Harvard University Press, 1973.

Shore, John, Lord Teignmouth. *Memoirs of The Life, Writings and Correspondence of Sir William Jones.* London: John Hatchard, 1806.

Simpson, David. "Raymond Williams: Feeling for Structures, Voicing 'History.'" *Social Text* 10 (1992): 9–26.

———. *Wordsworth's Historical Imagination.* New York: Methuen, 1987.

Siskin, Clifford. *The Historicity of Romantic Discourse.* New York: Oxford University Press, 1988.

———. "The Lyric Mix: Romanticism, Genre, and the Fate of Literature." *The Wordsworth Circle* 25 (1994): 7–10.

Smith, Charlotte. *The Banished Man.* 4 vols. London: T. Cadell, Jr. and W. Davies, 1794.

Stanton, Judith Phillips. "Charlotte Smith's 'Literary Business': Income, Patronage, and Indigence." In *The Age of Johnson,* edited by Paul J. Korshin, 375–401. New York: AMS Press, 1987.

———. Introduction to *The Old Manor House,* by Charlotte Smith, edited by Anne Henry Ehrenpreis. Oxford: Oxford University Press, 1989.

Storey, Mark, ed. *Clare: The Critical Heritage.* London: Routledge & Kegan Paul, 1973.

Tate, W. E. *The English Village Community and the Enclosure Movements.* London: Victor Gollancz, 1967.

Taylor, John. Introduction to *Poems Descriptive of Rural Life and Scenery,* by John Clare. 4th ed. London: Taylor and Hessey, 1821.

———. Introduction to *The Village Minstrel, and Other Poems,* by John Clare. London: Taylor and Hessey, 1821.

Thelwall, John. *Poems, Chiefly Written in Retirement.* London: Richard Phillips, 1801.

Thompson, E. P. *Customs in Common*. New York: New Press, 1993.

———. "Disenchantment or Default?: A Lay Sermon." In *Power and Consciousness*, edited by Conor Cruise O'Brien and William Dean Vanech, 149–81. London: University of London Press, 1969.

———. *The Making of the English Working Class*. New York: Vintage, 1966.

Thompson, T. W. *Wordsworth's Hawkshead*. Edited by Robert Woof. London: Oxford University Press, 1970.

Tibble, John, and Anne Tibble. *John Clare: His Life and Poetry*. Melbourne and London: William Heinemann, 1956.

Todd, Janet. *Sensibility: An Introduction*. London: Methuen, 1986.

Vendler, Helen. "*Tintern Abbey*: Two Assaults." In *Wordsworth in Context*, edited by Pauline Fletcher and John Murphy, 173–90. Lewisburg, Pa.: Bucknell University Press, 1992.

Weiner, Margery. *The French Exiles, 1789–1815*. London: John Murray, 1960.

Williams, Merryn, and Raymond Williams. *John Clare: Selected Poetry and Prose*. London: Methuen, 1986.

Williams, Raymond. *The Country and the City*. New York: Oxford University Press, 1973.

Wolfson, Susan J. "Individual in Community: Dorothy Wordsworth in Conversation With William." In *Romanticism and Feminism*, edited by Anne K. Mellor, 139–66. Bloomington: Indiana University Press.

Woodring, Carl. *Wordsworth*. Boston: Houghton Mifflin, 1965.

Wordsworth, Dorothy. *The Journals of Dorothy Wordsworth*. Edited by Ernest de Selincourt. 2 vols. Oxford: Oxford University Press, 1941.

Wordsworth, William. *The Poetical Works of William Wordsworth*. Edited by William Knight. Vol. 7. London: Macmillan, 1896.

———. *The Prelude, 1799, 1805, 1850*. Edited by Jonathan Wordsworth, M. H. Abrams, and Stephen Gill. New York: Norton, 1979.

Yeats, William Butler. *Autobiographies*. London: Macmillan, 1961.

[Young, Arthur.] *General Report on Enclosures, Drawn up by Order of the Board of Agriculture*. 1808. Reprint, edited by Sir John Sinclair. New York: A. M. Kelley, 1971.

Zimmerman, Sarah M. "Charlotte Smith's Letters and the Practice of Self-Presentation." *Princeton University Library Chronicle* 53 (1991): 50–77.

Index

Abrams: on audience, 77, 197n. 14; critical influence of, x–xi, 1–2, 15–20, 25, 32; definition of "greater Romantic lyric," xiv, 15–16, 42, 62, 74, 85–86, 94, 196n. 1; definition of lyric, 186–87n. 3; on disinterestedness, 186n. 1, 196–97n. 8; identification with Romantic poets, 2, 4–5; influenced by Mill, 4, 188n. 23; on memory, 25, 62; on nature, 148–49; political disillusionment of, 6, 187n. 7; political action divorced from poetry, 18; on subjectivity, x–xi, 3, 15–19, 41, 80. Works: "English Romanticism: The Spirit of the Age," 18, 74; *Glossary of Literary Terms*, 186–87n. 3; *The Mirror and the Lamp*, 1, 16, 186n. 1, 188n. 23; *Natural Supernaturalism*, xiv, 5, 18–19; "Structure and Style in the Greater Romantic Lyric," xiv, 15–18, 74

Adorno, Theodor W., 8–9, 28

Alexander, Meena, 21–22, 122

Alfoxden Journal (Dorothy Wordsworth), 116–18, 121–29

Analytical Review: review of *The Banished Man* (Smith), 70; review of *Elegiac Sonnets* (Smith), 68–69; review of *The Emigrants* (Smith), 66

Antijacobin: notice of *Letters of a Solitary Wanderer* (Smith), 110; review of *Poems Descriptive of Rural Life and Scenery* (Clare), 181

Arnold, Matthew: canon-building, 198n. 21, 205n. 5; emphasis on sincerity, 14; on nature and poetic truth, 13–14. Works: Preface to *The Poems of Wordsworth* (1879), 14

atemporality, xv, 52–54

Auden, William H., 5. Works: "New Year Letter of 1940," 5

audience: characterization of, in critical tradition, 32–34, 41, 77, 197n. 14 engaged by interiority, 32–37, 47–48; of soliloquy, 12, 15–17, 96–97. *See also* readers

autobiography: as "egotism," 70; and poetic persona, 36–37; as risk for poet, xvi–xvii, 66–72, 113–14, 182–83; as site of social engagement, 36–37, 43–51; as site of sympathetic identification, 35–36, 39–40, 57–66, 116; as verification of sincerity, 55–56. *See also* biography

Bahti, Timothy, 191n. 72, 193–94n. 24

Baillie, Joanna: Introductory Discourse to *A Series of Plays* (1798), 33–34

228   INDEX

literary career *(continued):*
Wordsworth's, 77–84, 100–101, 108–
11. *See also* income; literary marketplace
literary marketplace: Clare's experience of,
149–50, 177–183, 211–12 n.
51; consequences of entering, xvi–xvii,
115–16, 145–46; disinterestedness as
response to, 36–37; Dorothy
Wordsworth's experience of, 118–21;
shift to, from system of patronage,
101; as site of exposure, xvi–xvii,
115–16; as site of social engagement,
36–37; Smith's experience of, 37, 39–
41, 51, 66–72, 108–11; William
Wordsworth's experience of, xvi, 77–
84, 100–101, 108–11. *See also*
income; literary career; readers
Liu, Alan, 20, 21, 23, 25, 27, 74, 89, 93–
94, 195 n. 42, 201 n. 49, 203–4 n. 74
local contexts, as site for social engagement, xii, 86–92
Lockhart, John Gibson, 144, 152
Lokke, Kari, 192–93 n. 7
Lucas, John, 209 n. 11
lyric mode: antithetical definitions of, 2,
19–24, 36–37; disinterestedness in, 2,
5–6, 14–19, 36–37, 113–14; as
dynamic exchange with readers, 40–
41; as eloquent, x; as lamentation, 39–
40, 151–72; opposed to narrative, 27,
85; and poetics of presence, 31–32;
and privacy, 148; sense of audience in,
32–34; as site of contradictory
impulses, 9, 93–94, 111; as site of
social engagement, 27–32, 86–93;
sympathy, use of, 40–41; and
theatricality, 201–2 n. 53
Lyrical Ballads (William Wordsworth), xvi,
83–84, 125, 131; political engagement
in, 75–76; position of "Tintern
Abbey" within, 94–96

Macaulay, Thomas Babington, 186 n. 1
Mackenzie, Henry, *The Man of Feeling,* 31
Macovski, Michael, 190 n. 51
Magnuson, Paul, 36–37
Marshall, David, 29–30, 49, 133
masculinism: in canonical definitions, 122;
in critical tradition, xiii, 16, 21, 99

McGann, Jerome J., xiv, 2–3, 20, 186 n. 5,
186 n. 6, 191 n. 65, 202 n. 58, 202
n. 60
melancholy: Dorothy Wordsworth's use of,
130, 137; and mourning, 106; as site
of social engagement, 54, 61–62;
Smith's use of, 53–56; William
Wordsworth's use of, 90, 106
Mellor, Anne K., 22, 99–100
memory: in canonical definitions of
lyricism, xii–xiii, 80; consequences of,
25–27, 106–7; as consolation, 62–63;
and cult of personality, 63–64; as
history, 64–65; and identity, 24–27,
95–96, 174–75; and local contexts,
24–27; and melancholy, 106;
prescribed to audience, 97–99; as
psychic defense, 25–27; relation to
experience, 26; as site of social
engagement, 20, 25–26, 62–66, 86,
102–7; as site of sympathetic
identification, 63–64; Smith's use of,
37, 62–66; subject's control of, 25–27;
William Wordsworth's use of, 95–97,
203–4 n. 74
Mill, John Stuart: critical influence of, ix–
x, 4, 14–19, 23; "eloquence" defined
by, 1, 11–13; emphasis on disinterestedness, 8; novel defined by, 23; poetry
defined by, 10–13, 23, 32; poetry
divorced from social engagement, 12–
13; political disillusionment of, 6, 7–8;
William Wordsworth's influence on, 7–
8, 11–12, 73–74. Works: "What is
Poetry?," ix–x, 75
Milton, John, 80
mimeticism, as standard for social
engagement, xi, 22–25
Monthly Magazine: memoir of Smith, 51;
review of *The Emigrants* (Smith), 66;
review of *Poems Descriptive* (Clare),
211 n. 45
More, Hannah, 59
Murphy, Peter, T., 77, 81, 197 n. 17

narrative: as entertainment, 91–93; as
mode of social engagement, 22–23,
27, 28; as opposed to lyric, 27, 85,
199 n. 30
Narrative Concerning George and Sarah